"This brilliant book should be compulsory reading for all church musicians and clergy. John Shepherd's lifelong experience gives a rare authenticity to an historical account which also resonates with our own time. Uncompromising in its analysis of the past, it shows the power of music to bring people closer to God."

— **Stephen Darlington**, *Christ Church Cathedral, Oxford*

—

"A remarkable synthesis. John Shepherd employs the pen of a scholar, the eye of an aesthete, the ear of a musician and the heart of a priest to demonstrate how in Anglican worship appreciation of the numinous and of the holiness of beauty became gateways to the mystery that is God."

— **Michael Burrows**, *Bishop of Tuam, Limerick and Killaloe*

—

"John Shepherd's challenging and fascinating book shows dramatically the impact of the Reformation on worship within the fledgling Church of England and thereafter in the centuries following. As a music scholar and cathedral dean his contribution here is unique with sharp lessons for us in the contemporary church."

— **Stephen Platten**, *retired bishop and theological writer*

—

"John Shepherd's eloquent exploration of liturgical worship is much more than mere remembrance, but a gateway not least through music and the arts to a share in divine mystery. He not only states an authentic Anglican position, but offers a pathway that has profound and welcome ecumenical implications."

— **Roderick Strange**, *St Mary's University Twickenham*

Worship and the Mystery of God

*The Anglican Divines and the
Reality of Divine Presence*

— JOHN SHEPHERD —

Sacristy Press

Sacristy Press
PO Box 612, Durham, DH1 9HT

www.sacristy.co.uk

First published in 2025 by Sacristy Press, Durham

Copyright © John Shepherd 2025
The moral rights of the author have been asserted.

All rights reserved, no part of this publication may be reproduced or transmitted in any form or by any means, electronic, mechanical photocopying, documentary, film or in any other format without prior written permission of the publisher.

Scripture quotations, unless otherwise stated, are from the New Revised Standard Version Bible: Anglicized Edition, copyright © 1989, 1995 National Council of the Churches of Christ in the United States of America. Used by permission. All rights reserved worldwide.

Every reasonable effort has been made to trace the copyright holders of material reproduced in this book, but if any have been inadvertently overlooked the publisher would be glad to hear from them.

Sacristy Limited, registered in England & Wales, number 7565667

British Library Cataloguing-in-Publication Data
A catalogue record for the book is available from the British Library

ISBN 978-1-78959-388-4

Contents

Acknowledgments..iv
Introduction..1

Chapter 1. Worship—Embodying the Divine 4
Chapter 2. Worship—Remembering the Divine 22
Chapter 3. Worship—Edification in Faith......................... 44
Chapter 4. Worship—An Exercise in the Spirit 59
Chapter 5. Understanding Enhanced by Music.................... 87
Chapter 6. Ceremonial of Worship Affirmed 111
Chapter 7. Participation in Christ's offering...................... 124
Chapter 8. Turning Earth into Heaven 144
Chapter 9. The Experience of Transcendence 166
Chapter 10. Worship united with Christ's offering................ 196
Chapter 11. Christ's Offering—A Present Reality 212
Chapter 12. Participation in the Worship of Heaven 231
Chapter 13. The Beauty of Holiness and the Holiness of Beauty.... 243

Conclusion 268
Index 272

Acknowledgments

My thanks are due to those who have inspired me to engage with the cohesion of the divine and human in the context of the offering of worship. Implicit in this engagement is the mystery of the intersection of the realms of nature and grace and the hope of worship being a means of transcendence, of enabling an experience of something beyond the ordinary, and to find, not only beauty in holiness, but holiness in beauty.

Initially these instincts were encouraged by Denis Stevens in New York, then Peter le Huray in Cambridge. More recently I am grateful to Diarmaid MacCulloch for reviewing my early attempts, and then for the support and advice of Stephen Platten, Hugh Benham, Stephen Darlington and Gary Macy. Their musical and liturgical scholarship within the area I have examined is profound and I have been a welcome beneficiary of their wisdom and encouragement.

I am also indebted to Natalie Watson—a gracious and insightful editor.

I have been privileged to be associated with both Christ Church Cathedral Oxford and St George's Cathedral Perth, institutions where the achieving of transcendence in worship has remained a priority. Both are places where the beauty of liturgy and its accompanying music is unfailingly evident and continues to transform the ordinary into the sublime, enabling us to look beyond the mundane, through the glass and, in the words of the great poet-saint George Herbert, "then the heaven espy".

Introduction

A critical aspect of the theological warfare of the Reformation was centred on the question of how it is possible to be made righteous or accounted righteous before God. Did the life, death and resurrection of Christ establish a hope, albeit a supremely confident one, or did it create a new relationship of being between God and man?

In terms of liturgical worship, the question took the form of a clear alternative: did one remember Christ in faith and thereby be accounted righteous, or was one brought into living contact with the substance of the divine life and, in the language of the patristic writers, divinized?[1] These two contrary strands became the defining issues of the Reformation debates concerning the nature and function of worship.

The decisive imperative of the worship of the mediaeval Church had been to embody the living presence of the divine. Worship therefore became the means of unity with a transcendent reality, described variously as the numinous, the wholly other, a *magisterium*.[2] Such a coherence of the divine and the human defied rational analysis. It was a mystery that confounded the resources of language to express. It could at best be revealed figuratively, through imagery, symbol and metaphor.

The most potent image of this divine–human unity was the coincidence of Christ's offering of his life on the cross and the offering of the bread and wine in the Mass on the altar.

On the cross, Christ had offered his body and blood to be slain; in the eucharist the bread and wine were offered to be broken and shed. The physical, embodied presence of Christ was confirmed in spatial and local

---

[1] B. Marshall, *The Holy Eucharist in the Church*, unpublished paper, 1966.

[2] Rudolf Otto, *The Idea of the Holy: An Inquiry into the Non-Rational Factor in the Idea of the Divine and Its Relation to the Rational*, tr. John W. Harvey, 2nd edn (Oxford: Oxford University Press, 1958).

terms and the reality of the divine presence in the offering of worship was manifest[3] United with Christ's offering on the cross, this offering was able to plead before God with the authority of Christ's offering itself.

The reformers of the mid-sixteenth century comprehensively overturned this understanding of worship and in doing so effectively demolished the liturgical and musical tradition of the established Church. Their default theological setting was that sin had so deeply perverted the human condition as to render impossible any offering of worship becoming united with Christ's offering to the Father. Further, to invoke divine forgiveness on the basis of such a proposed unity was abhorrent. The only offering acceptable to God was the sacrifice made by Christ on the cross. As a result, worship was no longer to be a living experience which embodied the reality of the divine presence, but a remembrance of Christ's once-for-all offering. Moreover, to avoid contamination by any physical, corrupted component it was to be a spiritual offering of the heart and mind.

Consequently, there was no attempt in worship to create a sense of the numinous, of transcendence or otherness. No effort was made to embody the divine presence. The priority turned instead to edification in the faith, for if worship were to be a remembering rather than an embodiment of Christ's offering, then it had to be clear what was to be remembered, and such edification required clarity of expression. Worship was no longer an engagement with a mystical dimension where various forms of artistic expression—ritual, ceremonial, art, architecture and in particular music—invoked a reality beyond the ability of words to describe. The role of the arts as facilitators in embracing the presence of the divine was diminished to the point of extinction.

A number of theologians were stirred into action at such an abandonment of the understanding of liturgical offering which had underpinned the liturgy for centuries before. To varying extents, the basic theological positions held by the reformers were either revised

---

[3] B. J. Kidd, *The Later Mediaeval Doctrine of the Eucharistic Sacrifice* (London: SPCK, 1898), p. 98; Council of Trent 13th Session; The Catechism of Trent; John Macquarrie, "Eucharistic Presence", in *Paths in Spirituality* (London: SCM Press, 1972).

or reversed. The view that humanity was so irredeemably corrupt as to render futile the inclusion of works in the offering of worship was demolished by arguments acknowledging the all-embracing authenticity and efficacy of divine forgiveness. With works then deemed to be acceptable, restriction of worship to the offering of the spirit was demonstrably untenable. Further, the narrow definition of edification which had led to the denigration of liturgical rites, including music, was shown to be inadequate.

The recasting of these attitudes made it possible for worship once more to be appreciated as the embodiment of the divine presence. This was achieved by means of the offering of worship being united with Christ's offering, and attitudes were expressed that granted a close affiliation of the bread and wine with the body and blood. As a result, the worship of the Church became united with the worship of heaven and the works which were offered became possessed with the divine holiness, which holiness, of necessity, embraced all that is beautiful.

It followed that works of beauty must embody the divine. So it became possible to speak not only of the beauty of holiness but the holiness of beauty, whereby the divine was able to be discerned in works of beauty. This acknowledgement enabled the arts once more to enrich worship with a sense of the sublime, the numinous.

1

Worship—Embodying the Divine

The fundamental dynamic of mediaeval eucharistic worship was to embody the reality of the divine. As a result, attention concentrated on the relationship between Christ's offering of his body and blood on the cross and the offering of the bread and wine on the altar. If the sacrifice of the cross could be identified with the sacrifice of the altar, Christ's offering of his body to be slain and his blood to be shed would be united with the bread and the wine being offered. Christ's body could then be said to exist in the consecrated bread and his blood in the consecrated wine. The physical, embodied presence of Christ would be confirmed in spatial and local terms and the reality of the divine presence in the offering of worship would be manifest.[1] Moreover, this offering could claim propitiatory authority to plead before God in the name of Christ on behalf of all humanity. Much mediaeval eucharistic scholarship was concerned to identify the precise relationship between the body and blood and the bread and wine as the essence of the unity of the human with the divine and the consequent reality of the divine presence.[2]

---

[1] B. J. Kidd, *The Later Mediaeval Doctrine of the Eucharistic Sacrifice* (London: SPCK, 1898), p. 98. Council of Trent 13th Session; The Catechism of Trent; John Macquarrie, "Eucharistic Presence", in *Paths in Spirituality* (London: SCM Press, 1972).

[2] G. Macy, "The Medieval Inheritance", in Lee Palmer Wandel (ed.), *A Companion to the Eucharist in the Reformation* (Leiden and Boston: Brill, 2014), p. 29.

Scholarship and the divine presence

Paschasius Radbertus (*c*.790–860), a ninth-century monk of Corbie, insisted that the body of Christ presented in the Mass was identical to the historical body of Christ that was born of Mary, sacrificed on the cross and resurrected from the tomb. In the sacrament of the altar was to be found the true body of Christ, not a figure of it.

On the other hand, Ratramnus of Corbie (*d.c.*868), whilst affirming that there was indeed a true presence of Christ at the eucharist, argued that this did not imply an identity of substance. The eucharistic elements, he maintained, became Christ's body and blood "in truth", but that "truth" was spiritual, not physical.[3] Ratramnus thereby distinguished between literal truth and figurative truth. Literal truth (*veritas*) he understood to be "the manifestation of the reality itself . . . not veiled by shadows or figures". Figurative truth, on the other hand, was a shadow or representation of that reality, "setting forth what it signifies under certain veils".[4] So the body and blood of Christ were figures of the truth, not according to their visible nature but according to their invisible substance. What they outwardly signified was one thing; what they inwardly and invisibly effected was another.[5] The body and the blood which the Church celebrated was a pledge, an image, a representation. As for the actual reality, it shall be "when neither pledge nor image shall appear, but the thing itself".[6]

For Berengar of Tours (*c*.1000–88), the body and blood present in the sacrament could not be the same as the historical body of Jesus, because this body retains its human characteristics and can exist only in heaven. The elements of bread and wine must therefore be a figure and likeness

---

[3] C. Radding and F. Newton, *Theology, Rhetoric, and Politics in the Eucharistic Controversy, 1078–1079* (New York: Columbia University Press, 2003), pp. 4–5.

[4] *The Book of Bertram, Monk of Corbie, A.D. 840 on The Body and Blood of the Lord*, tr. W. F. Taylor (London: Simpkin Marshall, 1880), p. 5.

[5] Taylor, *The Book of Bertram*, p. 33.

[6] Taylor, *The Book of Bertram*, pp. 56–7.

of the body and blood, a symbol of the spiritual presence of Christ.[7] Berengar's views provoked critical responses, most notably from Alberic of Monte Cassino (d.1088) and Lanfranc of Bec (c.1010–89), who berated Berengar for denying the transformation of the elements into the actual nature and substance of the body and blood.[8] Various interpretations were held by other theologians, amongst them Hrabanus Maurus (780–856) and Gottschalk of Orbais (808–67), thereby emphasizing the diversity of opinion concerning the nature of the reality of Christ's body and blood in relation to the bread and wine.[9] Assumptions that the Church of the mediaeval period was irrevocably aligned with a single version of the real presence and impatient of anything other than a monochrome view of so-called transubstantiation have been shown to be unfounded.[10] Even the views of the Dominican theologian Thomas Aquinas (d.1274) were vigorously contested, not least by the Archbishop of Canterbury Robert Kilwardby (1215–79).[11]

---

[7] A succinct account of Berengar's position is given by Gary Macy, "The Medieval Inheritance", in Lee Palmer Wandel (ed.), *A Companion to the Eucharist in the Reformation* (Leiden and Boston: Brill, 2014), p. 23.

[8] J. Pelikan, "The Growth of Medieval Theology (600–1300)", in *The Christian Tradition: A History of the Development of Doctrine*, Vol. 3 (Chicago, IL: University of Chicago Press, 1978), pp. 186–204.

[9] Radding and Newton, *Theology, Rhetoric, and Politics in the Eucharistic Controversy*, pp. 3–31.

[10] Macy, "The Medieval Inheritance" and *Treasures from the Storeroom* (Collegeville, MN: Liturgical Press, 1999), Chapter 1. Macy's findings endorse the earlier work of Francis Clark (*Eucharistic Sacrifice and the Reformation* (Oxford: Blackwell, 1967)), who similarly challenged what he perceived to be a caricature of mediaeval eucharistic theology as static and one-dimensional.

[11] Macy refers to James Weisheipl, *Friar Thomas D'Aquino: His Life, Thought and Works* (Washington D.C.: Catholic University of America Press, 1983), pp. 335–8, for an account of criticisms of Aquinas's views.

Councils and the divine presence

However, whilst scholarship is patient of exploration, even ambiguity, ecclesiastical councils tend to be conservative and defensive, intent on eradicating doubt and encouraging uniformity. In consequence, the mediaeval controversy concerning the eucharist proceeded at differing levels: the wide-ranging intellectual discourses amongst scholars and the more narrowly focussed ecclesiastical debates of church councils intent on establishing orthodoxy. A further distinction between these two environments was the intellectual capacity of the participants. With a degree of irony, it has been noted that councils were inevitably dominated by abbots, archbishops and bishops, "not all of whom necessarily grasped the philosophical and theological issues involved".[12]

Accordingly, the Fourth Lateran Council of 1215, presided over by Pope Innocent III, set out to establish certainty concerning the presence of Christ in the eucharist and had no appetite for accommodating the varying insights of scholarship. An uncompromising statement was issued declaring that the body and blood of Jesus Christ "are truly contained in the sacrament of the altar under the forms of bread and wine, the bread and wine having been changed in substance, by God's power, into his body and blood".[13] It has been found extraordinary that a single phrase of the opening creed of this council, *transsubstantiatis pane in corpus et uino in sanguinem potestate diuina*, was ever taken as an authoritative definition of the dogma of transubstantiation, given that during the late twelfth and early thirteenth centuries there was no common understanding of substance, much less agreement on the exact

---

[12] Radding and Newton, *Theology, Rhetoric, and Politics in the Eucharistic Controversy*, pp. 2–3.

[13] N. Tanner (ed.), *Decrees of the Ecumenical Councils*, Vol. I (London: Sheed & Ward, 1990), p. 230. For a general summary of the emergence of the doctrine of transubstantiation see Wandel, *The Eucharist in the Reformation: Incarnation and Liturgy* (Cambridge: Cambridge University Press, 2006), pp. 14–45, which includes reference to this text. A detailed analysis is given by Kidd, *The Later Mediaeval Doctrine of the Eucharistic Sacrifice*, and Macy, *Treasures from the Storeroom*, pp. 1–19, 36–58, 81–121, 142–72.

meaning of transubstantiation.[14] It is now more clearly understood that this phrase was never intended as a formal definition, nor understood to be, by the majority of thirteenth-century theologians.[15]

The definition provided by the Council of Trent over 300 years later in 1562 was more sympathetic to scholarly insights. It declared the sacrifice of the Mass not to be an absolute sacrifice in the sense of being a reiteration of Calvary, but a relative sacrifice whereby Christ's past offering to the Father was re-presented—the word *repraesentatio* was used—and made effective in the present as his body and blood were offered to the Father in the substance of bread and wine.[16] In essence, the language of theological scholarship was not easily accommodated within the language of ecclesiastical decree and the edicts promulgated by the councils cannot be taken as unerringly representative of mediaeval eucharistic thought, which was multi-layered, varied and alien to easy characterization.

Worship embodies the divine reality

However, it was beyond scholarship and decrees, unencumbered by attempts at rational explanation, that the reality of the divine presence could be experienced most directly and vividly, and that was within the liturgy—the offering of worship itself.

Lex orandi, lex credendi was a tag attributed to a lay monk, Prosper of Aquitaine (390–455), from a capitulum annexed to a letter of Pope Celestine I (422–32), written between 435 and 442. The phrase originally read *legem credendi lex statuat supplicandi*, "Let the law of prayer

---

[14] Macy, *Treasures from the Storeroom*, pp. 81–7.
[15] Macy, "The Medieval Inheritance", p. 26. Macy identifies three key issues concerning eucharistic change upon which debate focussed: coexistence, substitution and transmutation, pp. 26–7.
[16] Kidd, *The Later Mediaeval Doctrine of the Eucharistic Sacrifice*, p. 98; Council of Trent 13th Session; The Catechism of Trent; John Macquarrie, "Eucharistic Presence", pp. 82–93.

establish the law of belief",[17] signifying that the offering of worship shapes Christian belief.

So the essence of the divine presence becomes embodied and experienced through the offering of worship. United with the offering of Christ, worship engages with a reality which defies rational analysis and is beyond the power of words to evoke or describe. The phenomenon of becoming united with the heart of God was not a puzzle to be solved, but a mystery, enigmatic, incomprehensible, more able to be apprehended than comprehended[18] and testimony to an inductive rather than a deductive theological logic.[19] As a result, worship found effective expression through symbolism, imagery, metaphor and works of great beauty—music, art and architecture—all of which provided an experience of transcendence, described as the *numinous*, the wholly other, a *magisterium*, the sense of a reality *mysterium tremendum et fascinans*.[20]

The most powerful and dramatic image of the uniting of the human and the divine was the simple, direct equivalence of the offering of Christ on the cross and the offering of the bread and wine on the altar. This was evident in the foremost eucharistic rites of the English Church—Salisbury (Sarum), York, Hereford, Bangor and Lincoln.[21] As the Offertory sentences were said by the priest or sung by the choir,

---

[17] A concise analysis is given in W. Taylor Stevenson, "Lex Orandi—Lex Credendi", in S. Sykes, J. Booty and J. Knight (eds), *The Study of Anglicanism* (London: SPCK, 1998), pp. 187–202. See also C. Baumstark and B. Botte (rev.), *Comparative Liturgy* (London: Mowbray, 1958) and C. Baumstark, *On the Historical Development of the Liturgy*, tr. F. West (Collegeville, MN: Liturgical Press, 2011).

[18] K. Ward, *God: A Guide for the Perplexed* (Oxford: Oneworld, 2002), pp. 24–6.

[19] Stephen Platten, miscellaneous papers.

[20] Rudolf Otto, *The Idea of the Holy: An Inquiry into the Non-Rational Factor in the Idea of the Divine and Its Relation to the Rational*, tr. John W. Harvey, 2nd edn (Oxford: Oxford University Press, 1958).

[21] High Mass was usually celebrated after Terce on Sundays and the principal Feasts, after Sext on weekdays and lesser Feasts, and after None during Advent, Lent and Vigils; J. D. Chambers, *Divine Worship in England in the Thirteenth and Fourteenth Centuries* (London: Pickering, 1877), p. 309.

the bread was laid on the altar and the chalice was made by mixing the water with the wine, which signified the blood and water running out of Christ's side.[22] Said by the priest before the preface to the prayer of consecration, the Secret for the Third Sunday after Trinity asked for the gifts offered to God to be sanctified "that... they may become the Body and Blood of Thy only-begotten Son".[23] The Canon of the Mass contained a forthright declaration of the unity of the bread and wine with the body and blood:

> Which oblation, we beseech thee, O Almighty God, that thou wouldest vouchsafe, in all respects, to bless, approve, ratify, and make reasonable and acceptable, that it may become to us the Body and Blood of thy most dearly beloved Son our Lord Jesus Christ.[24]

The reality of Christ's presence was reinforced through ritual actions which provided visual representations of Christ's sacrificial journey to Calvary and his offering on the cross.[25] The role of gesture and symbol assumed critical importance, in particular for worshippers either unfamiliar with the language or unable to discern what was said because of the architectural dynamics of the building.

The origin of the treatment of the liturgy as a re-enactment of the passion of Christ has been attributed to Amalar of Metz (c.775/780–850), Bishop of Trier (812–13) and Bishop of Lyon (835–8). In his *Expositiones*

The Sarum Missal was first printed at Paris in 1487. Subsequent printings occurred at Basle (1489), Rouen (1492), Venice (1494) and London (1498).

[22] C. S. Cobb (ed.), *The Rationale of Ceremonial 1540–1543*, Alcuin Club Collections XVIII (London: Longmans, Green, 1910), p. 22. The short title, *Rationale of Ceremonial*, now in common usage, does not appear in either of the manuscripts of the *Book Concerning Ceremonies to be Used in the Church*.

[23] A. Harford Pearson (ed.), *The Sarum Missal* (London, 1884), p. 228.

[24] *Sarum Missal*, p. 310. Also T. F. Simmons (ed.), "The Use of York", in *The Lay Folks' Mass Book or the Manner of Hearing Mass*, Early English Text Society (EETS), Orig. Series 71 (London, 1879), p. 107.

[25] A. Ryrie, *Being Protestant in Reformation Britain* (Oxford: Oxford University Press, 2013), p. 345.

Missae, Amalar embarks upon a riot of allegory in which every prayer, ceremony and person is made to refer to the life of Christ—his ministry, passion, suffering, death, resurrection and ascension. The movements, placing and posture of the ministers, the vestments, linens and adornment of the altar were endowed with symbolic significance.[26] The Offertory marked the entrance of Christ into Jerusalem and from this point the Mass was identified as a progress to suffering and death, culminating in Christ's sacrifice offered on the cross being represented by the sacrifice offered by the priest at the altar.

That Christ was truly and personally present was demonstrated with dramatic effect at the elevation of the elements at the moment of consecration. Reinforced by the ringing of bells, this liturgical action provided dramatic assurance of the actual presence of the body and blood of Christ on the altar. Ritual became a manifestation of the reality of Christ's presence.

Devotions and the divine presence

Devotional books available as companions to the offering of the Mass enhanced the immediacy of Christ's presence. It is estimated that the *Hours of the Blessed Virgin Mary* were in use from the eleventh century and the *Hours of the Cross* from at least the fourteenth century.[27] In regular devotional use were also the *Hours of the Breviary*.[28] Some Hours

---

[26] J. M. Hanssens (ed.), *Amalarii Episcopi Opera liturgica omnia* (Città del Vaticano: Biblioteca apostolica vaticana, 1948–50). P. Jacobson, *Ad memoriam ducens: The development of liturgical exegesis in Amalar of Metz's Expositiones Missae*, Dissertation (ProQuest Dissertations Publishing, 1996), p. 244.

[27] By the early sixteenth century, there is thought to have been at least 50,000 Books of Hours in circulation. There is a full discussion of the devotional content of the Primers in E. Duffy, *The Stripping of the Altars: Traditional Religion in England c.1400–c.1580* (London: Yale University Press, 1992), Chapter 7, pp. 233–65.

[28] R. Morris (ed.), *Legends of the Holy Rood: Symbols of the Passion and Cross Poems*, EETS Orig. series 46 (London, 1871), pp. 222f.; C. Horstman (ed.), *The*

carried both Latin and English versions.[29] All these devotions invited contemplation on the passion and at the moment of the priest's elevation of the consecrated sacrament the worshipper was instructed to meditate solely on Christ's offering on the cross: "Call to remembrance and imprint inwardly in your heart by holy meditation, the whole process of the Passion, from the Maundy until the point of Christ's death."[30] As with the *Hours*, the *Lay Folks' Mass Book or Manner of Hearing Mass* similarly invited personal reflection on the suffering and death of Christ.[31] The stated purpose of Langforde's *Meditations in the Time of the Mass* was "to stir the worshipper to the diligent and compendious remembrance of the passion of Christ". The set of 15 prayers beginning with the exclamation "O", known as the "Fifteen Oes of St Bridget" and possibly the most popular of all prayers in late mediaeval England,[32] recreated with striking realism all aspects of Christ's suffering throughout the period of the crucifixion. *A Treatise of the Manner and Mede of the Mass*,[33] a meditation on the life of Christ which accompanied the recitation of the Canon, culminated at the consecration with a devotion on the passion: "Between the Sanctus and the sakring [consecration] you shall pray standing... Then should you kneel down and think upon his passion".[34] A final prayer reminded the worshipper that it was Christ's offering on the cross which brought salvation: "God hath died upon the Rood that bought us with his precious blood upon the hard tree."[35]

Minor Poems of the Vernon MS, EETS Orig. series 98 (London, 1892–1901), pp. 37–43; T. F. Simmons (ed.), *Cursor Mundi* (Part V), EETS Orig. series 68 (London, 1878), pp. 1458–67; *The Lay Folks' Mass Book*, pp. 81–7.

[29] *Horae Beatae*, pp. 111 and 116 (Wynkyn de Worde, Westminster, 1494).

[30] *Tracts on the Mass* XXVII (London: Henry Bradshaw Society, 1904), p. 24.

[31] K. Stevenson, "The Prayer Book Noted", in C. Hefling and C. Shattuck (eds), *The Oxford Guide to the Book of Common Prayer: A Worldwide Study* (Oxford: Oxford University Press, 2006), p. 50.

[32] Duffy, *Stripping of the Altars*, p. 249.

[33] *The Lay Folks' Mass Book*, pp. 128ff.

[34] *The Lay Folks' Mass Book*, pp. 143–4.

[35] *The Lay Folks' Mass Book*, p. 147.

So dramatically were the events of the passion presented that the effect of each day's devotion was to experience afresh Christ's offering on the cross. Little wonder that when the kneeling congregations saw the Host held up above the priest's head at the sacring they were transported to Calvary itself. In his *Instruction for Parish Priests*, John Myrc (*c*.1450) directs the worshippers to kneel with great devotion before the priest, "Goddes body wyth hym beryge".[36]

The offering of Christ continued at the altar

The unity of the human and divine offerings was so profound that the worshipper was informed "the priest signifieth Christ; the altar the Cross".[37] The priesthood of Christ was understood not to have terminated with Christ's death but to have continued through the apostles and their successors. This was vividly represented with the equation of the eucharistic vestments worn by the priest with those worn by Christ on his journey towards death. The amice represented the veil with which Christ's face was covered during his beating; the alb the white garment with which Herod clothed Christ when he was sent to Pilate; the girdle the whip with which Christ was scourged; the maniple the cord which bound Christ's left arm when taken in the Garden and led to Annas; the stole the rope with which Christ was bound to the pillar when he was scourged; the chasuble the mantle with which the soldiers dressed him after his scourging.[38] Other interpretations of the significance of the vestments also recreated the reality of Christ's offering on the cross:

---

[36] John Myrc, *Instructions for Parish Priests*, ed. E. Peacock, Early English Text Society (London, 1868, rev. 1902), Sections 304–11; Wandel, *The Eucharist in the Reformation*, pp. 37–8. Lee Palmer Wandel itemizes the familiar inventory of eucharistic vessels, vestments, books and artefacts which affirm the present experience of Christ at the eucharist.

[37] *Tracts on the Mass* XXVII, p. 19.

[38] Cobb, *The Rationale of Ceremonial*, pp. 16–18.

> When the maniple is put on the left hand remember the ropes with which the knights did bind our Saviour's hands when they did lead him from tyrant to tyrant... When the priest casteth on his outermost vestment called a chasuble remember the purple mantle wherein they did clothe our Saviour in great scorn, and how they crowned and sceptred him with a robe, and beat and mocked him.[39]

Not only the vestments but the actions of the priest corresponded to moments of significance at the crucifixion. In praying to the Father to accept the gifts prepared for consecration, the priest inclined his body, made a cross on the altar and kissed it, "signifying thereby the humble inclining and willing obedience of Christ to his Father's will to suffer his passion upon the altar of his cross for our salvation".[40] The worshipper was informed that immediately after the consecration the priest would spread out his arms "in the manner of a cross, signifying the press of the Passion of Christ".

Humanity united with the divine

The unity of the bread and wine with the body and blood made it possible for humanity to be "found in the likeness of Him in whom we are united... Jesus Christ our Lord"[41] and to be made a partaker of the one supreme Divine Nature.[42] In consequence, that which was offered in the eucharist became united to Christ's eternal gift presented to the Father and thereby assumed the redemptive authority of Christ himself.[43] The offering of the eucharist would have the same effect as Christ's offering: "Mercifully accept, O Lord, the offering which Thou hast willed to be

---

[39] *Tracts on the Mass* XXVII, p. 21.
[40] "Ceremonies Used in the Mass", *Ceremonies to be Used in the Church of England*, 8, Lambeth MS. 1107, in Cobb, *The Rationale of Ceremonial*, p. 24.
[41] Secret, Christmas Day at Midnight, *The Sarum Missal*, p. 20.
[42] Secret, 19th Sunday after Trinity, *Sarum Missal*, p. 248.
[43] Secret, Trinity Sunday, *Sarum Missal*, p. 221.

for a propitiation before Thee ... that salvation should be restored to us in the might of Thy loving-kindness."[44] Being adopted into the holy mysteries, the offering would be carried by the hands of God's holy angel on high before the sight of the divine majesty so that "as many as should partake at the altar and receive the most sacred Body and Blood of Thy Son may be fulfilled with all grace and heavenly benediction".[45] Being united to the Paschal mysteries the offering made at the eucharist would be profitable "for our health to all eternity".[46] With confidence it was possible to plead before God "to look down on the offerings we lay on Thy holy Altar; that they may be to the honour of Thy Name, by obtaining abundant pardon for us".[47] In consequence, forgiveness could be received and reconciliation granted: "Favourably behold, O Lord, Thy people and their offerings: that being reconciled by this oblation, Thou mayest bestow upon us pardon, and grant our petitions."[48] In perpetuating the one atoning sacrifice of Christ, the offering of the eucharist was "profitable to our salvation, both cleansing us from our sins and reconciling us to Thy loving-kindness".[49]

The offering of the eucharist thus became established as a continuation of the work of redemption, a decisive instrument of mediation between God and humanity by which the Church was able continually to participate in the salvific work of Christ and to become an active co-operator in the work of divine salvation. Its virtue could be applied to the welfare of the living and the dead in a variety of ways, such as deliverance from the ravages of the destroyer, guidance to the land of new promise[50] and the strengthening of human frailty.[51] Further, this

---

[44] Secret, 22nd Sunday after Trinity, *Sarum Missal*, p. 252.
[45] *Sarum Missal*, p. 312. Also "The Use of York", *The Lay Folks' Mass Book*, p. 109.
[46] Secret, Holy Saturday, *Sarum Missal*, p. 173.
[47] Secret, 13th Sunday after Trinity, *Sarum Missal*, p. 241.
[48] Offertory Sentence, 14th Sunday after Trinity, *Sarum Missal*, p. 242.
[49] Secret, 15th Sunday after Trinity, *Sarum Missal*, p. 243.
[50] Secret, Palm Sunday, *Sarum Missal*, p. 120.
[51] Secret, 11th Sunday after Trinity, *Sarum Missal*, p. 238.

work of redemption was not to be meted out sporadically but came into force every time the sacrifice was offered:

> Grant us, O Lord, we beseech Thee, frequently and worthily to approach these mysteries: seeing that as often as this commemorative sacrifice is celebrated, the work of our redemption is carried on.[52]

"As Christ satisfied fully, so by participation we also satisfy"

In his *A Declaration of such true articles as George Joye hath gone about to confute as false*, Stephen Gardiner, Bishop of Winchester, affirmed this eucharistic imperative.[53] As the offerings of humanity became united with the perfect offering of Christ they assumed the character of Christ's offering: "For so much as we do participate, we have also the thing in deed." Therefore, argued Gardiner, "as God is goodness itself, we by participation from him be good. As God is light itself, we by participation from him be light. As God is wisdom itself, we by participation from him, be wise." This participation in the divine nature neither infringed the integrity of God's being nor compromised the uniqueness of Christ's works. "As our goodness, light, and wisdom by participation is no addition or derogation to God's goodness, light or wisdom, in essence or being", Gardiner declared, "no more is our meriting, deserving, or satisfaction a derogation or supplement to the merits of Christ's passion, but only a due using of them, by the gift of his grace".[54] By this "due using" of the divine characteristics, God's glory and honour were neither lessened

---

[52] Offertory Sentence, 10th Sunday after Trinity, *Sarum Missal*, p. 237.

[53] Stephen Gardiner (*c.*1490–1555): Master of Trinity Hall, Cambridge 1525–49; Bishop of Winchester 1531–51 and 1553–55. Deprived of his bishopric in 1551, he was released on the arrival of Mary, restored to Winchester and appointed Lord High Chancellor.

[54] Stephen Gardiner, *A Declaration of such true articles as George Joye hath gone about to confute as false* (London, 1546), f. 13r.

nor diminished, but amongst us "more set forth and spread abroad".[55] Thus incorporated in Christ's offering, human offering elicited the same satisfaction from God as though it were Christ's: "As Christ merited and deserved thoroughly, we by participation in using his gifts, merit and deserve. And as Christ satisfied fully, so by participation we also satisfy."[56]

Offering physical as well as spiritual

Further, it was clear that Christ's offering of his life was by no means a spiritual offering only. Its presence in the form of his body and blood was testimony enough to that. Similarly, just as this offering was physical and tangible, the offering of worship was to include gifts that were physical and tangible. Gardiner made this clear:

> Jesu, that was in Bethlehem born
> And three kings came before you,
> They offered gold, incense, and myrrh,
> And you forsook none of them,
> But blessed them well all three
> Home again to their country,
> Right so our offerings that we offer,
> And our prayers that we proffer,
> Take Thou, Lord, to Thy loving,
> And be our help in all things.[57]

A Treatise of the Manner and Mede of the Mass included prayers to be said during the Offertory ceremonies which referred to the offering of physical gifts as an inherent part of the sacrifice offered to God:

---

[55] Gardiner, *A Declaration*, f. 59r.
[56] Gardiner, *A Declaration*, f. 13r.
[57] Gardiner, *A Declaration*, p. 22. Cf. Matthew 2:11.

God that was in Bethlehem born,
Three kings kneeled before you,
And their offering brought,
You took the offering of all three,
So receive this of me,
And forget me not,
That I may ever dwell with Thee.[58]

This inclusion of gifts or works within the offering of the eucharist was supported by Gardiner. That "true worshippers shall worship in spirit and in truth" (John 4:23) was never intended, he insisted, to exclude the offering to God of the works of the body, for the body and the spirit had been united at creation: "By the text of the gospel is not denied outward adoration with the body, which body is with the soul created of God, and shall be hereafter glorified with the soul."[59] In any case, that the offering of worship should be restricted to a spiritual offering was contradicted by Christ himself in the Garden of Gethsemane, where his prayer involved a physical aspect: "Christ's [be]haviour in the time of his praying teacheth the contrary, for he fell down on his face and prayed."[60]

With the offering of such "outward adoration", as Gardiner had it, embracing not just spiritual but physical gifts, and because that which was offered was united with the offering of Christ, these gifts became integral to the embodiment of the divine presence in worship, which in turn claimed an equivalence with the propitiatory status of Christ himself.

---

[58] *A Treatise of the Manner and Mede of the Mass*, in *The Lay Folks' Mass Book*, pp. 142–3.

[59] Stephen Gardiner, *A Detection of the Devils Sophistrie, wherewith he robbeth the unlearned people of the true byleef, in the most blessed Sacrament of the aulter* (London, 1546), f. 60v.

[60] Gardiner, *A Detection of the Devils Sophistrie*, f. 61r.

Music and the *mysterium tremendum*

Amongst the most prominent of these gifts to be incorporated into the offering of worship was music. Its significance turned principally on the presentation of the sound itself, there being no liturgical compulsion for the words which were sung to be heard distinctly or even understood. The experience of the divine was beyond the ability of words to describe or convey, so composers encountered no impediment to words being sublimated beneath a maze of extended and often elaborate counterpoint. The words of settings of the Mass, Magnificats, motets and hymns were routinely broken up, with a consequent loss of intelligibility. It was not uncommon for texts to be diluted as individual vowels were stretched over many notes.[61] Even the words sung to plainsong chants were regularly elongated to the point of obscurity. This characteristic of textually oblique lines was sometimes bound up with the use of geometric dimensions of ratio and proportion as compositional structures. The ratios of 1:2, 2:3 and 3:4, which correspond to the perfect intervals of octave, fifth and fourth, were regularly employed, particularly with the use of isorhythmic tenors; for example, John Dunstable's (*d*.1453) progressive diminution (3:2:1) of the three statements of an isorhythmic tenor in *Veni sancte Spiritus/Veni creator*.[62]

Many works were troped—extended with extra verses—and some motets incorporated textless tenors or carried the text only in the upper parts. Some of these melismatic elaborations were based on one or two words only, sometimes just a syllable. An additional challenge to discerning the text was that whole phrases in Mass settings were sometimes completely omitted. Parts of the *Credo* were routinely excluded and there are sections without text in the *cantus firmus* parts

---

[61] Taverner's *Missa Corona spinea* provides many examples of this technique.
[62] H. Benham, *Latin Church Music in England c. 1460–1575* (London: Barrie & Jenkins, 1977), pp. 44–7, gives an authoritative account of the occurrence of numerical equality with reference to works of Dunstable, Taverner, Fayrfax and, in the mid-sixteenth century, Tallis and Whyte. A structural analysis of a typical isorhythmic Mass is given in F. L. Harrison, *Music in Medieval Britain* (London: Routledge & Kegan Paul, 1958), p. 251.

in the *Gloria* and *Credo* of Ashewell's Mass *Jesu Christe*, and likewise John Browne's *O regina mundi clara* and *O Maria salvatoris mater*.[63] These omissions, together with the lack of particularity regarding textual underlay, encourage the speculation that the fitting of words to notes was occasionally left to the spontaneous inclination of the singers.

Whilst there is some evidence of words being presented in very nearly a syllabic fashion and of musical lines attempting to depict the sense of the text, this is uncommon. There are notable instances of such treatment. Throughout sections of a five-part *Salve regina* by John Hampton (*c*.1455–after 1520), the words are presented in a clear, almost syllabic fashion. The nine-part setting of *Salve regina* by Robert Wylkynson contains instances of syllabic treatment. In the opening sections of Taverner's *Gaude plurimum*, rising figures appear to portray the resurrection, ascension and assumption. There are also instances of varying combinations of voice parts and contrasting rhythmic patterns which invest individual words with dramatic colour. In his *Stabat mater*, John Browne has the word *crucifige* sung by the full choir before and after music for fewer voice parts, and in his *O Maria salvatoris mater* it is, rather similarly, the full choir which enters to "*En!*" ("Behold!"). In Tallis's *Gaude gloriosa*, all the voices are used for the words "*omnia servient*", and Browne's second *Salve Regina* has the words "*et pro nobis flagellato/Spinis puncto*" sung by the full choir. Examples of the colouring of individual words are "*citius*" ("quickly") with quicker notes than immediately before or after, in Fawkyner's *Gaude virgo salutata*; "*florida*" (the flowering or blossoming of Aaron's rod) in Banester's *O Maria et Elizabeth*; and "*stabas*" ("you were standing") with very long notes in the opening two voices, to suggest absence of movement, in Browne's six-part *Stabat virgo mater Christi*.[64]

Nevertheless, such examples are few and far between. Genuinely imaginative treatment of words is sparse. The instances that do exist testify more to spasmodic flights of fancy than to a serious concern to illuminate the text. For example, the rendering of "*serpentem*" in John Fawkyner's

---

[63] Identified by Benham, *Latin Church Music in England c. 1460–1575*, p. 52.

[64] These examples are identified by Timothy Symons in his textual commentary accompanying Stephen Darlington's recording, *More Divine than Human*.

Gaude rosa sine spina might, with undulating melodic movement, possibly suggests the writhing of a serpent, and the diminished fourth at "*hac lacrimarum valle*" in William Cornysh's *Salve regina* for five voices might well portray the vale of tears.

These associations, however, are tentative, bordering on illusory. The liturgical music of the period spanned by Henry VII and Henry VIII, acknowledged as the true zenith of Tudor polyphony, remained "sublimely indifferent to the audibility of the texts".[65] With consummate irony, the attitude of composers of this period to textual clarity has been described as "very casual".[66] These musical techniques were anathema to the reformers of the Edwardian and the early Elizabethan periods, as they set about such a reorientation of crucial elements of the doctrinal landscape as would have an immediately pulverizing effect on the purpose and practice of the offering of worship.

---

[65] Benham, *Latin Church Music in England c. 1460–1575*, p. 37.
[66] D. Stevens, *Tudor Church Music* (London: Faber & Faber, 1961), p. 50.

2

Worship—Remembering the Divine

The first Edwardian Act of Uniformity (2 & 3 Edward VI, cap.1) was passed by Parliament on 21 January 1549 and from "the feast of Pentecost next coming" (9 June) authorized the exclusive use of *The Booke of the Common Praier and Administracion of the Sacramentes, and other Rites and Ceremonies of the Churche after the Use of the Churche of England.* The second Edwardian Act of Uniformity (5 & 6 Edward VI, cap.1) passed through Parliament on 14 April 1552 and introduced the use of the second Book of Common Prayer with effect from the feast of All Saints (1 November) following.

Remembering Christ

The fundamental principle underpinning these Books of Common Prayer was that worship no longer embodied Christ; it remembered Christ. The gravity of sin prevented any offering of humanity being united with the offering of Christ, thereby eliminating worship as a means of integration with the divine. Further, worship was no longer able to assume any propitiatory value for, in respect of the irrevocability of human fallenness, the only offering that could plead authentically before God was Christ's alone. The best that could be attributed to worship was to remember Christ's saving actions, not to become identified with them. In consequence, the offering of worship became, not the means of becoming united with the divine and participating in Christ's continuing offering of salvation, but one of praise and thanksgiving in remembrance of that offering.

The Books of Common Prayer and human corruption

Human sin, depravity and corruption therefore became a dominant and persistent theme permeating the Books of Common Prayer, the accompanying Homilies and the writings of prominent theologians and divines. That humanity had erred and strayed from a state of grace was a prominent *leitmotif* of the new Prayer Books. People were lost sheep, selfish and constant breakers of God's law. They followed too much the devices and desires of their own hearts. "We have offended against thy holy laws", they confessed. "We have left undone those things which we ought to have done, and we have done those things which we ought not to have done, and there is no health in us."[1] Sin was rampant, incurring God's anger:

> ... we acknowledge and bewail our manifold sins and wickedness, which we from time to time most grievously have committed, by thought, word, and deed, against thy divine majesty: provoking most justly thy wrath and indignation against us.[2]

Humanity was inherently evil and could plead only that God would not "enter into judgement with thy servants, O Lord, for no flesh is righteous in thy sight".[3] The *Ministration of Baptism* included the debilitating reminder of the inherent evil of humanity's sinful conception and birth, and *Of Them that be Baptised in Private Houses* referred to the stain of Original Sin and its provocation of God's eternal wrath. The *Order for the Burial of the Dead* emphasized humanity's instability, transitoriness and inherent weakness:

> Man that is born of a woman hath but a short time to live, and is full of misery: he cometh up and is cut down like a flower; he fleeth as it were a shadow, and never continueth in one stay.

---

[1] Confession, Morning Prayer.
[2] Confession, The Communion.
[3] Sentence, Morning Prayer, 1552.

Evil had become so corrosive that "In the midst of life we be in death"; a devastation brought about by God's displeasure with human sin.

The Books of Homilies and human corruption

Embedded within the liturgy, the *Book of Homilies* cemented the theme of human corruption.[4] First published 31 July 1547, it contained a preface and 12 sermons. The 1549 Prayer Book directed that after the creed had ended, a sermon or homily, or "some portio[n] of one of the Homelyes, as thei shalbe herafter deuided", should be delivered.[5] Their public reading was enforced in various Visitation Articles and Injunctions. In his *Articles concerning Christian Religion*, Bishop John Hooper even demanded that they displace sermons on Sundays and holy days, and be read in order and in full.[6] Issued in 1553 and drafted predominantly by Thomas Cranmer (1489–1556), Archbishop of Canterbury from 1532, Article 34 of the *Forty-Two Articles* required that the Homilies be "receiued of all menne, and therefore are to be readde to the people diligentlie, distinctlie, and plainlie". Subsequently the *Thirty-Nine Articles* of 1563 commended the Second Book of Homilies together with the First and ordered them to

---

[4] G. E. Corrie (ed.), *Certain Sermons, or homilies, appointed by the King's Majesty, to be declared and read, by all Parsons, Vicars or Curates, every Sunday in their Churches, where they have Cure* (Cambridge: Parker Society, 1850).

[5] In order to facilitate their more practicable reading, in 1549 they had been subdivided into 32 parts.

[6] "Articles concerning Christian Religion", in "A true Coppey of Bishop Hooper's Visitation Booke made by him in Anno Dom. 1551, 1552", in Charles Nevinson (ed.), *Later Writings of Bishop Hooper, together with His Letters and Other Pieces* (Cambridge: Parker Society, 1852), p. 123. John Hooper (c.1485–1555): returned from Zurich 1549; chaplain to the Protector Somerset 1559; Bishop of Gloucester 1550; Bishop of Worcester 1552.

be read "in churches by the ministers diligently and distinctly that they may be understanded of the people".[7]

Entitled *A Sermon on the Misery of all Mankind, and of his Condemnation to Death Everlasting, by his own Sin*, the Second Homily invoked the Book of Genesis where it was stated that God had given a name to our great grandfather Adam and it was simply "dust". To the question "what we be, whereof we be, from whence we came, and whither we shall go" the answer was also unequivocal—the earth. We are dust, to dust we shall return, and we must "learn to know ourselves to be but ground, earth and ashes and that to earth and ashes we shall return". Man's correct name and title was therefore to be "earth".[8] Such a tarnished origin rendered humanity weak, ineffectual and transitory. Simply by being born, humanity was rendered unclean and in consequence was miserable, universally given to sin and totally estranged from God. The result of such a diseased seed, humanity was so infected with sin that his entire being, his nature and works were inherently evil and so deeply ingrained that God was understood to have regretted ever creating mankind, which had become damnable with "no hope of salvation".[9] The degeneration into vileness and depravity was so catastrophic that human life had become death.[10]

Theological scholarship and human corruption

This theme of corruption expressed so vividly in the Homilies was taken up individually by various theologians and divines, both before and after the time many of them spent in exile during the Marian years.

In 1550, John Hooper produced *A briefe and clear confession of the Christian faith, according to the order of the Creede of the Apostles*, the Ninth Article of which confronted the reader with the devastating

---

[7] E. C. S. Gibson (ed.), *The Thirty-Nine Articles of the Church of England* (London: Methuen, 1910), Article 35, p. 722.
[8] Gibson, *The Thirty-Nine Articles*, pp. 11–12.
[9] Gibson, *The Thirty-Nine Articles*, p. 18.
[10] Gibson, *The Thirty-Nine Articles*, p. 16.

assertion that "all men after their own nature are corrupt, unjust, liars, ignorant, unkind, and imperfect in all things, and have no power of their own nature to do, think, speak, or will anything that may please God". This corruption of nature, added Hooper in his Tenth Article, was otherwise called Original Sin and was the fountain and root of all other sins.[11]

Thomas Becon had no compunction in declaring everyone by nature to be sinners and children of wrath. He characterized human imperfection with chilling ferocity: humanity had become repulsive and had entirely forfeited the benefits and pleasures once enjoyed by familial right as a child of God.[12] John Jewel regarded every person as having been born in sin and as now living in sin with unclean hearts. Even the most seemingly righteous person was an unprofitable servant: "There is no one mortal creature which can be justified by his des[s]erts in God's sight."[13]

A further calamity was that this evil was not a passing depression but a deeply ingrained stigma that had bred and settled until it had become completely identifiable with the very essence of being. Born and begotten in sin, humanity had become utterly warped. "By nature we are the children of wrath," wrote Edwin Sandys. "Corruption is bred and settled within our bones; ... we are both born and begotten in it; that with it all the powers and faculties of our nature are infected ... Such corruption yet cleaveth fast unto our souls," and with ominous certitude Jewel declared that "there it sticketh as long as life doth endure,

---

[11] "A briefe and clear confession of the Christian faith, according to the order of the Creede of the Apostles", in *Later Writings of Bishop Hooper*, p. 25.

[12] John Ayre (ed.), *The Works of Thomas Becon*, Vol. III (Cambridge, 1842–4), pp. 326–7. Becon (c.1513–67) was expelled from St Stephen's Walbrook on the accession of Mary 1553, fled to Strassburg 1554, Frankfurt 1555, Canon of Canterbury Cathedral 1559.

[13] John Ayre (ed.), *The Works of John Jewel, Bishop of Salisbury*, Vol. III (Cambridge: Parker Society, 1845–50), p. 578. Jewel (1522–71) returned from Frankfurt, Strassburg and Zurich 1559, then Bishop of Salisbury 1560.

so irksome and so grievous, that it forceth the most upright and perfect to cry, Miserable man, who shall deliver me?"[14] The abysmal condition of human nature was held responsible for further calamity. So completely had humanity become the prisoner of perversion, they could no longer distinguish the ways of God from the ways of evil. Corruption had so distorted human judgement that nothing remotely spiritual or heavenly could ever be ventured without succumbing to fleshly desires. Edmund Grindal concluded that when we consider and examine our whole life, "we find nothing in ourselves that deserveth any other thing but eternal damnation".[15]

There being no escape from this dread existence, the challenge was how to react to it. According to Alexander Nowell, the only viable option was to treat life as "a shadow, passing and fleeing away, as a fading flower, as a bubble rising on the water", and to assume a contempt of this wretched existence "with all her trifling and uncertain joys, and all manifold and horrible evils".[16] Thus devoid of any good whatsoever, it stood to reason that humanity was powerless to effect its own cleansing. Branded as a child of God's wrath, born not for glory but for shame and alienation, there was no possibility of doing anything which could allay God's anger or effect restoration to God's favour.[17]

---

[14] John Ayre (ed.), *The Sermons of Edwin Sandys, D.D.* (Cambridge: Parker Society, 1842), p. 21. Edwin Sandys (1516–88): Master of Catharine Hall Cambridge 1547; prebendary of Peterborough 1549; Vice-Chancellor of Cambridge University 1553; exiled in Antwerp, Augsburg, Strassburg and Zurich; Bishop of Winchester 1559–70; Bishop of London 1570–5; Archbishop of York 1575–88.

[15] W. Nicholson (ed.), *The Remains of Edmund Grindal* (Cambridge: Parker Society, 1843), p. 87. Grindal (1519–83): exiled in Frankfurt; Bishop of London 1559; Archbishop of York 1570; Archbishop of Canterbury 1575.

[16] *An Homily concerning the Justice of God*, in W. Nicholson (ed.), *The Remains of Edmund Grindal* (Cambridge: Parker Society, 1843), p. 109. Alexander Nowell (1507–1602), exiled in Frankfurt, Dean of St Paul's Cathedral 1560–1602.

[17] *Certain Sermons or Homilies*, p. 16.

Humanity incapable of effective offering

This desolate understanding of human nature became the bedrock of reformed theology. Its immediate effect was to negate any possibility of worship embodying the presence of Christ by becoming united with Christ's offering and thus constituting an acceptable offering to God. Barren and despoiled, as the Second Homily had it, humanity could offer nothing of any good: "We be of ourselves of such earth, as can bring forth but weeds, nettles, brambles, briars, cockle, and darnel."[18] In fact, if these weeds were to be offered to God, then this act would constitute a foolish and arrogant conceit, for not even the most highly regarded of human offerings could be so free from imperfection as to contribute in the slightest to the achieving of reconciliation.

Regrettably such conceits had already been committed. Failing to appreciate humanity's rightful status, calling and title, which was that of a child of the divine wrath, the Pharisees had offered their own counterfeit holiness with the intention of pleasing God, hoping thereby to justify themselves for their sin. That these offerings may have emanated from those claiming to be just, learned, wise, perfect and holy constituted no commendation in the eyes of God. Such conceits served only as warnings against further hypocrisy and vain-glory.[19] This was made abundantly clear in the Third Homily, *A Sermon of the salvation of all mankind, by only Christ our Saviour, from sinne and death everlasting*, thought to have been written by Cranmer himself.[20] Merely to contemplate the offering of these human works as an attempt to please God constituted "the greatest arrogancy and presumption of man that antichrist could set up against God, to affirm that a man by his own works take away and purge his sins, and so justify himself".[21]

---

[18] *Certain Sermons or Homilies*, p. 15.

[19] *Certain Sermons or Homilies*, pp. 15, 18.

[20] *Certain Sermons or Homilies*, p. xi. Stephen Gardiner's letters to the Lord Protector, the Duke of Somerset, identify Cranmer as the author. To Cranmer has also been attributed, but without evidence other than stylistic similarity, the first, fourth and fifth homilies.

[21] *Certain Sermons or Homilies*, p. 26.

John Hooper went further. He declared that all human works, merits, deservings, doings and obedience were so corrupted as to be of no validity, worthiness or merit before God even though they be done by the Spirit of God, in the grace of God. Although empowered by the Holy Spirit they remained as unworthy as ever.[22] That not even the Holy Spirit was deemed capable of rehabilitating human works was chilling testimony to the reformers' intransigence concerning the irreversible fall of mankind. All good works done by man in their greatest perfection remain imperfect, stipulated Hooper, for they forever lack any grace to pardon their imperfection.[23] Human works were therefore deemed to be completely invalid as a means of reconciliation with God. Article 10, *Of Free Will*, confirmed this stark reality. "The condition of man after the fall of Adam", it declared, is such

> that he cannot turn and prepare himself by his own natural strength and good works, to faith and calling upon God: Wherefore we have no power to do good works pleasant and acceptable to God.[24]

Christ's offering unique

This deeply ingrained fixation was the necessary pre-condition for a single-minded affirmation of Christ's offering being the only offering acceptable for the achieving of reconciliation. *The Order for the Administration of the Lord's Supper, or Holy Communion*, at what is known as the Comfortable Words, declared that: "If any man sin, we have an advocate with the Father, Jesus Christ the righteous, and he is the propitiation for our sins." This unique sufficiency of Christ's sacrifice was stated unequivocally at the outset of the prayer before the reception of communion:

---

[22] *Certain Sermons or Homilies*, p. 25.
[23] *A Godly Confession and protestacion of the christian faith* (London, 1550), in *Later Writings of Bishop Hooper*, p. 73.
[24] *Later Writings of Bishop Hooper*, p. 378.

> Almighty God our heavenly Father, which of thy tender mercy didst give thine only Son Jesus Christ to suffer death upon the cross for our redemption, who made there (by his one oblation of himself once offered) a full, perfect and sufficient sacrifice, oblation, and satisfaction for the sins of the whole world.

It was Christ's offering alone, without any hint of human works being united with that perfect offering, which constituted any hope of reconciliation with God. The only offering with any propitiatory authority was that of Christ's and no works of any kind could be tolerated. Only the righteousness of Christ could meet the price set by God to be paid for the remission of sin. This unique status of Christ's sacrifice was taken up with alacrity by John Jewel:

> We say also "that he by the same one only sacrifice which he once offered upon the cross, hath brought to effect and fulfilled all things, and that for that cause he said, when he gave up the ghost, 'It is finished;' as though he would signify that the price and ransom was now full paid for the sin of mankind."[25]

Should there be any who imagined this sacrifice to be insufficient and needful of other offerings to be joined to that of Christ's, Jewel challenged them to find a superior. Contentment with Christ's sacrifice was such that we "look for none other". So, he concluded, "we have no meed [reward] at all by our own works and deeds but appoint all the means of our salvation to be in Christ alone".[26] Only through the mediation of Jesus Christ, insisted Edwin Sandys, are we "ransomed out of the hands of our enemies, pulled out of the jaws of Satan, freed from the servitude of anti-christ, of ignorance, and of sin". Christ alone had defeated the power

---

[25] John Jewel, "An Answer to a Certain Book lately set forth by M. Harding, and Entituled, A Confutation of the Apology of the Church of England" (referred to as *The Defence of the Apology*), Chapter Xix, Division 1, in John Ayre (ed.), *The Works of John Jewel* (Cambridge: Parker Society, 1845–50), p. 579.

[26] Jewel, "An Answer to a Certain Book lately set forth by M. Harding", Chapter xx, Division 1, p. 582.

of sin which held humanity captive and so Christ's sacrifice alone was the means of achieving human redemption.[27] To have believed the work of sinful man could ever have been considered a propitiatory, satisfactory, expiatory sacrifice for the sin of so many and "of greater strength and virtue than the sweet-smelling sacrifice of the high bishop Christ Jesu" was for Thomas Becon a foolish paradise into which the gullible had been led through the crafty juggling of spiritual sorcerers.[28] For the extinguishing of all doubt in the Diocese of Gloucester, John Hooper specified in Article 15 of his *Articles Concerning Christian Religion* that

> the oblation of Christ once made on the cross is a full satisfaction for all manner of sins, be they original, actual, present, past, or to come, to all men believing in the same sacrifice; and that there is no other means, propitiation, redemption, satisfaction, or sacrifice for sin.[29]

There was to be no room for doubt or dissension. Hooper made the Article binding on all deans, parsons, prebends, vicars, curates "and other ecclesiastical ministers". Any other interpretation "but the only death of Christ" was for Hooper an ungodly doctrine,[30] and in Article 27 of his *Brief and Clear Confession* he established that Christ's offering "wholly performed the work of our salvation, and hath abolished and made an end of all other sacrifices".[31] Hope for the future rested in abandoning all illusions of self-worth and placing one's trust entirely in the offering of Jesus Christ.

---

[27] *The Sermons of Edwin Sandys*, p. 179.

[28] *Later Writings of Bishop Hooper*, I, p. 414.

[29] "Articles concerning Christian Religion", in "A true Coppey of Bishop Hooper's Visitation Booke made by him in Anno Dom. 1551, 1552," in *Later Writings of Bishop Hooper*, p. 123.

[30] John Hooper, "An Oversight and Deliberation upon the Holy Prophet Jonas", in Samuel Carr (ed.), *Early Writings of John Hooper, D.D.* (Cambridge: The Parker Society, 1843), p. 488.

[31] *Later Writings of Bishop Hooper*, p. 32.

Propitiatory offering rejected

With the inadequacy of any human offering acknowledged and the sole efficacy of Christ's sacrifice established, any idea of the offering of worship having a propitiatory status was untenable. In his fifth book of *A defence of the true and catholike doctrine of the Sacrament*, entitled *Of the Oblation and Sacrifice of our Saviour Christe*, Thomas Cranmer made this abundantly clear. "One kind of sacrifice there is", he wrote, "which is called a Propitiatory or merciful sacrifice," and this was a sacrifice which "pacifieth God's wrath and indignation, and obtaineth mercy and forgiveness for all our sins, and is the ransom for our redemption from everlasting damnation".[32] However, noted Cranmer, this was a sacrifice impossible for humanity to offer. Christ's offering was the only sacrifice whereby sins could be pardoned. As a result, the offering of a sacrifice whereby the priests make their Mass a sacrifice propitiatory was the greatest blasphemy and injury that could be made against Christ.[33] Under pretence of holiness, Cranmer noted, "the papistical priests have taken more upon them to be Christ's successors, and to make such an oblation and sacrifice as never creature made but Christ alone".[34] If the death of Christ be "the oblation, sacrifice and price wherefore our sins be pardoned, then the act or ministration of the priest cannot have the same office". To give that office or dignity to a priest Cranmer found to be nothing less than an abominable blasphemy.[35]

Further, because a propitiatory sacrifice could be offered only by Christ, it could only be offered once, for if Christ had made any oblation for sin more than once, he should have died more than once, which he did not. Since there was no oblation for sin but only his death and since

---

[32] John E. Cox (ed.), *Writings and Disputations of Thomas Cranmer* I (Cambridge: Cambridge University Press, 1844), p. 345. *A defence of the true and catholike doctrine of the sacrament of the body and bloud of our saviour Christ, with a confutation of sundry errors concerning the same, grounded and stablished upon Goddes holy woorde* ... (London, 1550), f. 106v.

[33] *Writings and Disputations of Thomas Cranmer* I, p. 345. *A defence*, f. 106v.

[34] *Writings and Disputations of Thomas Cranmer* I, p. 345.

[35] *Writings and Disputations of Thomas Cranmer* I, p. 347.

his death could not be repeated, the Mass which repeated his death was illegitimate.[36] The propitiatory sacrifice made by the priest in the Mass is "a great abomination before God", set up by antichrist and to be abhorred by all who truly profess Christ.[37]

Article 30 of the Forty-Two Articles of 1553—*Of the perfect oblation of Christ made upon the cross*—roundly condemned as forged fables and dangerous deceits the sacrifices of Masses in which the priest offers Christ for the quick and the dead for remission of pain or sin.[38] If the death of Christ be of full force, argued Thomas Becon, and sufficiently perfect as to take away the sins of the whole world, "what need we the missal sacrifice, lately brought in by the devil and antichrist?"[39] John Jewel kept up the attack. "Where they say, and sometimes do persuade fools," he railed,

> that they are able by their masses to distribute and apply unto men's commodity all the merits of Christ's death ... this is a mockery, an heathenish fancy, and a very toy. For it is our faith that applieth the death and cross of Christ to our benefit, and not the act of the massing priest.[40]

The offering by the priest of the daily sacrifice was a pitiful defacing of the death and passion of Christ, declared Thomas Cooper, for it usurped Christ's role as the one and only means of reconciliation between God and his people. Therefore "when your priests take upon them his office to offer sacrifice propitiatory, they go beyond their commission, and

---

[36] *Writings and Disputations of Thomas Cranmer* I, p. 346.
[37] *Writings and Disputations of Thomas Cranmer* I, p. 355.
[38] Gibson, *The Thirty-Nine Articles*, p. 84. This Article held its place as Article 31 of the Thirty-Nine Articles of 1563—*Of the one oblation of Christ finished upon the cross*—with the substitution of "guilt" for "sin". Gibson, *The Thirty-Nine Articles*, p. 687.
[39] *Works of John Jewel* II, p. 247.
[40] Jewel, *Apologia* II.

take more upon them than their duty, not without just reprehension of arrogancy and presumption".[41]

Non-propitiatory offering

The devastation of human sin, the consequent inability of a corrupted humanity to offer anything acceptable to God, the acknowledgement of the pre-eminence of Christ's offering and the subsequent denigration of any offering of works being united with the propitiatory offering of Christ set the scene for a total reappraisal of what could be offered in worship. Accordingly, Thomas Cranmer presented an alternative, non-propitiatory interpretation of sacrifice. It was a sacrifice which could not of itself achieve any reconciliation between the divine and human. It was styled a sacrifice of praise and thanksgiving and was to be offered solely in recognition of the offering already accomplished by Christ. "Another kind of sacrifice there is", he declared, "which doth not reconcile us to God, but is made of them that be reconciled by Christ, to testify our duties unto God, and to shew ourselves thankful unto him".[42] Sacrifices of this sort "be not called propitiatory, but sacrifices of justice, of laud, praise and thanksgiving".

Cranmer argued that when the early Fathers referred to the offering of the Mass or the supper of the Lord as a sacrifice, they were not ascribing to it any propitiatory quality but purely that of a remembrance of Christ's sacrifice. Therefore, when the Fathers called the Mass or supper of the Lord a sacrifice, they meant that

> it was a sacrifice of laud and thanksgiving (and so as well the people as the priest do sacrifice,) or else that it was a remembrance of the very true sacrifice propitiatory of Christ; but they meant

---

[41] Thomas Cooper, *An answere in defence of the truth. Against the Apologie of Private Masse* (London, 1562), p. 88. Thomas Cooper (c.1517–94): Dean of Christ Church Oxford 1567–69; Dean of Gloucester 1569–71; Bishop of Lincoln 1571–84; Bishop of Winchester 1584–94.

[42] *An answere in defence of the truth*, p. 346. *A defence*, f. 107v.

in no wise that it is a very true sacrifice for sin, and applicable by the priest to the quick and dead.[43]

This reconstituted interpretation of sacrifice was made clear in the prayer after communion in the reformed service books: "O Lord and heavenly Father, we thy humble servants entirely desire thy fatherly goodness, mercifully to accept this our Sacrifice of praise and thanksgiving." According to John Jewel it was our duty to "offer up unto God thanks and praises for that great sacrifice once made upon the cross", which oblation alone had succeeded in "making possible the salvation of us all". In response, we are obliged "to offer continually unto God a remembrance instead of a sacrifice".[44]

Moreover, it was only the understanding of sacrifice as one of praise and thanksgiving which could accommodate the fundamental tenet of reformed theology: human weakness and corruption. "What is it to offer the sacrifice of praise?" asked Becon. It is "to confess and unfeignedly to grant that whatsoever is naught cometh of ourselves", and again:

> that all that ever good is, cometh of God only, as he saith by the prophet: "O Israel, thy destruction cometh of thyself, but thy health and salvation cometh only of me."[45]

God could only be delighted with this reformed interpretation of sacrifice, Becon added, because it affirmed humanity's inability to offer anything that would achieve salvation. It was an oblation that gave a goodly odour towards God and made God "well pleased with him that doth offer it, inasmuch as by the oblation hereof he confesseth himself to be able to do nothing".[46] Paraphrasing from Eusebius, Thomas Cooper expressed his pleasure that now "we offer to the most high God a sacrifice of praise:

---

[43] *Writings and Disputations of Thomas Cranmer* I, p. 355. *A defence*, f. 115v.
[44] *The Works of John Jewel* II, p. 716.
[45] *Works of Thomas Becon* I, pp. 298–9. Cf. Hosea 13:9: "O Israel, thou hast destroyed thyself; but in me is thine help."
[46] *Works of Thomas Becon* I, p. 299.

we offer a full, sweet, and holy sacrifice, after a new sort, according to the New Testament".[47]

The reformers therefore condemned the worship of the mediaeval liturgy as nothing but an upstart, illegitimate offering which had unlawfully perverted the integrity of the one true sacrifice of Jesus Christ. The correct interpretation of Christ's offering to the Father, Cooper declared, is made clear by Christ himself, who said: "Take, eat, do this in remembrance of me." He did not say "give, offer, and sacrifice for your sins".[48] Therefore the Mass could not justly be called the Lord's Supper for "the Lord's supper ... is a gift of God to us, which we must receive with thanksgiving". Rightly considered, Cooper concluded, the Lord's Supper is "a remembrance of one perfect sacrifice, whereby we were once sufficiently purged from sin, and continually are revived by the same". In dire contrast, the mediaeval sacrifice, which consisted of a daily offering for our sins, presumed that Christ's original sacrifice had not been perfectly done.[49] The sacrifice that we celebrate, insisted Cooper, is "the remembrance of his death and passion; which was the only true and perfect sacrifice".[50] For the reformers, the difference underlying the purpose of worship was stark: the one sought to reiterate a sacrifice; the other to remember a sacrifice.[51]

Offering to be spiritual

The new sacrifice of praise and thanksgiving had an important characteristic fundamental to the subsequent form of worship. Given the unacceptability of human works it was crucial that this offering be entirely spiritual, not physical. Unlike the bloody sacrifices of the

---

[47] *An answere in defence of the truth*, p. 92. Eusebius, *The Proof of the Gospel being the Demonstratio Evangelica of Eusebius of Caesarea*, tr. W. J. Ferrar (London: SPCK, 1929), Vol. I, Chapter 10, p. 62.

[48] *An answere in defence of the truth*, p. 88.

[49] *An answere in defence of the truth*, p. 98.

[50] *An answere in defence of the truth*, p. 93.

[51] *An answere in defence of the truth*, p. 99.

Old Testament, this sacrifice was unbloody and being unbloody it was therefore spiritual.[52] The "bloody" sacrifice had been abolished; it was now to be the sacrifice of the soul and the spirit which was to be offered to God. Jewel quoted Chrysostom, who held that what we offer is

> not now the fat or blood of beasts. All these things are abolished. And instead thereof there is brought in a reasonable or spiritual duty. But what is this duty that we call reasonable or spiritual? That it is that is offered by the soul and spirit.[53]

The reformers pressed this point consistently. The sacrifice of praise and thanksgiving was a purely spiritual offering: "We offer and present unto thee, O Lord, ourselves, our souls and bodies to be a reasonable [spiritual], holy, and lively Sacrifice unto thee."[54] This offering now being refashioned as a spiritual offering, the invisible prayer of the heart, meant that nothing could be offered to God of a material nature. As James Calfhill had it, "To compare a gift of God, which is in the mind, to the work of man, made with the hand, is *canibus catulos conjungere, matribus haedos*: to join the whelps and hounds, the kids and goats together."[55] Jewel insisted that "we make our sacrifices, not by smoke, smell, and blood, but by the grace of

---

[52] *Works of John Jewel* II, p. 735.

[53] *Works of John Jewel* II, p. 735. *Works of John Chrysostom* (London, 1718–38), Vol. XII, p. 115. Also, *The Homilies of St. John Chrysostom, Archbishop of Constantinople, on the Epistle of S. Paul the Apostle to the Hebrews*, in *A Select Library of the Nicene and Post-Nicene Fathers of the Christian Church*, ed. Philip Schaff (New York: The Christian Literature Company, 1890), p. 420. "No longer sheep and oxen, no longer blood and fat. All these things have been done away; and there has been brought in in their stead 'the reasonable service.' (Rom.xii.1.) But what is 'the reasonable service?' The [offerings made] through the soul; those made through the spirit."

[54] John Jewel subsequently treated "reasonable" as "spiritual", *Works of John Jewel* II, p. 734, but Jeremy Taylor as "according to right reason".

[55] James Calfhill, "An Answer to John Martiall's Treatise of the Cross", The First Article (London, 1565), p. 86. James Calfhill (*c*.1530–70): Canon of Christ Church Oxford 1560; Rector of St Andrew Wardrobe London 1562; Lady

the Holy Spirit".[56] Therefore works of art whose beauty had once been considered pleasing to God had now to be eliminated. As Jewel noted, since the true sacrifice to be offered is spiritual and grows only from the mind, none of the arts once offered in the hope of securing God's favour could be permitted. Assuming to himself the words of Christ, Calfhill maintained that "by your Imagery you have excluded My word: by your Roods, Crosses, and Crucifixes... utterly defaced the glory of My death".[57] Edwin Sandys robustly condemned the offerings made by Saul, who believed that the beauty of his works would be pleasing to God. He was utterly deluded, said Sandys. In fact, the effect of his sacrifice was the opposite to that which was intended: "Saul thought that sacrifice had been service, but God had liked better of his obedience." Uzza had supposed he had done God "very good service in holding up the ark which was like to fall: but God taught him that it was far otherwise". He struck him dead.[58] Demanding only inward holiness, the sacrifice previously offered by the scribes and Pharisees, which had included arts of great beauty, was an illegitimate sacrifice, for nowhere had God prescribed this kind of worship.[59] Consequently, the offering of worship was no longer to include any works as would formerly have contributed to any offering of a sacrifice of propitiation. To the contrary, God would respond positively, not to any such works, but to the very opposite: the acknowledgement of humanity's inability to create any works of beauty whatsoever. In any case, that works of beauty could be representative of humanity was logically impossible, claimed Sandys. He argued that it was God, not man, who in the first place was the creator of beauty. In terms of offering something representative of humanity, anything of beauty was therefore impossible since anything of beauty could only have been created by God and was not mankind's to give. It was only by denying that human works could give pleasure to God that God could

---

Margaret Professor of Divinity Oxford 1564; Archdeacon of Colchester 1565; Bishop-designate of Worcester 1570.

[56] *Works of John Jewel* II, p. 734.
[57] Calfhill, "An Answer to John Martiall's Treatise of the Cross", pp. 124–5.
[58] Cf. 2 Samuel 6:3–8; 1 Chronicles 13:7–11.
[59] *Sermons of Edwin Sandys*, p. 189.

be properly perceived to be the sole source of beauty, magnificence and glory. Striving for beauty in worship therefore became irrelevant. More than irrelevant, such striving was an impediment to the true worshipping of God. Regardless of how splendid such an offering may have appeared and how much skill that offering may have represented, it was invalid. God is not delighted in outward shows, proclaimed Sandys, nor "in gorgeous pomps, in beautiful buildings, in painted sepulchres . . . ".[60] Such art was the work of the harlot and the Pharisee. "It is the inward beauty of the king's daughter and not the outward beauty of the harlot of Babylon wherewith God is pleased", continued Sandys. "It is the contrite heart of the prostrate publican, and not the proud ostentation of the Pharisee, wherein he doth delight."[61] All such pretended works of beauty were nothing but "external shews". They were but as "the beauty of a painted wall, not only not acceptable, but even loathsome unto God".[62] They were futile attempts at self-adornment, being "outwardly arrayed in purple and scarlet, gilded with gold, precious stones, and pearl, like the strumpet that sitteth upon many waters".[63]

Works of beauty condemned

Equally despicable were efforts to include the so-called "amorous arts" in worship as they obscured the proper declaration of the faith. "The thing which we must learn", said Sandys, "is the word of God; not the decrees and decretals of popes, not the quiddities of too curious schoolmen, not lying legends, not amorous arts . . . ".[64] Far from performing "hearty and sincere service", Sandys believed that those who offered works of beauty as a sacrifice to God were indulging in hypocritical and painted shows of religion because their offering consisted not of sincerity and truth but the external beauty of their material temple. He was appalled

---

[60] *Sermons of Edwin Sandys*, p. 347.
[61] *Sermons of Edwin Sandys*, pp. 347–8.
[62] *Sermons of Edwin Sandys*, p. 348.
[63] *Sermons of Edwin Sandys*, p. 29.
[64] *Sermons of Edwin Sandys*, p. 116.

that they "wondered at the stones and goodly buildings, at the gorgeous furniture and precious gifts, wherewith [the temple] was both outwardly and inwardly adorned and enriched".[65]

Alexander Nowell regarded such amorous arts with equal disfavour and had only harsh words for those that "set all our delight in gathering together and heaping of worldly muck".[66] Calfhill's solution was brutal: "Every image, made by painter's wicked art of any kind of matter, is to be removed forth of the church of Christians, as that which is strange and abominable."[67] The flesh, noted Calfhill, "hath made us prone ... to superstition and wicked worshippings".[68] The house of God is not the material church of lime and stone, he stressed, "but the congregation of faithful people, in whose hearts he dwelleth: nor the beauty hereof consisteth in outward garnishing, but spiritual values; not in Imagery, but in piety".[69] The face of this Church is not corporal, he added, but spiritual: "Not by proportion of Imagery, but by properties of virtue to be discerned."[70] God so disliked the superstitious ceremonies of the temple that he would not allow the stones of it to stand. "Better a naked service, with the word", he urged, "than a gorgeous solemnity, not commanded by the word".[71]

Such pleasures and delights were reviled by John Jewel as "orient colours", doing nothing but obscuring the true principles of faith instituted by Christ himself. Many playthings had illegitimately become

---

[65] *Sermons of Edwin Sandys*, p. 347.

[66] *An Homily Concerning the Justice of God*, in *The Remains of Edmund Grindal*, p. 100.

[67] James Calfhill, The Preface to "An Answer to John Martiall's Treatise of the Cross", Third Article (London, 1565), p. 151.

[68] Calfhill, The Preface to "An Answer to John Martiall's Treatise of the Cross", p. 23.

[69] Calfhill, The Preface to "An Answer to John Martiall's Treatise of the Cross", p. 163.

[70] Calfhill, The Preface to "An Answer to John Martiall's Treatise of the Cross", Third Article, pp. 165–6.

[71] Calfhill, The Preface to "An Answer to John Martiall's Treatise of the Cross", Second Article, pp. 123–4.

a part of worship: "Salt, water, oil-boxes, spittle, palms, bulls, jubilees, pardons, crosses, censings, and an endless rabble of ceremonies, and ... pretty games to make sport withal." In these things, he complained, "have they set all their religion, teaching the people that by these God may be duly pacified, spirits be driven away, and men's consciences well quieted".[72] "How gilded we images," railed Becon, "painted their tabernacles, and set up candles before them, thinking in so doing to do a more meritorious deed than if we had bestowed our goods in helping the poor members of Christ".[73]

Becon unleashed a waspish attack upon the "popish prattling of monstrous monks, and the mumbling masses of those lazy soul-carriers". He bemoaned the trust previously placed in "masking masses of the momish [foolish] mass-mongers, believing to have as plenteous remission of all our sins in them, as in the precious death of our Lord and Saviour Jesu Christ".[74] In a more restrained yet no less potent style, John Merbecke asserted that works had no place in the sacrifice of propitiation, "which doth only pertain to our Saviour Jesus Christ, whereof all the Levitical sacrifices were but shadows and signs".[75] Offer the sacrifice of righteousness, he declared, "that is, serve God purely, and not with outward ceremonies".[76]

According to Cooper, the problem was that the old Church "toward the end did forsake the law and right use of God's ceremonies, and being divided in sundry sects, devised new worshippings according to their own phantasies".[77] Indeed, any offering of inventions and fantasies negated the true means of redemption, observed Sandys, for they had so "filled the mass, [and] were so many and so gross, that they quite covered and shadowed the death of Christ and the holy mysteries of

---

[72] John Jewel, *Apologia* V, in *Works of John Jewel* III, p. 89.
[73] "The Jewel of Joy", in John Ayre (ed.), *The Catechism of Thomas Becon, S.T.P.* (Cambridge: Parker Society, 1844), p. 413.
[74] *Works of Thomas Becon* I, p. 414.
[75] John Merbecke, *A Book of Notes and Common Places* (London, 1581), p. 940.
[76] *A Book of Notes and Common Places*, p. 943.
[77] *An answere in defence of the truth*, p. 181.

our salvation".[78] Throughout scripture, he observed, God had given no indication of pleasure derived from any human works—a sure sign that God found them all unpleasurable, and common sense decreed that God would never reward that which he found unpleasurable. Worship was therefore meaningless whilst it preferred human offerings to the offering of Jesus Christ.[79] "Will ye invent new things of your own fantasy", asked Becon, "and offer them to God of a good intent, that by this means he may be the more merciful to you?" Such an action was deceitful and vain, "for if things prescribed and commanded of God himself cannot obtain for you remission of your sins, what shall then your dreams, your fantasies, your inventions, your good intents, your godly zeals, do in this behalf?"[80]

Remembrance to be spiritual

That which could be offered to God was a dilemma which confronted King David, noted Becon: "What will he give God? What amends will he make to God? In what things will he shew himself thankful again unto the Lord?"[81]

David considered offering works of beauty:

> Will he give him mountains of gold? Will he bring him heaps of precious stones? Will he fetch him frankincense, and other sweet savours out of Araby? Will he offer unto him fat oxen, lusty heifers, well-liking sheep?

Unsurprisingly, the answer was no. Such gifts were not to be offered. God had no need of them and had already indicated his displeasure with them. In any case, whatever gifts humanity was capable of had been bestowed by God and were not to be offered back, for they were inadequate for this purpose anyway. God had no need of David's offering for God had heaven

---

[78] *Sermons of Edwin Sandys*, p. 24.
[79] *Sermons of Edwin Sandys*, p. 20.
[80] *Works of Thomas Becon* I, p. 49.
[81] *Works of Thomas Becon* I, p. 298.

and earth at his pleasure and all that is contained in them." Without works, "What will he give God then?"

The answer for Becon was predictable: "Verily, the sacrifice of praise and of thanksgiving." This was the sacrifice with which God was well pleased. It is this oblation, and none other, that gives "so goodly an odour before God".[82] Calfhill had nothing but contempt for those who had been obsessed with traditions, ceremonies and outward solemnities to the neglect of the inward true service of God. As a result, these superfluities, the long train of ceremonies, must be cut off, for they hindered the course of godliness. Jewel agreed. All those works of beauty which had formed such an integral part of the mediaeval liturgy had to be suppressed: "Everything that may delight or move the mind is not therefore meet for the church of God."[83]

Worship conceived as an offering which could be united to the perfect offering of Christ and so be received with satisfaction by God, move God to forgiveness and achieve reconciliation, was comprehensively dismissed and replaced by a spiritual remembrance of the perfect offering of Jesus Christ. Christ's offering could not be replicated; it could only be remembered. Worship was no longer to embody the presence of God. It was unable to become incorporate in the divine and engage with the mystery of God, thereby relinquishing the impetus to seek something beyond itself. Worship became a simple act of remembrance whose duty was to pay respects to God.

Here was a revolutionary recasting of the offering of worship which succinctly expressed a key Reformation principle—the need never to confuse heaven and earth. In such a religion of the spirit, there was no place for human actions as causes in the realm of grace.

---

[82] *Works of Thomas Becon* I, p. 299.
[83] *Works of John Jewel* II, p. 662.

3

Worship—Edification in Faith

As well as separating itself completely from any sense of unity with Christ's offering, the newly minted definition of the offering of worship as one of praise and thanksgiving required the words which were used, both said and sung, to be coherently expressed and clearly understood. If the point of worship was now to remember with thanksgiving Christ's offering, then that remembering had to be made possible. This priority accounts for the emphasis given to propositional declaration in worship. The purpose of worship was now not to embody the divine but to convey information regarding the benefits of Christ's offering. Edification became a crucial element of worship, and any sense of engagement with the *mysterium* of God, so much a feature of pre-reformed worship, was now obliterated.

Vernacular essential for edification

An immediate priority was therefore the insistence of language in the vernacular. With the appearance of *The Order of Communion*, a companion to the Latin Mass of the Sarum Rite and authorized for use from Easter 1548, the use of the vernacular had already secured a foothold. The sections of the Mass deemed necessary for the worthy reception of the sacrament were all presented in English—the exhortation, the charge to the intending communicants, the general confession and absolution, the Comfortable Words, the prayer of humble access and the words of administration.[1]

---

[1] H. Wilson, *The Order of the Communion, 1548* (London: Henry Bradshaw Society, 1908).

Although permission was granted in the Act of Uniformity of 1549 for the use of Greek, Latin and Hebrew, their use was granted only to those professing to understand those languages and was applicable only to the services of Matins and Evensong and then only when said in private. The Preface to the Prayer Book of 1549 specified that languages other than English could be used for Matins and Evensong "from tyme to tyme, in Cathedrall and Collegiate Churches, Parishe Churches, and Chapelles to the same annexed" as it shall "serve the congregacion". However, this concession was removed in the Preface of the 1552 Prayer Book, which restricted the saying of Matins and Evensong in a language other than English to private use only.[2] With the use of Latin therefore restricted to the point of extinction, a significant barrier to edification in the faith was removed.

Style of singing to enable edification

The next obstacle to be overcome, given that music had occupied such a substantial place in the liturgy, was the style of singing. Initially Thomas Cranmer showed no desire to eliminate choirs and choral music, provided the words that were sung were able to be understood. In a letter to Henry VIII, he commended music's ability to stimulate a sense of prayer and holiness to the enrichment of the spoken word. Of his translations of Latin processions, he proposed that "if your grace command some devout and solemn note to be made thereunto... I trust it will much excitate and stir the hearts of all men unto devotion and godliness". Later in the same letter he allowed for "they that be cunning in singing to make a much more solemn note" as an alternative for music he had himself composed to accompany his verse translation of *Salve festa dies*.[3] His facility with prose was exquisite; his success with verse

---

[2] The use of Latin in the Edwardian period is discussed by Hugh Benham, "Latin Church Music under Edward VI", *The Musical Times* 116 (May 1975), pp. 477–80.

[3] J. Cox, *Miscellaneous Writings and Letters of Thomas Cranmer* (Cambridge: Parker Society, 1846); F. E. Brightman, *The English Rite, being a synopsis*

less so and his attempt at a metrical version of the *Veni Sancte Spiritus* in the Ordinal was replaced by John Cosin for the Prayer Book of 1662.

Moreover, Cranmer did nothing to prevent the singing of the parts of the Mass, provided they were in English. Provision was made for Introits, Offertory sentences, Communion sentences and anthems to be sung by a choir of clerks. His allowance for music of "a much more solemn note" has even fuelled speculation that some of the simpler works of the later mediaeval composers, such as the *Playnsong Mass* and *Small Devotion* of John Taverner, being adapted to the English text, might have been in use during the Edwardian period, as well as his arrangement of the antiphon *Mater Christi*, reissued as *O God, be merciful unto us*.[4]

The overriding concern, however, was that the words set to music needed to be discernible and capable of being understood. So Cranmer duly recommended that the words of the Litany sung should not be full of notes, "but as near as may be, for every syllable a note".[5] It was a principle which would apply to other sung parts of the liturgy, "as be in the Matins and Evensong, *Venite*, the Hymns, *Te Deum, Benedictus, Magnificat, Nunc dimittis*, and all the Psalms and Versicles; and in the mass *Gloria in excelsis, Gloria Patri*, the Creed, the Preface, the *Pater noster*, and some of the *Sanctus* and *Agnus*".[6]

---

of the sources and revisions of the Book of Common Prayer Vol. I (London: Rivingtons, 1915), p. lxi.

[4] H. Benham, *John Taverner: His Life and Music* (Aldershot: Ashgate, 2003), pp. 259–63.

[5] Cox, *Miscellaneous Writings and Letters of Thomas Cranmer*, p. 412. W. Maskell, *Monumenta Ritualia Ecclesiae Anglicanae*, Vol. I (London: Pickering, 1846), p. xcix. Much significance had been attributed to these proposals: P. le Huray, *Music and the Reformation in England 1549–1660* (Cambridge: Cambridge University Press, 1978), pp. 5–7; H. Benham, *Latin Church Music in England c.1460–1575* (London: Barrie & Jenkins, 1977), p. 164. Denis Stevens has described them as "Cranmer's precepts for the new style of church music", *Tudor Church Music* (London: Faber & Faber, 1961), p. 18.

[6] Cox, *Miscellaneous Writings and Letters of Thomas Cranmer*, p. 412. Brightman, *The English Rite*, Vol. I, p. lxi. The phrase "some of the *Sanctus* and *Agnus*" may suggest the omission of the *Benedictus* following the *Sanctus*

Immediate assistance was provided by John Merbecke. In 1550, he produced *The Booke of Common Prayer Noted*,[7] in which he set aside the melismatic elaboration of his earlier polyphonic works such as the mass *Per arma justitie* and votive antiphons *Domine Jesu Christe* and *Ave Dei patris filia* and adopted a style based on the flowing lines of late mediaeval plainsong, but which for the most part allowed only one note for each syllable. These melodic lines followed a simple mensural system which conformed to the various stresses demanded by the form of the words. The number of note values was restricted to four: breve, semi-breve, minim and the "close" to mark the end of a verse. A "prycke" or dot alongside the minim added half the value. Merbecke became an enthusiastic advocate for this more straightforward presentation and roundly condemned the ornate compositions of the past. In a work entitled *A Book of Notes and Common Places* published in 1581, but likely to have appeared before 1550,[8] he included the lines

> Non vox sed votum,
> non cordula musica sed cor,
> Non clamans sed amans,
> Cantat in aure Dei.

For which he provided a translation:

---

if they were thought of as one item, and of the second petition of the *Agnus Dei*, being a repetition of the first.

[7] John Merbecke (c.1510–85), *The Booke of Common Praier Noted 1550* (reprinted 1979, Nottingham Court Press in association with Magdalene College, Cambridge).

[8] The date of its first appearance is discussed by J. Eric Hunt, *Cranmer's First Litany, 1544 and Merbecke's Book of Common Prayer Noted, 1550* (London: SPCK, 1939), pp. 38–9.

> Not the voice but the desire,
> Not the pleasantness of music,
> But the voice not crying, but loving,
> Singeth in the ears of God.[9]

Music, he insisted, could be tolerated in worship only where it was possible "to let the voice of the singer so sing that not the voice of him that singeth, but the words that are read may delight".[10] Merbecke quoted Augustine's reference to Athanasius, which he rendered as: "When he sung, he should but little alter his voice, so that he should be like rather unto one that readeth, than to one that singeth."[11] Merbecke also welcomed Augustine's conclusion that "those do sin deadly which give greater heed to music than unto the word of God". It was never the case, Merbecke argued, that words were intended to be subservient to the music: "Measure and singing were brought in for the words' sake, and not words for music."[12] Sadly, he noted, this had proved not to be the case, for "what other thing doth the common people hear than voices signifying nothing?" The words could not be distinguished: "Only the sound beateth the ears."[13] Merbecke likened musicians who were complicit in this travesty to "a

---

[9] *A booke of notes and common places, with their expositions, collected and gathered out of the workes of diuers singular writers, and brought alphabetically into order. A worke both profitable and also necessarie, to those that desire the true vnderstanding & meaning of holy Scripture By Iohn Marbeck* (London: Thomas East, 1581), p. 756. A possible reference to Ambrose, more fully quoted by Thomas Becon, *The reliques of Rome contayning all such matters of religion, as have in times past bene brought into the Church by the Pope and his Adherentes* (John Day, 1563), EEBO edition, f. 117r.

[10] Merbecke, *A booke of notes and common places*, pp. 1016–19 (pagination error in text); Becon, *The reliques of Rome*, f. 118.

[11] Merbecke, *A booke of notes and common places*, p. 755; *The Confessions of St Augustine*, Book X, Chapter 33, tr. John K. Ryan (New York: Image Books, 1960), p. 227.

[12] Merbecke, *A booke of notes and common places*, p. 755; *The Confessions of St Augustine*, Book X, Chapter 33.

[13] Merbecke, *A booke of notes and common places*, p. 1020.

nurse that taketh away an apple from a child and eateth it herself; and because the child should not cry, she giveth it a puppet of clowts [clothes] to dandle with. Even so they have taken away the word of God."[14] He commended John Calvin's condemnation of frivolous chantings, which only "feedeth the ears with a vain sound".[15]

Robert Holgate, Archbishop of York (1545–54), lost no time in making this simpler style of singing obligatory for the choir of York Minster.[16] His *Injunctions* to the Dean and Chapter of 1552 enforced the style Merbecke had produced:

> We will and command that there be none other note sung or used in the said church at any service there to be had, saving square note plain, so that every syllable may be plainly and distinctly pronounced, and without any reports or repeating which may induce any obscureness to the hearers . . .

---

[14] John Strype, *Ecclesiastical Memorials Relating Chiefly to Religion and the Reformation of it*, Vol. I (Oxford: Clarendon Press, 1822), p. 321.

[15] Merbecke, *A booke of notes and common places*, p. 754. John Calvin, *Commentary on Psalm 33*. Merbecke's *Book of Common Prayer Noted* has been assessed within the broader intellectual and religio-cultural context of Renaissance humanism, particularly that espoused by Erasmus, with a view to testing Merbecke's reliance upon the scholarship and aesthetics of humanist ideals. Hyun-Ah Kim, *Humanism and the Reform of Sacred Music in Early Modern England: John Merbecke the Orator and the Booke of Common Praier Noted 1550* (Aldershot: Ashgate, 2008), p. 15. Merbecke's sympathetic treatment of the words and their rendition in the vernacular was certainly consistent with humanist principles, yet the impetus to produce this particular work was the need to reorder worship according to the Reformed theological principles. This was a theological imperative.

[16] Robert Holgate (1481/2–1555): Bishop of Llandaff 1537; Archbishop of York 1545–54; deprived 1554.

Faith made accessible and comprehensible

Having eliminated Latin, enforced English and established the need for what was sung to be understood, the next stage was to provide texts easily comprehensible, even allowing for congregations to participate. Consequently, versions of the psalms in metre began to appear.[17] Robert Crowley's *Psalter of David newly translated into Englysh metre* was published in 1549 and was the first complete metrical psalter in English. Simple four-part settings were provided, some being of considerable musical interest, with harmonies elaborating a plainsong chant in the tenor line. The extent to which this *Psalter* became available is unknown and its impact is thought to be modest.[18] However, Thomas Sternhold (1500–49) published his first collection of 19 *Certayn Psalmes* between 1547 and 1549. As well, *Al such psalmes of David as Thomas Sternhold… didde in his life time draw into English Metre* was printed posthumously in 1549 and included 37 translations by Sternhold and seven psalms by John Hopkins. Reprints of this later edition appeared in 1550 and 1553. In 1553, Christopher Tye produced a metrical version of the first 14 chapters of the Acts of the Apostles entitled *The Actes of the Apostles, translated into Englyshe Metre, and dedicated to the kynges moste excellent Maiestye … with notes to eache Chapter, to synge and also to play upon the Lute*. This work was intended solely for domestic use and had no liturgical potential, yet nevertheless provided four-part choral settings of great beauty, characterized by elegantly moving melodic lines and notable points of imitation with some intriguing canonical treatment.

---

[17] A comprehensive and scholarly account of the emergence of English metrical psalms is given in R. Zim, *English Metrical Psalms: Poetry as Praise and Prayer, 1535–1601* (Cambridge: Cambridge University Press, 1987). His guide to English psalm versions printed 1530–1601 (pp. 211–59) is particularly valuable.

[18] Le Huray, *Music and the Reformation in England*, pp. 371–2.

Edification of musicians

In a bid to advance edification and understanding of the texts, attention turned to the edification of the musicians themselves. Whereas priority for filling choral vacancies had been musical expertise, a requirement now being advanced was for singers to be selected on the basis of their good character and biblical expertise. Noting that "whereas heretofore, when descant, prick-song and organs were too much used and had in price in the church, great search was made for cunning men in that faculty", who in any case were widely believed to be given to licentiousness, the *Injunctions* of 1550 for St George's Chapel, Windsor jettisoned musicianship as the basis of selection. God was now to be "praised with gentle and sober quiet minds and with honest hearts".[19] Even though an acquaintance with Latin was required, personal virtue and biblical competence took precedence over musical ability:

> When the room of any of the clerks shall be void, the Dean and prebendaries of this church shall make search for quiet and honest men, learned in the Latin tongue, which have competent voices and can sing, apt to study and willing to increase in learning: so that they may be first deacons and afterward admitted priests; having always more regard to their virtue and learning than to excellency in music.[20]

Once selected, the burden of proficiency in the faith was far from over. The singing-men and choristers had a daunting biblical challenge ahead of them. Holgate's 1552 *Injunctions* to the Dean and Chapter of York gave instructions that all vicars-choral under the age of 40 were required to memorize a chapter of one of St Paul's epistles in Latin every week, beginning at the first chapter of the Epistle to the Romans. Those over the age of 40 had age on their side and were granted a token respite.

---

[19] Frere and Kennedy, *Visitation Articles and Injunctions*, Vol. II, p. 225. *Injunctions* for St George's Chapel, Windsor, 8 February 1550, paragraph 30.
[20] Frere and Kennedy, *Visitation Articles and Injunctions*, Vol. II, pp. 225–6.

They were to memorize merely "the sum" of the appointed chapter,[21] and if the choristers ever imagined their youth would render them exempt, they were in for a shock. They were required to "learn without book" every week or at least every fortnight, a chapter of the Gospels and the Acts of the Apostles in the English tongue beginning at the first chapter of St Matthew.[22] Here was a blatant effort to enforce a priority of the reformers—the knowledge of scripture as the basis of faith—a priority which was administered in such a demanding way as inevitably to jeopardize the level of musical expertise required to undertake more complex repertoire.

Any hopes that the Prayer Book of 1552 might have treated music more sympathetically were comprehensively dashed. The rubrics of the 1549 Book, which had permitted the presence of a choir and specifying parts of the Mass which could be sung, were simply expunged.[23]

Marian respite

However, in 1553, and before the 1552 Prayer Book had a chance completely to settle in, Edward died. He was buried with bleak Prayer Book honours and Bishop Gardiner said a Requiem in the Tower of London in the presence of Mary and those members of the Privy Council wisely not involved in the Lady Jane Grey party. The First Act of Repeal (1 Mary, Statute 2, cap.2)[24] was passed in the first Parliament of Mary's reign and enacted that "from and after the twentieth day of December

---

[21] Frere and Kennedy, *Visitation Articles and Injunctions*, Vol. II, p. 317.

[22] Hyun-Ah Kim's speculation that these requirements reflect the impact of contemporary humanist ideas in which morals were the essential part of the education of the young is strained. The idea that memorizing large swathes of scripture would inspire moral virtue amongst members of choral establishments, then and now, is remarkably aspirational.

[23] The rubrics of the two rites as they affect the role of the clerks are tabled comparatively in Le Huray, *Music and the Reformation in England*, p. 27.

[24] H. Gee and W. J. Hardy, *Documents Illustrative of English Church History* (London: Macmillan, 1896), pp. 377–80.

[1553] all such divine service and administration of Sacraments as were most used in the realm of England in the last year of the reign of our late Sovereign Lord King Henry VIII shall be ... used and frequented ...". Pre-Reformation services were thus officially restored, and composers responded with Latin-texted works of great proficiency and beauty. Christopher Tye's *Missa Euge Bone* and his impressive antiphon for seven voices, *Peccavimus cum patribus nostris*, are likely to be from this period, as is John Sheppard's *Gaude, gaude, gaude Maria virgo*, a *cantus firmus* setting of the Respond for the 2nd Vespers of the Feast of the Purification of the Blessed Virgin Mary, as well as his monumental votive antiphon *Gaude Virgo Christiphera*. Other significant compositions associated with this Marian period include Thomas Tallis's Mass setting *Puer natus est nobis*, responsory *Loquebantur variis linguis* and votive antiphon *Gaude Gloriosa*; William Mundy's votive antiphon *Vox Patris coelestis* and *Magnificat Secundi Toni*; and Robert White's *Tota pulchra es, amica mea* and *Exsurge, Christe, defende nos*. This remarkable output of elaborate polyphony was perfectly integrated with the return of worship as an offering united with the offering of Christ, and therefore able to claim propitiatory significance. Once more the primary focus of music was to support the liturgy's engagement with the reality of the divine, unhindered by the necessity for words to be clearly declaimed and understood.

Euphoria of 1559—the reformers' optimism

After a period marked by the persecution of Protestants, the death of Mary and Cardinal Pole on the same day in 1558 prepared the way for Elizabeth's accession to the throne on 17 November. The same people went on to lead the Elizabethan Church, less those eliminated by the Marian purges. Exiles returned, jostling for higher office and determined to restore the Edwardian reforms with all their liturgical and ceremonial authority. The process of reinstating the Second Prayer Book of Edward VI began. With few modifications it was finally presented to Parliament and a new Act of Uniformity (1 Elizabeth, cap.2) was passed on 28 April 1559, requiring that the Book should be used from the Feast of St John

Baptist following, 24 June.²⁵ Presumably until that date most cathedrals, churches and chapels worshipped as they had done in the Marian period.

The 1559 Prayer Book made no alterations to the Book of 1552 concerning what was said or sung. In both books, the *Creed, Sursum Corda, Benedictus* and *Responses* were to be said; the *Gloria in Excelsis, Venite* and *Quicunque vult* could be sung. Critically, in both 1552 and 1559, instructions are given in Morning Prayer that were unchanged from 1549:

> to thend the people may the better hear, in such places where thei do sing, there shal the lessons be song in a plain tune after the maner of distinct reading: and likewise the Epistle and Gospell.²⁶

The 1559 Book was rendered in Latin in 1560 with the title *Liber Precum Publicarum*, presumably to facilitate the saying of Offices privately by those familiar with the language and for worship in Cambridge and Oxford chapels. However, the general restrictions placed on the use of languages other than English in the 1549 and 1552 Prayer Books remained in place.

Elizabeth's arrival marked a period of intense euphoria amongst the reformers. John Parkhurst (c.1512–75), soon to become Bishop of Norwich, wrote gleefully to the Swiss reformer Heinrich Bullinger (1504–75) on 21 May 1559 that the Mass was abolished and "The Book of Common Prayer, set forth in the time of King Edward, is now again in general use throughout England, and will be every where, in spite of the struggles and opposition of the pseudo-bishops."²⁷ The following day, John Jewel expressed his pleasure at the restoration of the Prayer Book and acknowledged the support Bullinger had given:

---

²⁵ Gee and Hardy, *Documents Illustrative of English Church History*, pp. 458–67.

²⁶ The implication that the Epistle and Gospel could be sung, albeit in the style of distinct reading, is absent from the Communion service, where they are ordered to be said.

²⁷ H. Robinson (ed.), *The Zurich Letters I, A.D.1558–1579* (Cambridge: Parker Society, 1842), p. 29. In 1531, Bullinger succeeded Huldrych Zwingli as Head of the Zurich Church and pastor at the Grossmünster.

Religion is again placed on the same footing on which it stood in King Edward's time; to which event, I doubt not, but that your own letters and exhortations, and those of your republic, have powerfully contributed.[28]

John Jewel found it encouraging that sympathetic appointments were made to various bishoprics—Cox to Ely, Scory to Hereford, Allen to Rochester, Grindal to London, Barlow to Chichester, and with the protestation of modesty not unfamiliar amongst those receiving ecclesiastical preferment, Jewel added that there was "I, the least of the apostles, to Salisbury". He rejoiced to hear of progress being made in Scotland, where "all the monasteries are every where levelled with the ground: the theatrical dresses, the sacrilegious chalices, the idols, the altars, are consigned to the flames" and "not a vestige of the ancient superstition and idolatry is left".[29]

Reformers' frustrations

Despite this initial euphoria, however, the final cleansing was nowhere near completion. Jewel may have claimed to Peter Martyr that doctrine is everywhere most pure, but he had to concede that "as to ceremonies and maskings, there is a little too much foolery".[30] What he described as his good hopes for religion faced a formidable challenge. "It is no easy matter", he confessed, "to drag the chariot without horses, especially up hill".[31] As he had bemoaned in an earlier letter to Martyr, the ceremonial, or "the scenic apparatus" of divine worship, was still very much "under agitation".[32]

He refers to what continued to be a source of frustration for the reformers—the sovereign's partiality to the ceremonial practice of

---

[28] Robinson, *Zurich Letters* I, p. 33.
[29] Robinson, *Zurich Letters* I, pp. 39–40.
[30] Robinson, *Zurich Letters* I, p. 55.
[31] Robinson, *Zurich Letters* I, p. 45.
[32] Robinson, *Zurich Letters* I, p. 23.

pre-reformed worship. This was highlighted by her toleration of a crucifix and candles at a eucharist presided over by the traditional three-fold ministry of priest, deacon and sub-deacon, all strikingly redolent of the offering of a propitiatory sacrifice. To Thomas Sampson's fury, the three ministers concerned were not only "three of our lately appointed bishops" but were wearing the traditional vestments for these roles—chasuble and dalmatics—all richly adorned—the "golden vestments of the papacy". "What hope is there of any good", he complained, "when our party are disposed to look for religion in these dumb remnants of idolatry and not from the preaching of the lively word of God?"[33] With consummate irony, he then enquired of Martyr, "Is my warmth of feeling carrying me away?"

Edwin Sandys's own warmth of feeling was exposed in a later grumble to Martyr concerning abuses that were still to be removed. The inconvenient difficulty for Sandys was that his views were not shared by the queen. She had made it clear that it was "not contrary to the word of God, nay, rather for the advantage of the church, that the image of Christ crucified, together with Mary and John, should be placed, as heretofore, in some conspicuous part of the church, where they might more readily be seen by all the people". In a moment of circumspection, Sandys admitted to being rather vehement in this matter and conceded that "I was very near being deposed from my office and incurring the displeasure of the queen".[34] Nevertheless he continued to lament that the "little silver cross, of ill-omened origin . . . still maintains its place in the queen's chapel". "Wretched me!" he bemoaned, "This thing will soon be drawn into a precedent." Like Jewel, he resorted to a vehicular allusion: "The slow-paced horses retard the chariot."[35] In liturgical matters, however, the queen was beyond persuasion and had no compunction in publicly admonishing preachers who questioned her devotional preferences, once lambasting Alexander Nowell, Dean of St

---

[33] Robinson, *Zurich Letters* I, p. 63. Peter Martyr Vermigli (1499–1562): Oxford 1547–53.

[34] Robinson, *Zurich Letters* I, pp. 73–4.

[35] Robinson, *Zurich Letters* I, p. 55.

Paul's, for attacking the cross and saints in an Ash Wednesday sermon.[36] There is no doubt that Elizabeth withstood persistent pressure from the more bullish reactionaries, especially those who had been marinating in continental Reformation ideology to relinquish the cross and candles for services, together with other ritual and ceremonial components of the now displaced propitiatory offering. Further, she resisted pressure to take the 1559 Book in an even more reformed direction than had already been established in 1552. The queen's regular attendance at sung services in the Chapel Royal every Sunday and feast day is well documented and her encouragement of an elaborate though vernacular choral tradition is acknowledged.[37]

Concerning music, although cut loose from any suggestion of it being part of an offering united to that of Christ and therefore instrumental in engaging with the presence of the divine, a set of *Royal Injunctions*, issued in July 1559 as a supplement to the Acts of Supremacy and Uniformity, afforded some comfort to those hoping for music to maintain a significant place in worship. Collegiate and parish churches which allocated livings to men and children for singing in church were to continue unhindered, conceding that it was due to this practice that "the laudable science of music hath been had in estimation and preserved in knowledge" and no measures would be introduced which could cause "in any wise the decay of anything that might conveniently tend to the use and continuance of the said science".[38]

---

[36] Alexander Nowell (1517–1602): exile in Strassburg and Frankfurt; Archdeacon of Middlesex, Canon of Canterbury Cathedral 1561, and Dean of St Paul's 1561–1601.

[37] P. McCullough, *Sermons at Court: Politics and Religion in Elizabethan and Jacobean Preaching* (Cambridge: Cambridge University Press, 2011), p. 156.

[38] 'The Royal Articles of Queen Elizabeth 1559, Article 49', in Frere and Kennedy, *Visitation Articles and Injunctions* Vol. III, pp. 22–3. Also H. Gee (ed.), *The Elizabethan Clergy and the Settlement of Religion 1558–1564* (Oxford: Clarendon Press, 1898), p. 60.

Rationality triumphs

Nevertheless, the overall message was clear. Music was not to be "so abused in the Church that thereby the Prayer should be the worse understanded of the hearers". Were there to be any singing it was to be a modest and distinct song, so used in all parts of the Common Prayers in the Church, that the same may be as plainly understood as if it were read without singing. Affirmation of a sort was forthcoming to those who valued music in worship and to the musicians who provided it, with permission being granted "for a hymn or such-like song" to be sung at the beginning or end of Common Prayers, either at morning or evening, "in the best sort of melody and music that may be devised". This came, however, with the strict proviso that the sentence of the hymn may be understood and perceived.[39]

A fundamental principle of the offering of praise and thanksgiving therefore remained intact. The importance of worship as a conveyer of meaning rather than mystery was clearly established. Rationality had ousted symbolism. Clarity had trumped imagery and metaphor. Worship as a means of embracing that which transcends the ordinary and probes that divine *mysterium* which is beyond the ability of words to encapsulate was now extinct.

---

[39] Gee, *The Elizabethan Clergy*, p. 23.

4

Worship—An Exercise in the Spirit

In order comprehensively to embed the newly imposed offering of praise and thanksgiving, the reformers embarked on a highly charged campaign of discreditation of any previous ritual or ceremonial testifying to the offering of worship being united to the offering of Christ and therefore embodying the divine presence. Any element of worship which testified to the presence of the divine was condemned and ordered to be expunged.

An obvious initial strategy was to utilize Diocesan Articles and Injunctions to legislate the banishment of all ceremonies, vestments and ecclesiastical artefacts which previously had invested the liturgy with the present reality of God. Accordingly, the *Lambeth Articles* agreed on by the archbishops of Canterbury and York, and the bishops of those Provinces, 12 April 1561, specified that "all old service-books, grails, antiphoners and other be defaced and abolished by order in visitations".[1] Thomas Bentham, Bishop of Coventry and Lichfield, issued *Injunctions* in 1565 requiring all books redolent of so-called idolatry and superstition to be "abolished and put clean away".[2] These instructions were still being reinforced in later sets of Articles when Grindal, Sandys and Guest all required the obliteration of the books of pre-Reformation ceremonial. Article 6 of Grindal's Articles for the Province of York enquired whether

---

[1] "The Lambeth Articles, 1561", Article 6, in W. H. Frere and W. M. Kennedy (eds), *Visitation Articles and Injunctions of the Period of the Reformation* Vol. III, 1559–1575 (London: Longmans, Green & Co., 1910), p. 96.

[2] "Bentham's Injunctions for Coventry and Lichfield Diocese", Article 21, in Frere and Kennedy, *Visitation Articles and Injunctions* Vol. III, p. 169. Thomas Bentham (1513–78): Marian exile at Zurich and Basle; Bishop of Coventry and Lichfield 1560–78.

all and every antiphoners, mass-books, grails, portesses, processionals, manuals, legendaries, and all other books of late belonging to your church or chapel, which served for the superstitious Latin service, be utterly defaced, rent and abolished, and if they be not, through whose default that is, and at whose keeping they remain.³

This Article left nothing to chance. It specifically outlawed "vestments, albs, tunicles, stoles, fanons, pixes, paxes, handbells, sacring bells, censers, chrismatories, crosses, candlesticks, holy water stocks, images and other such relics and monuments of superstition and idolatry as items to be utterly defaced, broken and destroyed". Add the removal of altars, rood-lofts, copes, chalices and the "superstitious" ringing of bells and worship is denuded of any of the ritual involved with the real presence of Christ in the eucharist and the offering of a propitiatory sacrifice. Article 33 of Sandys's 1571 *Articles* for the London Diocese sought to discover whether "there be any mass-books, portesses, or other books of the Latin popish service ... reserved in your church, chapel, or elsewhere, or in the hands or custody of any person or persons, which yet are not defaced and destroyed".⁴

A similar Article was included in Guest's 1571 *Articles* for Rochester.⁵ The requirement that mass books, vestments or other "massing gear"– images, candlesticks, holy-water vats or other ornaments be not only defaced but destroyed reveals a determination bordering on the fanatical to obliterate any vestige of the liturgy implying the presence of the divine. These ceremonial elements of the liturgy were similarly condemned by John Bale. In a riot of explosive language, he identified copes, cruets,

---

3   "Grindal's Articles for the Province of York", Article 6, in Frere and Kennedy, *Visitation Articles and Injunctions* Vol. III, p. 255.
4   "Sandys' Articles for London Diocese 1571", Article 33, in Frere and Kennedy, *Visitation Articles and Injunctions* Vol. III, p. 311.
5   "Guest's Articles for Rochester Diocese 1571", Article 2, in Frere and Kennedy, *Visitation Articles and Injunctions* Vol. III, p. 332. Edmund Guest (1514–77): Archdeacon of Canterbury 1559–64, Bishop of Rochester 1560–71, Bishop of Salisbury 1571–7.

candlesticks, mitres, crosses, censers, chrismatories, corporasses and chalices as perverse indicators of "whorish holiness". Just as surely as Babylon perished, he predicted, so "the continual light of lamps before the high altars, the burning cressets at triumphs in the night, the torches at burials and solemn processions, tapers at high masses, and the candles at offerings, shall never more burn in thy sinful synagogues".[6]

Ornate polyphony condemned

As these ritual components were being unearthed and destroyed, the music with which they were associated was also condemned. The ornate polyphony, intricate textures and florid melismatic passages which had allowed the words of faith to be lost in a maze of sound, already dismissed as an impediment to edification, were now identified as unwelcome remnants of a liturgy which pretended to embody the divine reality, thereby usurping the perfect propitiatory offering of Christ. "To this foolish and ungodly kind of singing", expostulated Bullinger, "as to a heavenly or meritorious work, there is more attributed than true faith doth allow".[7] Such musical offerings he declared to be nothing but illegitimate attempts to force an invalid contract with God by offering that which it was not possible to offer. "Let no man think that prayers sung with man's voice are more acceptable unto God than if they were plainly spoken or uttered", he warned, "for God is neither allured with the sweetness of man's voice, neither is he offended though prayer be offered in a hoarse or base sound".[8] Augustine himself confessed it a sin when

---

[6] *The Image of Both Churches, Being an Exposition of the Most Wonderful Book of Revelation of St John the Evangelist*, in H. Christmas (ed.), *Select Works of John Bale, D.D. Bishop of Ossory* (Cambridge: Parker Society, 1849), pp. 536–7. Bale (1495–1563): fled to Antwerp 1540; Bishop of Ossory 1552; escaped to Frankfurt and Basle on the accession of Mary; returned on the accession of Elizabeth; Prebendary of Canterbury 1560.

[7] T. Harding (ed.), *The Decades of Henry Bullinger* (Cambridge: Parker Society, 1849–52), Fifth Decade, Sermon 5, p. 197.

[8] *The Decades of Henry Bullinger*, Sermon 4, pp. 190–1.

he found himself more delighted with the sweetness of the voices than with the sense of the words and demanded that all the melodious tunes of sweet songs, wherewith the Psalter of David is replenished, might be removed from his ears and the hearing of the Church.[9]

Bullinger commended Rabanus, the ninth-century bishop of Mainz, who claimed that singing in church had been introduced "for fleshly-minded men's sake, and not for such as are guided by the Spirit".[10] This style of music was characterized by Bullinger as *operosam*, and he urged its immediate extinction. Bullinger did concede that the practice of singing in worship was of great antiquity; after all, the Levites in the ancient Church sang. However, he countered, whilst their singing was performed according to God's commandment, the *operosam* style of singing was not, and its abandonment was legitimate, necessary and long overdue. It was indistinguishable from the other superstitious ceremonies of the ancient temple, many of which had unfortunately been instituted by David but fortuitously abolished with the temple and its ill-advised associated ceremonies.[11]

Any thought of music endorsing the reality of the divine or being a part of the disgraced propitiatory offering raised the ire of John Merbecke. He railed: "All the sleights and grounds of the Pope's intentions which wholly consisteth in false superstitious worshipping, filthy Idolatry, fained hypocrisy, [and] foolish scrupulosity" are "clearly sifted and bolted

---

[9] *The Decades of Henry Bullinger*, Sermon 5, p. 194. *The Confessions of St Augustine*, Book X, Chapter 33, tr. John K. Ryan (New York: Image Books, 1960), p. 227. Bullinger's translation of Augustine is: "However, when it so happens that I am moved more by the singing than by what is sung, I confess that I have sinned, in such wise as to deserve punishment, and at such times I should prefer not to listen to a singer."

[10] *The Decades of Henry Bullinger*, pp. 195–6. Rabanus Maurus (776 or 784–856): Abbot of Fulda 822; Archbishop of Mainz 847, *De clericorum institutione* VI, p. 28. [*Propter carnales in ecclesia, non propter spirituales, consuetudo cantandi est institute, ut qui verbis non compunguntur, suavitate modulaminis moveantur.*]

[11] *The Decades of Henry Bullinger*, p. 191.

out" by all the "infinite godly and learned writers".[12] It was therefore anathema that music should claim a place in worship because of its supposed appeasing effect on the divine and any thought of it being offered as a work of beauty for the pleasure and satisfaction of the divine was abhorrent. For this reason, he noted, St Gregory was appalled that deacons of the church in Rome, who rather than preaching the gospel and providing for the poor, had "set all their pleasure on pleasant singing".[13] In his own account of this incident, Thomas Becon grimly added that Gregory ordered these reprobate deacons to forgo such singing on pain of excommunication.[14]

It was obvious to all but the most perverse, claimed Becon, that "God hath no pleasure in these external sacrifices, but rather abhorreth them".[15] Moreover, of all the arts ever offered in worship, he identified music as the most frivolous, inconsequential and illegitimate. Unworthy even of human attention, how could music ever have been deemed worthy of being associated with the divine presence and offered to God? Moreover, music in worship not only afforded God no pleasure but created the opposite effect of arousing God's anger. For Becon, the belief that music could ever become part of a propitiatory offering effective for salvation was ludicrous: "The noise of the mouth, the mumbling of the lips, the roaring of the throat, the shaking of the head, the knocking on the

---

[12] J. Eric Hunt, *Cranmer's First Litany, 1544 and Merbecke's Book of Common Prayer Noted, 1550* (London: SPCK, 1939), pp. 38–9.

[13] *A booke of notes and common places, with their expositions, collected and gathered out of the workes of diuers singular writers, and brought alphabetically into order. A worke both profitable and also necessarie, to those that desire the true vnderstanding & meaning of holy Scripture By Iohn Marbeck* (London: Thomas East, 1581), p. 1016. Hyun-Ah Kim, *Humanism and the Reform of Sacred Music in Early Modern England: John Merbecke the Orator and the Booke of Common Praier Noted 1550* (Aldershot: Ashgate, 2008).

[14] Thomas Becon, *The reliques of Rome contayning all such matters of religion, as have in times past bene brought into the Church by the Pope and his Adherentes* (John Day, 1563), EEBO edition, f. 118r.

[15] T. Becon, "The News out of Heaven", in John Ayre (ed.), *The Early Works of Thomas Becon, S.T.P.* (Cambridge: Parker Society, 1843), p. 49.

breast, the kneeling on the ground, and whatsoever can be reckoned more, is vain, unfruitful, and nothing to the purpose, rather bringing damnation than salvation." Those indulging in these despicable practices were beyond contempt: "They never leave babbling, their minds being utterly drawn from their prayers and altogether set upon transitory and worldly things."[16] "Nowe a dayes Musicke is growne to such and so greate licentiousnesse", he bemoaned, "that even at the ministration of the holy Sacramente all kynde of wanton and leude trifelyng songes with pipyng of Organs have theyr place and course".[17] As for the divine service and common prayer,

> it is chaunted, mynsed [minced] and mangled of oure costlye hired, curious and nice Musitions (not to instructe the audience withal, nor to stirre up mens minds unto devotion but with an whorythe [h]armonye to tickle theyr eares) that it may justly deme not to be a noyse made of men, but rather a bleating of brute beastes.[18]

With extraordinary overreach, Becon paraphrased a passage from Heinrich Cornelius Agrippa von Nettesheim, which he then embellished to give the raucous farmyard references a more inflammatory aspect:

> the children ney [neigh] discant *as it were a sorte coltes*: other bellowe a tenoure *as it were a companye of oxen*: other barke a counterpoint *as it were a number of dogges*: other roare out a treble *lyke a sort of bulles*: other grunte out a base, *as it were a number of hogges, so that a foule evel favoured noyse is made*, but as for the words and sentences, and the very matter it selfe is nothing understanded at all, but the authorite and power of

---

[16] "The Pathway Unto Prayer", in *The Early Works of Thomas Becon, S.T.P*, p. 134.

[17] Becon, *The reliques of Rome*, f. 121.

[18] Becon, *The reliques of Rome*, f. 121r.

judgemente is taken awaye both from the eares and from the mynde utterlye.[19]

Predictably Becon concluded that music was "a more vain and trifling science than it becometh a man, born and appointed to matters of gravity, to spend much time about it". Whilst some kings and philosophers found minstrelsy a remedy against the tediousness of their painful labours, for many it was considered a worthless, depraved art. This was confirmed for Becon by King Philip, father of Alexander the Great. Far from commending Alexander for his musical skill, Philip had made a point of rebuking him. Upon hearing Alexander play very pleasantly, his father had only one question to put to him: "Art thou not ashamed that thou canst play and sing so cunningly?" Not only King Philip, but Sextus Nero the Emperor had also displayed a laudable distaste for music. Languishing on his death-bed Nero had greatly lamented that he was so excellent in the science of music and wished that he had rather spent his time in good letters and virtuous exercises. Had he taken this more appropriate course, judged Becon, he might have been more able justly and truly to govern his realm.[20] Music being so disgraced as a vain and worthless indulgence, it was inappropriate even to contemplate it as an acceptable offering. Such a despicable art would never find favour with God and should therefore never be permitted in worship.

James Calfhill fuelled the hostility towards music with a lively account of the dedication of a church. According to Augustine, noted Calfhill, all that was needed for such a service was a sermon, prayers and perhaps the sign of the cross. However, on this occasion, after the bishop had

---

[19] Becon, *The reliques of Rome*, f. 121r. Heinrich Cornelius Agrippa von Nettesheim (1486–1535), *De incertitudine et vanitate scientiarum atque atrium declamatio invectiva* (Declamation Attacking the Uncertainty and Vanity of the Sciences and the Arts), 1526; Cologne, 1527); *Of the Vanitie and vncertaintie of Artes and Sciences*: Englished by James Sandford (London: Henrie Bynneman, 1575; EEBO Editions ProQuest), p. 30v. Becon's additions are in italics.

[20] T. Becon, "The Jewel of Joy", in John Ayre (ed.), *The Catechism of Thomas Becon, S.T.P.* (Cambridge: Parker Society, 1844), p. 429.

knocked on the church door, "presumably with his crozier", he proceeded to perambulate twice about the church with as much devotion as a horse. The choir then sang *Erexit Jacob lapidem*, one of the texts prescribed for the hallowing of a church, the biblical context of which Calfhill judged the members of the choir to be disgracefully ignorant (Genesis 28:18, 20, 22). He then condemned the poor translation provided; "Jacob erected a stone" being rendered as "Jacob reared up a stone". As though this were not enough, the choir continued "bleating out with wide throats" a setting of *Ibi est Benjamin adolescentulus, in mentis excessu* (Psalm 68:27). Calfhill was infuriated that the more accurate translation "There is Benjamin, a youth, in ecstasy of mind" had been discarded for the comic "There is little Benjamin, out of his wits." In essence, he bemoaned, the entire Mass was notable chiefly for "renting of throats, and tearing of notes, chanting of Priests, howling of Clerks, slinging of coals, and piping of organs. This they continue a long while in mirth and jollity: many mad parts be played."[21]

Necessity for words to be understood

The need for the words which were sung to be understood continued to be pressed. Since the sacrifice of praise and thanksgiving consisted of a thankful remembrance of Christ's offering, it was necessary for the remembrance of that divine offering to be made explicit. Jewel recalled Augustine's observation that when the sound of the voice obliterated the sense of the mind, worship was reduced to the meaningless chatter of birds: "People should know what they pray, and so sing with reason agreeable to a man, and not chatter with voice as birds do. For if they sing or pray they know not what, [Augustine] saith that, for their sound of voice and want of sense, they may be well compared with ousels or popinjays."[22] This passage from Augustine was embellished in the homily

---

[21] James Calfhill, "An Answer to John Martiall's Treatise of the Cross", Fourth Article (London: 1565), pp. 209–10.

[22] John Ayre (ed.), *The Works of John Jewel*, Vol. I (Cambridge: Parker Society, 1845–50), p. 283. "Second Discourse on Psalm 18", *St Augustine on the Psalms*

"Of Common Prayer and Sacraments", the ninth homily of the *Second Tome of Homilies*, released in 1571. St Augustine, it was noted, writing upon the eighteenth Psalm, said:

> What this should be, we ought to understand, that we may sing with reason of man, and not with chattering of birds. For ousels, popinjays, ravens, pies, and other such like birds, are taught by men to prate they know not what: but to sing with understanding is given by God's holy will to the nature of man.[23]

Words to be in the vernacular

Condemnation of Latin continued. Singing with understanding would clearly be jeopardized using Latin and so Jewel had no time for those who "mumble up all their service, not only with a drowned and hollow voice, but also in a strange and barbarous tongue".[24] Such obfuscation had become so blatant that Jewel concluded it was a deliberate attempt to deprive worshippers of the means of faith. "These men," he railed, "like sounding metal, yell out in the churches unknown and strange words without understanding, without knowledge, and without devotion; yea, and do it of purpose because the people should understand nothing at all."[25] All that is heard, claimed Bullinger, "is a long sound, quavered, and strained to and fro, backward and forward, whereof a man cannot understand one word", and not being able to understand one word made a nonsense of worship.[26] Often the singers strove among themselves to produce the most excellent sound, he added, whereby "the whole church ringeth with a hoarse kind of yelling, and through the strife that riseth

---

Vol. I, tr. Scholastica Hebgin and Felicitas Corrigan (London: Longmans, Green, 1960), p. 182.
[23] *The Second Tome of Homilies*, Homily IX.
[24] *Apologia* V, in *Works of John Jewel* III, p. 89.
[25] *Apologia* V, in *Works of John Jewel* III, p. 89.
[26] *The Decades of Henry Bullinger*, Fifth Decade, Sermon 5, p. 197. "Quavered" is the translation of Bullinger's *suspensus*.

about their voices the hearers little understand what is sung".[27] In his *Exposition of Psalm 23*, John Hooper expressed his disdain for the ungodly colleges of priests that "daily bo-o and roar the holy scriptures out of their mouths and understand no more the meaning thereof than the walls which they sing and speak unto".[28]

Becon recorded his admiration for the Emperor Justinian, who enacted that all bishops and priests should speak "in the tongue which the people understand that they might thereby be the better edified and also be the more fervently stirred unto devotion and praying to God".[29] Bullinger could also be relied on for his support: "They sing moreover in a strange tongue which few do understand, and that without any profit at all to the church."[30] Robert Wisdom, Archdeacon of Ely, agreed: "It is utterly to be reproved that the people shall come to the churches, and tarry there three or four hours, and have nothing taught them of God, or of his word, but only hear a noise in a foreign tongue, that unneth [scarcely] the singers themselves understand."[31] In his *Articles Concerning Christian Religion* for the Diocese of Gloucester, Hooper declared that

> it is not lawful for any man to sing or say in the church in any kind of tongue other than such as the people shall be able to understand; and that it is not sufficient to speak or read in

---

[27] *The Decades of Henry Bullinger*, Fifth Decade, Sermon 5, p. 197.

[28] "An Exposition upon the 23. Psalme of David full of frutefull and comfortable doctrine ... " (London, 1562), in *Certeine comfortable Expositions of the constant Martyr of Christ, M. John Hooper, Bishop of Glocester and Worcester, written in the time of his tribulation and imprisonment, upon the XXIII, LXII, LXIII, and LXXVII psalmes of the prophet David* (London, 1580); Charles Nevinson (ed.), *Later Writings of Bishop Hooper* (Cambridge: Parker Society, 1852).

[29] Becon, *The reliques of Rome*, f. 118, 118r.

[30] *The Decades of Henry Bullinger*, Fifth Decade, Sermon 5, p. 197.

[31] Robert Wisdom (d.1568): in exile in Bremen 1546; Rector of Settrington, Yorkshire 1550; abroad, possibly Geneva, during Marian period; Archdeacon of Ely 1559. John Strype, *Ecclesiastical Memorials Relating Chiefly to Religion and the Reformation of it*, Vol. I (Oxford: Clarendon Press, 1822), p. 321.

the English, or mother-tongue, but there be due and distinct pronunciation, whereby all the people may have true knowledge."[32]

A set of *Interrogatories* for July 1560 had more generally enquired of the clerks "whether that the song in the church be modest and distinct, so devised and used that the ditty [text] may plainly be understood, or no?"[33] John Parkhurst's *Injunctions and Interrogatories* for Norwich of 1561 copy this wording.[34] By 1565, Edmund Guest's *Articles* for Rochester Diocese wanted to know "whether you sing the said service openly in the church in any other language or tongue than in the English according to the laws of the realm".[35] There was a further issue. Not all words which were sung were from the Scriptures. They were taken "out of I know not what kind of legends", lamented Bullinger, and "out of the traditions of men". Even where the words were scriptural, they were mostly "so wrested and corrupted that there remaineth no part of the heavenly sense of meaning".[36]

Length of music condemned

Also, extended choral settings detracted from the time which should have been allocated for the declaration and cultivation of faith by means of readings, prayers and sermons. "Neither is there any end or measure in their singing", Bullinger objected: they sing day and night with musical settings that "so occupied the whole time of divine service in the church,

---

[32] "Articles concerning Christian Religion", in "A true Coppey of Bishop Hooper's Visitation Booke made by him in Anno Dom. 1551, 1552," in Nevinson, *Later Writings of Bishop Hooper*, pp. 122–3.

[33] "Interrogatories, July 1560", Article 42, in Frere and Kennedy, *Visitation Articles and Injunctions* Vol. III, p. 87.

[34] "Parkhurst's Injunctions and Interrogations for Norwich 1561", Article 3, in Frere and Kennedy, *Visitation Articles and Injunctions* Vol. III, p. 105.

[35] "Guest's Articles for Rochester Diocese 1565", Article 3, in Frere and Kennedy, *Visitation Articles and Injunctions* Vol. III, p. 148.

[36] *The Decades of Henry Bullinger*, Fifth Decade, Sermon 5, p. 196.

that very little or none was left for true prayers, and for the holy and heavenly preaching of the word of God".[37] The place of preaching in worship was inviolable and not to be compromised by music.

An inconvenient setback had been the queen's distinct lack of enthusiasm for sermons, about which Thomas Sampson vented his ire to Peter Martyr: "Oh! My father, what can I hope for, when the ministry of the word is banished from court?"[38] Becon ventured memorably, if indiscreetly, into a more strident criticism. "It becometh kings, princes, and rulers rather to hear the preacher of God's word", he expostulated, "than to hearken to the sound of vain instruments, and to delight in hearing the filthy and trifling songs of drunken musicians, which rather provoke unto fleshly fantasies than unto virtuous exercises".[39] According to Becon, whilst the words of the preacher inspired virtue, music encouraged nothing but vice: "the one getteth the favour of God, the other provoketh his wrath, indignation and vengeance; the one lifteth up into heaven, the other detrudeth and thrusteth down into hell-fire".[40] Those worshipping faithfully in accordance with biblical truth had never allowed elaborate singing to be offered to God and it was imperative that it be banned so that the true sacrifice of the spirit—prayer, preaching and the word of God—could be offered uncontaminated.[41]

Singing in the Spirit

Given the seemingly intractable problems attached to singing in worship, consideration was even given to the possibility of singing without music. A foundational element of the sacrifice of praise and thanksgiving was that the sacrifice consisted, not of any physical aspect which would include the offering of works, but the offering of the spirit—the heart and

---

[37] *The Decades of Henry Bullinger*, p. 197.
[38] H. Robinson (ed.), *The Zurich Letters I, A.D. 1558–1579* (Cambridge: Parker Society, 1842), p. 63.
[39] Becon, "The Jewel of Joy", pp. 429–30.
[40] Becon, "The Jewel of Joy", p. 429. Detrudeth: force down.
[41] *The Decades of Henry Bullinger*, Fifth Decade, Sermon 5, p. 197.

the mind. This, it was argued, was the only offering which was acceptable to God. For support, Jewel cited the determinations of the Council of Acon [Macon] where it was resolved that "the voice and mind of them that sing unto the Lord in the church must agree together".[42] This was consistent with the words of St Paul: "I will sing with my spirit, I will sing with my mind."[43] Neither the spirit nor the mind, it was argued, were dependent on vocal expression. Thomas Becon claimed he could produce many notable sayings of the doctors of the Church which would establish beyond doubt that "prayer is not the work of the mouth but of the heart, not of the voice but of the thought, not of the lips but of the mind".[44] This was a fundamental truth manifestly evident in scripture, he declared. When Moses led the people of Israel out of Egypt, he considered how he might lead them to safety. Placing his confidence in God, he "prayed nothing at all with his mouth, but only uttered his cause secretly in his heart unto God, and he was heard". His crying was not the voice of the mouth but the affection of the heart. He cried with a pure mind to God and as a result he was heard, although the mouth kept silence. Becon added the story of Hannah, who at Shiloh prayed to God for the gift of a child. Under the watchful eye of Eli the priest, she prayed for a long time before the Lord and her prayers were silent: "She spake in her heart ... her lips only moved, but her voice was heard nothing at all."[45] Mary Magdalene also prayed in her heart, not with her lips and mouth. When

---

[42] *The Works of John Jewel* I, p. 309. The Synod of Macon commonly refers to the Second and Third Councils of Bishops held in Macon, France, 581 or 582, and 585. "*Psallentium in ecclesia Domino mens concordare debet cum voce, ut impleatur illud apostoli, Psallum spiritu, psallam et mente.*" (*Concil. Aquisgr.* Cap. 132, in *Crabb. Concil. Col. Agrip.* 1551. Tom. II, p. 698.)

[43] *The Works of John Jewel* I, p. 309; 1 Corinthians 14:15.

[44] Becon, "The Pathway Unto Prayer", p. 134.

[45] Becon, "The Pathway Unto Prayer", p. 132. "Hannah was praying silently; her lips were moving although her voice could not be heard." Cf. 1 Samuel 1:13.

she washed Christ's feet with the tears of her eyes and wiped them with the hair of her head, her plea for forgiveness was made in her mind only.[46]

When speaking with the woman of Samaria, Christ predicted the time when the true worshippers shall worship the Father in spirit and truth. This was enough for Becon to conclude that since God is a spirit he must be worshipped in spirit.[47] It is the inward and spiritual, not the outer and physical, which must worship God. The basis of this argument, he claimed, is the common assumption that "like will to like" and that "everyone desireth such as he is himself". According to this principle, since God is a spirit, "therefore requireth he a spiritual manner of worshipping, which doubtless proceedeth from the heart, and not from the stentorious and crying voice of the mouth". What God requires is the pure affection of the heart, not the whispering noise of the lips.[48]

That Christ himself had said "This people honour me with their lips, but their heart is far from me . . . verily they worship me in vain" was proof enough for Becon that prayer is the work of the heart, the spirit, the mind, and not of the mouth and lips.[49] Those who wished to worship fruitfully must "pray in heart, in spirit, in mind, in thought, in affection, in the soul, in the inward man".[50]

Becon's preference was that psalms, hymns and spiritual songs, which might have seemed to have required musical settings, were to be recited, not sung. The only singing that was required was the singing of the heart. "Let the voice of the singer so sing", he said, referring to Jerome's commentary on the *Epistle to the Ephesians*, "that not the voice of him that singeth, but the words that are read, may delight". It is not the voice but the desire, he added, not the musical instrument but the heart, not the crier but the lover that sings in the ear of God.[51] This was a new way of singing and more appropriately called reading. Any modulation

---

[46] Becon, "The Pathway Unto Prayer", p. 132. Cf. Mark 14:3–7, Matthew 26:6–11, John 12:3–8.

[47] Becon, "The Pathway Unto Prayer", p. 132. Cf. John 4:23.

[48] Becon, "The Pathway Unto Prayer", p. 132.

[49] Becon, "The Pathway Unto Prayer", p. 132. Cf. Mark 7:6–7; Matthew 15:8–9.

[50] Becon, "The Pathway Unto Prayer", p. 134.

[51] Becon, *The reliques of Rome*, f. 117r.

or ornamentation that disturbed the normal intonation associated with reading was not to be tolerated. The inevitable conclusion for Merbecke was that "we ought to sing, to make melody, and to praise the Lord rather in mind than in voice". Those whose office it was to sing in the Church must sing to God, not in the voice, but in the heart.[52] Unfazed by the challenge of singing without using the voice, Merbecke pressed on with a version of Colossians 3:16: "Let the word of the Lord abound plenteously in you, teach and admonish ye one another, in Psalms, Hymns, and spiritual songs, singing in your hearts with grace."[53] From this verse, Merbecke concluded that "it is the duty of a devout mind to pray to God, not with the voice, or with the sound of the voice, but with the devotion of the mind and with the faith of the heart." Merbecke's interpretation sits uneasily with Paul's actual meaning, which was that the singing of psalms, hymns and spiritual songs must be heartfelt with the grace of God, not that there should be no singing. Nevertheless, Merbecke concluded that "the crying of the voice is not the work in prayer unto God" and that authentic worship is "the crying of faith and the devotion of a godly and pure mind".[54]

Bullinger rose to the challenge of accounting for two potentially troublesome passages of scripture where Christ and his disciples were reported to have sung a hymn.[55] In both instances, the key word was ὑμνήσαντες, being translated "having sung a hymn". Undeterred by what might seem to be obvious, Bullinger maintained that "having sung a hymn" constituted no proof that the verb ὑμνέω implied such modulation of the voice as would constitute singing as distinct from saying. In any case, even if the disciples did sing, there is no indication that Jesus also sang with them. "For that which is read in Matthew and Mark", he argued:

> κάι ὑμνήσαντες εξήλθον εἰς τό ὄρος τῶν ελαιών (which may be Englished, "And when they had sung an hymn, or psalm, then went out into the Mount of Olives"), is such a kind of saying, as

---

[52] Merbecke, *A booke of notes and common places*, p. 1016.
[53] Merbecke, *A booke of notes and common places*, p. 1015.
[54] Merbecke, *A booke of notes and common places*, p. 1019.
[55] Cf. Matthew 26:30; Mark 14:26.

doth not necessarily force us to understand, that the Lord sang with his disciples; for a hymn, which is the praise due unto God, may be humbly uttered without quavering of the voice.[56]

Bullinger found comfort in his proposition that it is possible to say rather than sing a hymn by citing the Latin version, claiming it to be the old translation, which rendered ὑμνήσαντες as *hymno dicto*:

> Truly, the old translation in both places, as well as Matthew as in Mark, constantly interpreteth it: *Et hymno dicto exierunt in montem Olivarum*; that is to say: "When they had said a hymn, they went out into the mount of Olives."

Bullinger also took advantage of an inconsistency in Erasmus's translation of ὑμνήσαντες as it appeared in Matthew and Mark. In Matthew, Erasmus used the Latin *Et cum hymnum cecinissent*: "And when they had sung an hymn", but in Mark he rendered the same phrase as *Et cum hymnum dixissent*: "When they had said an hymn." But in either place it is read ὑμνήσαντες.

However, claimed Bullinger, the most convenient translation of ὑμνέω is "to praise, or to set forth one's praise", for it is patient both of the sense of singing and saying.[57] So even though Jesus and his disciples may have praised God by means of a hymn, this was no proof for Bullinger that there had been any singing. Moreover, he insisted, all available evidence indicated that Christ neither sang in the temple nor outside the temple. There was also no indication that Christ encouraged singing amongst the apostles or that the apostles sang themselves or that they attributed any value to singing in the church. Further, the passage at 1 Corinthians 14:15 seemed to encourage the worshippers to sing with the spirit and the understanding, and this for Bullinger was further evidence that no musical sounds were involved.

---

[56] *The Decades of Henry Bullinger*, Fifth Decade, Sermon 5, p. 191. "Quavering" is the translation of Bullinger's *modulatione*.

[57] *The Decades of Henry Bullinger*, Fifth Decade, Sermon 5, p. 191.

As for the passages at Colossians 3:16 and Ephesians 5:19 which referred to the use of singing with psalms, hymns and spiritual songs, Bullinger claimed that they were accounts of activities at private occasions and were irrelevant to liturgical worship. The distinction between private and liturgical singing was best illustrated, he said, by the Ephesians passage with its admonition "be not drunken with wine, wherein is excess; but be fulfilled with the spirit; speaking unto yourselves in psalms, and hymns, and spiritual songs".[58] Since being drunk with wine could only have been an issue at private functions, it being unthinkable to be drunk during a service, clearly, he argued, this passage could not be referring to public worship. So if there actually had been singing it would have been in a private setting. However, just to be sure, Bullinger rendered "singing" as "speaking". It was the words of faith, not the works of faith, which were now what mattered in worship, and that their importance had been neglected was a matter of great regret.

Bullinger conceded one point. His assertion that there was no New Testament evidence to support singing in worship permitted one exception: the church at Corinth had sung and Paul did not appear to condemn it. Nevertheless, Bullinger was quick to add, the acceptance of singing in this instance was possible only because "their manner of singing differeth much from the old".[59] The singing of the ancient Church was a "far other kind of singing than that which at this day is used" and only on this basis was it tolerated. Searching for a description of this "far other kind" of singing, Bullinger confirmed Erasmus's judgement that "the singing used in the ancient churches was no other than a distinct and measured pronunciation".[60] This account of the form in which singing was tolerated coincided with the oft-quoted recollection of Augustine concerning Athanasius, Bishop of Alexandria, "who with so little straining of the voice made the reader of the psalm to utter it, so that he rather seemed to read than to sing".[61] As Bullinger affirmed from

---

[58] *The Decades of Henry Bullinger*, Fifth Decade, Sermon 5, p. 192.
[59] *The Decades of Henry Bullinger*, Fifth Decade, Sermon 5, p. 192.
[60] Erasmus, *Commentary on 1 Corinthians 14:26*.
[61] *The Decades of Henry Bullinger*, Fifth Decade, Sermon 5, p. 194. The passage to which Bullinger is referring is: "I think the safer course is what I remember

Rabanus Maurus, "the primitive church did so sing, that with a little altering of the voice it made him that sang to be heard the further; so that the singing was more like loud reading than song".[62] Becon's forthright solution was to cast out of the churches "such chattering and fanglyng ways, or else to appoint them, that when they sing, they should rather rehearse the songes after the manner of such as reade, than followe the fashion of chattering charmers".[63]

Singing to resemble speech

Preferably there would be no singing whatsoever. However, if some sort of singing were unavoidable then it must be as monotone as possible, subject only to the natural inflections of ordinary speech. Sandys's *Injunction* of 1571 therefore enquired

> whether there be a modest and distinct song, so used concerning the said parts of the Common Prayer which be sung, that the same may be as plainly understood as if they were read without singing, and whether in any church or chapel, if singing be there used, such parts only of the Common Prayer be sung as by the Book of Common Prayer are appointed to be sung.[64]

In 1571, the ultra-Protestant Horne issued *Injunctions* for Winchester, legislating that in the quire

---

> has often been related to me about Athanasius, Bishop of Alexandria. He made the reader of the psalm utter it with so slight a vocal inflection that it was more like speaking than singing." *The Confessions of St Augustine*, Book X, Chapter 33, tr. John K. Ryan (New York: Image Books, 1960), p. 227.

[62] *The Decades of Henry Bullinger*, Fifth Decade, Sermon 5, pp. 193–4.
[63] Becon, *The reliques of Rome*, f. 120r–121.
[64] Sandys's "Articles for London Diocese 1571", Article 4, in Frere and Kennedy, *Visitation Articles and Injunctions* Vol. III, p. 304.

no note shall be used in song that shall drown any word or syllable, or draw out in length or shorten any word or syllable otherwise than by the nature of the word [as] it is pronounced in common speech, whereby the sentence cannot well be perceived by the hearers. And also the often reports or repeating of notes with words or sentences whereby the sense may be hindered in the hearer shall not be used.[65]

Condemnation of organs and instrumental music

Special loathing was reserved for instrumental music for it constituted an offering of pure sound, completely textless. At least pre-Reformation vocal settings had words, or rather the semblance of words, mostly distorted. Instrumental music did not even have any words to distort. Musicians responsible for such music, declared Sandys, were "feeding men's eyes with all glorious and glittering shews ... they invent to themselves instruments of music to delight the ear, but of the work of the Lord, of instructing the heart, of building the faith ... who seeth not how little regard they have?"[66]

Whilst the initial effect produced by instruments might be one of exhilaration and comfort, claimed Becon, it was nevertheless a false one. With continued listening, the sound of the instruments soon became one of distaste and revulsion.[67] Even though the Psalmist mentioned the use of various musical instruments such as the tabret, harp and viol, Merbecke judged this practice to be nothing but an impediment to true worship. He contemptuously dismissed the people of the Old Testament as tender and childish, becalmed in the shadow of the Old Law where sacrifices for forgiveness of sin were still regarded as acceptable. The inclusion of instrumental music in those earlier times was understandable because

---

[65] "Bishop Horne's Injunctions for Winchester Cathedral 1571", Article 6, in Frere and Kennedy, *Visitation Articles and Injunctions* Vol. III, p. 319.
[66] "A Sermon made in Paul's, on the Day of Christ's Nativity", in John Ayre (ed.), *The Sermons of Edwin Sandys* (Cambridge: Parker Society, 1842), p. 29.
[67] Becon, "The Jewel of Joy", p. 429.

God was still guiding his people towards a more enlightened approach. However, the days of tolerant tutelage had passed. Christ had now come and the brightness of the gospel had dispelled the darkness of the Old Covenant. In any case, Christ had offered the only legitimate sacrifice so that the offering of music or of any work of art was no longer appropriate. Those sacrifices of the Old Law could now be seen as nothing but foolish and lewd superstitions and any attempt to replicate them would be anathema.[68] It was true that instrumental music had been a traditional ingredient of the law of schooling and a significant part of the furniture of the temple, but it was now unacceptable and the need for its removal urgent.

Pope Vitalian, bemoaned Merbecke, was a prime example of someone who had inflicted great damage on the Church, not only by his misguided support for "prick song, descant, and all kynde of sweete and pleasaunt melodye", but for his pampering of the "vayne, folysh, and the idle eares of fond and fantastical men" by "joining the Organs to the curious musike".[69] "When they haunt their holy assemblies", said Merbecke, "I think that musical instruments are no more meet for the setting forth of God's praises than if a man shall call again censing and lamps and such other shadows of the law".[70] John Jewel took issue with the Dean of St Paul's, Henry Cole,[71] who claimed the affirmation *Omnis spiritus laudet Dominum* (Let all spirits praise the Lord)—the last line of Psalm 150 (Let everything that hath breath, praise the Lord)—was incontrovertible proof that there must be organs in the church. "Logic was good cheap", Jewel concluded, "when these arguments were allowed."[72]

---

[68] Merbecke, *A booke of notes and common places*, p. 755.
[69] Merbecke, *A booke of notes and common places*, p. 1020; Becon, *The reliques of Rome*, f. 116r.
[70] Merbecke, *A booke of notes and common places*, p. 754.
[71] Henry Cole (c.1500–79 or 80): Doctor of Civil Laws 1540; Archdeacon of Ely 1554; Dean of St Paul's 1556; Dean of the Arches 1557/8; committed to the Tower of London 1560, then to the Fleet prison, until his death.
[72] "The Reply of the Bishop of Sarum to the Letter Above Written", in John Ayre (ed.), *The Works of John Jewel, Bishop of Salisbury*, Vol. I (Cambridge: Parker Society, 1845), p. 78.

John Bale relished the opportunity to liken the despicable city of Babylon with the blasphemous and "prostibulous [relating to prostitutes] church of antichrist" which was so dangerously corrupting the present-day children of God.[73] With ominous relish he predicted that retribution was near, for as the Babylon of the Book of Revelation was thrown by the mighty angel like a millstone into the sea (18:21), so the same fate awaited all who presently perverted the true worship of God. Unsurprisingly musicians featured conspicuously in this apocalyptic devastation. As soon as all harpists, minstrels, flautists and trumpeters were forever banished upon this overthrow of the licentious Babylon, the faithful would be granted a peaceful and fulfilling existence, "all quietous without troubles". Then would God's true reformed church be spared such diabolical impediments as

> the merry noise of them that play upon harps, lutes and fiddles, the sweet voice of musicians that sing with virginals, viols and chimes, the harmony of them that pipe in recorders, flutes and drones, and the shrill shout of trumpets, waites, and shawms.[74]

To the relief of those yearning for an end to such blasphemous worship Bale confidently predicted that in the future those sounds would no longer be heard: "Neither shall the sweet organs containing the melodious noise of all manner of instruments and birds be played upon, nor the great bells be rung after that, nor yet the fresh descant, pricksong, counterpoint and faburden be called for." These were all marks of the synagogue of Satan and were responsible for nothing but "lascivious harmony and delectable music, much provoking the weak hearts of men to meddle with thy abominable whoredom by the wantonness of idolatry".[75] As far as Bale was concerned, their fate was self-evident: everlasting damnation.

Textless sound, so much a part of the pre-reformed worship and the perceived enemy of edification in the faith, continued to rile the reformers to the point where Articles and Injunctions were instituted to

---

[73] Bale, *Image of Both Churches*, p. 535.
[74] Bale, *Image of Both Churches*, p. 536.
[75] Bale, *Image of Both Churches*, p. 536.

restrict the use of organs, either to that of accompaniment rather than solo performances, or to complete silence. Cathedral worship appears to have been unaffected as Sandys's *Articles* of 1569 for Worcester Cathedral required that "their master be able and willing to instruct the choristers in singing and playing on the organs according to the statutes".[76] Yet in his *Articles*, which would have affected the parishes of the London Diocese of 1571, Sandys enquired whether "in your church or chapel any organs be used in the time of Common Prayer or ministration of the Communion, otherwise than is appointed by the said Book of Common Prayer, or by the Queen's Majesty's *Injunctions*".[77] Since the Book of Common Prayer and the *Royal Injunctions* of 1559 make no mention of the use of organs, Sandys is likely to have been referring to the rubrics which specified those parts of the services which could be sung and where the organs could be used as accompaniment.

Robert Horne found organs intolerable and used his *Injunctions* for Winchester College 1571 to forbid them. Then, not content with having eliminated the instrument, Horne went on to eliminate the instrumentalist. The organist's salary, together with that of a chaplain, was reallocated in a manner believed to be more agreeable to the getting of faith:

> *Item*, that the organs be no more used in service time, and the stipend for the organ player and that which was allowed to a chaplain to say mass in the chapel in the Cloister shall be hereafter by the Warden and fellows with the consent of the Bishop of Winchester turned to some other godly and necessary purpose in the college.[78]

---

[76] Sandys's "Articles for Worcester Cathedral", Article 16, in Frere and Kennedy, *Visitation Articles and Injunctions* Vol. III, p. 230.

[77] Sandys's "Articles for London Diocese 1571", Article 4, in Frere and Kennedy, *Visitation Articles and Injunctions* Vol. III, p. 304.

[78] Horne's "Injunctions for Winchester College", 1571, Article 27, in Frere and Kennedy, *Visitation Articles and Injunctions* Vol. III, p. 330.

Antagonism to musical performers

The discrediting of music moved seamlessly into a general condemnation of the singers and performers. If the music was deplorable, so also must be those who produced it. As cantankerous as ever, Becon applauded the sneer of the Bishop of Mende, Guillaume Durand, that singing in worship was perpetrated by carnal and fleshly, not spiritual and godly, men.[79] It was a disgrace, said Becon, that so many present at worship should be content with

> such a noyse as delight their eares, care nothyng, so that nowe it is come to this point, that with the common sort of people, all the worshippyng of God semeth to be set in these singsters, although generally there is no kynde of people more light, nor more leud.[80]

Such depravity was irritatingly apparent even in the procedures the singers adopted to prepare their voices for performance. Becon sided with Durand in condemning singers who, in the words of Jerome, anointed their "throats and chaws with sweet ointments after the manner of gameplayers".[81] Through such pampering of their voices these self-absorbed musicians were seducing people into coming to church "as into a common gameplace ... to heare them bo[o]ing, bleating and yelling".[82] For Robert Wisdom, musicians who cared only for the beauty of the sound they were producing were to be utterly despised. "All the care", he complained, "is to maintain and uphold ceremonies, images, and singing,

---

[79] Becon, *The reliques of Rome*, f. 120. Guillaume Durand (*c*.1230–96): Bishop of Mende, *Rationale divinorum officiorum, Book IV, On the Mass and Each Action Pertaining to it (Orig. pub. 1459)*, ed. T. Thibodeau, Corpus Christianorum in Translation CCT 14 (Turnhout: Brepols, 2013).

[80] Becon, *The reliques of Rome*, f. 120r.

[81] Becon, *The reliques of Rome*, f. 117r; "The Pathway Unto Prayer", p. 134. Jerome, *Commentariorum Hieronymi in Epistolam ad Ephesios*, Ca.V, in *Omnium Operum Divi Eusebii Hieronymi*, Tom. IX, f. 115r. (Basle, 1516).

[82] Becon, *The reliques of Rome*, f. 120r.

and playing on organs. But as for God's word, preaching or reading, they care not at all."[83] Predictably, Thomas Becon was also dismissive:

> Many delight in music, but few in the love of wisdom: many covet to excel in singing, playing, and dancing, but in the knowledge of God's word, very few. Many can abide to spend whole days and whole nights in musical exercises, but in hearing or reading the holy scriptures, they think one holy day in a week a great matter.[84]

A sure point of ignition for the reformers was that members of musical establishments received a salary. Bullinger duly leapt to the fray. These fraudsters worshipped God not for faith but for money, he propounded: "They sing not of their own accord or good will, but upon constraint, yea, they sing for money, and to the end that they may get an ecclesiastical benefice, as they term it."[85]

They hire these singers, Becon assured his readers, "with money, they cherishe and feede them, yea to be short, they thinke them alone to be the ornamentes and precious jewels of Gods house".[86] Edwin Sandys judged the payment of musicians to be symptomatic of the overall corruption of cathedral-style worship. "These ... cubs, enemies to the cross of Christ", he objected, "have under pretence of long prayer ... gotten to themselves the riches and wealth of the whole world with false merchandise, selling that for bread which is no bread, making their gain of masses, merits, pardons, and such like stuff". Pre-eminent in the category of "such like stuff" music had become one of those inventions and fantasies that was now performed, not for the glory of God, but for personal gain. Sandys bitterly condemned "the little foxes ... [who] what with singing, and what with begging, have raked no small heaps together".[87] Bullinger

---

[83] Strype, *Ecclesiastical Memorials* I, p. 321.
[84] Becon, "The Jewel of Joy", p. 429.
[85] *The Decades of Henry Bullinger*, Fifth Decade, Sermon 5, p. 191.
[86] Becon, *The reliques of Rome*, f. 120r.
[87] E. Sandys, "A Sermon made before the Parliament at Westminster", in John Ayre (ed.), *The Sermons of Edwin Sandys, D.D.* (Cambridge: Parker Society, 1842), pp. 63–4.

bewailed the practice whereby "only clerks hired for that purpose do now-a-days sing; not the whole church of Christ, as in time past hath been accustomed". He urged this arrangement be quickly discontinued.[88]

It was inevitable that the perceived corruption of musical establishments should be extended to embrace the religious institutions which harboured them. These houses were rife with despicable qualities, declaimed Becon: "pride, ambition, vain-glory, covetousness, whoredom, swearing, stealing, polling, picking, envy, malice, fighting, flattery, superstition, hypocrisy, papistry, idolatry, and all kind of abomination".[89] Disgracefully there still remained those who allocate immense riches "in nourishing many idle singing-men to bleat in their chapels, thinking so to do God an high sacrifice, and to pipe down their meat and their drink, and to whistle them asleep". This lavishing of resources on music reprehensively displaced any concern for having "a learned man in their houses to preach the word of God, to haste them to virtue and to dissuade them from vice".[90]

In his usual cantankerous style, Bale called for all "palaces, temples, abbeys, colleges, convents, chantries, fair houses, and orchards of pleasure" to be abandoned and built no more. Their desolation would bring the added advantage of forcing the departure of the religious dignitaries who inhabited them, considered by Bale to be dross of the first order. "Though in their painted stories", he expostulated, "they put popes, cardinals, and bishops, monks, canons, and shaven priests, friars, nuns and hermits in heaven among the saints", yet there are actually none there, and never will be. Their final resting place would not be in heaven, but at the bottom of the sea.[91] As Jewel had expostulated to Peter Martyr, "The cathedral churches were nothing else but dens of thieves, or worse, if any thing worse or more foul can be mentioned."[92]

---

[88] *The Decades of Henry Bullinger*, Fifth Decade, Sermon 5, pp. 196–7.
[89] Becon, "The Jewel of Joy", p. 429. Reference given as Proverbs 29, but possibly Proverbs 1:24.
[90] Becon, "The Jewel of Joy", p. 429.
[91] Bale, *Image of Both Churches*, pp. 536–7.
[92] Robinson, *Zurich Letters*, p. 45.

Musicians to be taught in the faith

Short of closing cathedrals altogether, the reformers were left with the option of changing their undoubted unsatisfactory and malignant culture by reapplying pressure on the biblical and theological edification of the musicians. As a result, the inculcation of members of choral establishments with the principles of an approved understanding of the faith continued to be of paramount concern. Horne's 1562 *Injunctions* for Winchester Cathedral had instructed that the choristers were to be "taught diligently by their master not alonely to sing, but also the Catechism in English such as is or shall be set forth by the Queen's authority". Competence in knowledge of the Catechism was to be strictly monitored: the choristers were to be "monthly examined by one of the prebendaries".[93] By 1571, Horne had stiffened the *Injunctions*, increasing the examinations from monthly to fortnightly. The choristers "shall not only learn to sing but also shall learn without book the Catechism in English written by Mr Nowell Dean of Pawles, and every fortnight shall be examined how they profit therein".[94] These *Injunctions* contained similar requirements for the men of the Cathedral Choir, who "shall resort to the said divinity lecture and diligently hear and note the same as other priests of the College and the town parishes shall do". The singing-men were now exposed to the same level of theological study as clergy and were to be "monthly examined ... how they have marked and remembered such points of doctrine".[95]

Grindal's *Injunctions* for York 1572 placed equal emphasis on the education of the choristers in the principles of religion, stipulating that they be examined "thrice in every quarter of a year in the English Catechism now lately set forth and enlarged".[96] Vicars-choral were obliged

---

[93] "Horne's Injunctions for Winchester Cathedral 1562", Article 19, in Frere and Kennedy, *Visitation Articles and Injunctions* Vol. III, p. 138.

[94] "Horne's Injunctions for Winchester Cathedral 1571", Article 23, in Frere and Kennedy, *Visitation Articles and Injunctions* Vol. III, p. 322.

[95] "Horne's Injunctions for Winchester Cathedral 1571", Article 23, in Frere and Kennedy, *Visitation Articles and Injunctions* Vol. III, p. 321.

[96] "Grindal's Injunctions for York Minster 1572", Article 16, in Frere and Kennedy, *Visitation Articles and Injunctions* Vol. III, p. 351.

to attend a daily divinity lecture, and to give a monthly account of their grasp of the material to the Chancellor of the Minster or to the reader of the lecture.[97] The vicars-choral were also required to commit to memory a chapter of one of Paul's Epistles each week, beginning with the first to the Romans. Token relief was offered to those over the age of 40. Instead of memorizing a chapter a week, mastery of the overall content was all that was required. There was a penalty for failure: "Whosoever shall make default herein, after three several admonitions, if he do not amend the same, [is] to be displaced, and some better placed in his room."[98] No respite from biblical and theological learning was afforded. Those in commons in the Bederne

> shall daily by course immediately after dinner read one chapter of the four Evangelists: and every day after supper shall read one chapter of the Acts of the Apostles, or some chapter of S. Paul's Epistles: and the same to be read in order, one chapter after another unto the end of the said books.[99]

---

[97] "Grindal's Injunctions for York Minster 1572", Article 5, in Frere and Kennedy, *Visitation Articles and Injunctions* Vol. III, p. 347.

[98] "Grindal's Injunctions for York Minster 1572", Article 8, in Frere and Kennedy, *Visitation Articles and Injunctions* Vol. III, p. 348.

[99] "Grindal's Injunctions for York Minster 1572", Article 9, in Frere and Kennedy, *Visitation Articles and Injunctions* Vol. III, pp. 348–9. The impetus for this intense programme of edification was a religious one—that of inculcating musicians responsible for worship with the biblical and theological knowledge consistent with reformed principles. Any suggestion that the motive was a desire to improve musicians' learning and virtue in accordance with humanistic principles can only be a peripheral one.

Antagonism to worship as embodiment of the divine

The essential element underpinning this broad range of objection was the implacable opposition to any element of worship which might be construed to embody the divine or thwart the conveying of faith by means of direct and comprehensible dialectic: so-called rational declaration. The more extreme reformers concluded that music was so embedded in the concept of worship as an embodiment of the divine, and so complicit in the obliteration of the sense of the words, that it could only be summarily dismissed as illegitimate. The idea that the divine presence could be experienced in worship and that the words of faith could be appreciated in any other form than the spoken vernacular was unconscionable.

For other reformers, music was tolerable but only if dehydrated of ornamentation and reduced to such a bland accompaniment of the words as could scarcely be distinguished from reading. Yet such was the force of their apprehension that, as Bullinger acknowledged, it was always going to be a hard thing "so to limit and restrain singing, which otherwise is tolerable, lest at some time it exceed and go beyond the appointed bounds".[100] As Merbecke summed up, "lest some corruption should creep in, which doth defile the pure service of God, and also bind men with superstition", music in worship was always to be feared.[101]

---

[100] *The Decades of Henry Bullinger*, Fifth Decade, Sermon 5, p. 197.
[101] Merbecke, *A booke of notes and common places*, pp. 754–5.

5

Understanding Enhanced by Music

As well as harbouring a deep-seated and abiding apprehension of worship once more becoming a means of embodying the present reality of God, with all the implications of a propitiatory offering that would follow, the reformers maintained their insistence that the words of worship be understood. In this respect, some encouragement was to be found in the increasing participation in the singing of psalms. Not only was this an opportunity to become involved in the expression of faith, but the style of metrical verse allowed the words to be readily delivered, understood and remembered.

Metrical psalms

Metrical psalms were not sung in the context of Morning or Evening Prayer where the psalms of the day were observed in accordance with the prose text supplied by the Great Bible of 1539; and where they were sung rather than read, they would have followed the traditional tones of plainsong. Yet even though the metrical psalms could not have taken the place of the prose psalms, it was possible for them to be sung in church, albeit before or after Morning and Evening Prayer or before or after sermons. However, the expectation was for them to be used outside worship in church.

Even so, the metrical psalm was welcomed as evidence of the growing influence of the need for edification and exposition of the faith. As early as 5 March 1560, John Jewel had reported this progress to Peter Martyr: "Religion is now somewhat more established than it was... the practice of joining in church music has very much conduced to this."[1] With great satisfaction, Jewel informed Peter Martyr that "as soon as they had once commenced singing in public in only one little church in London, immediately not only the churches in the neighbourhood, but even the towns far distant, began to vie with each other in the same practice".[2] Particularly gratifying was the popularity of singing at gatherings outside churches. On one occasion at Paul's Cross, Jewel estimated, perhaps with a degree of optimism, that after one particular sermon 6,000 persons, old and young and of both sexes, all sang together. By such means, reflected Jewel, the disgraced pre-reformed liturgy was weakened and shaken. This is a practice which annoys the mass-priests and the Devil, he declared, "for they perceive that by these means the sacred discourses sink more deeply into the minds of men, and that their kingdom is weakened and shaken at almost every note".[3]

According to St Gregory Nazianzus, Jewel noted, the church where Basil preached resounded to the singing of all the worshippers, not just a few: when the emperor Valens entered the church where St Basil preached, he was "stricken with the psalmody, as if it had been with a thunder".[4] Inspired by Gregory's allusion to the "thundering roll of the psalms" and the "sea of heads of the congregation", Jewel warmed to the prospect of whole congregations singing together: "In our prayers that we make to God we raise up such a sound of the voices of men, women, and children praying together, as if it were the noise of the waves beating against the sea-banks."[5] Singing was to be the work of the whole body

---

[1] John Ayre (ed.), *The Works of John Jewel, Bishop of Salisbury*, Vol. IV (Cambridge: Parker Society, 1845–50), p. 1231.

[2] *Works of John Jewel* IV, p. 1231.

[3] *Works of John Jewel* IV, p. 1231.

[4] *Works of John Jewel* I, p. 266. "Select Orations of Saint Gregory Nazianzen, Sometime Archbishop of Constantinople", tr. C. Browne and J. Swallow, in H. Wace and P. Schaff (eds), *A Select Library of Nicene and Post-Nicene Fathers of the Christian Church*, Vol. VII (Oxford: Parker & Co., 1894), p. 412. St Gregory Nazianzus (*c.*329–*c.*389): Bishop of Sasima 372; Patriarch of Constantinople. Basil of Caesarea (*c.*330–79): Bishop of Caesarea 370.

[5] *Works of John Jewel* I, p. 290.

of worshippers, freed from any semblance of being channelled through a priestly filter, or undertaken by a choir on behalf of others or in any way associated with the trappings of a discredited propitiatory offering. The value of such wholesale participation in the expression of faith also enabled personal intimacy with God. "As it were with one mouth," Jewel quoted of Basil, "and from [the] heart, they offer up unto the Lord the psalm of confession, and the words of repentance every one of them applieth particularly unto himself."[6] This was possible because the people sang the psalms together and understood what they sang. Jewel praised St Gregory's admonition for singing in the church to be "fitter for the multitude of people than for the priest", noting that whilst Gregory expressly forbade the priest to sing in the church, he could not recall that he ever forbade the people.[7] The only musical role granted the priest was that of setting the psalm in motion. The priest "beginneth the holy psalmody", Jewel quoted from Dionysius, and "the whole body of the church singeth with him".[8]

Certainly, the quality of metrical psalms was improving. Thomas Sternhold's collection of 1549, published in Geneva in 1556 and used by the exiles, was unharmonized and of little musical substance.[9] By contrast, a revision by John Day in a collection of c.1563, entitled *The whole psalms in foure partes, which may be song to al musicall instruments, set forth*

---

[6] *Works of John Jewel* I, p. 290. *Tanquam ab uno ore, et ab uno corde, confessionis psalmum offerunt Domino, et verba poenitentiae eorum quisque proprie ascribit sibi.* Basil: *Ad. Cler. Neoc. Epist.* ccvii.

[7] *Works of John Jewel* I, p. 266.

[8] *Works of John Jewel* I, p. 115. Dionysius the Great (d.264): Bishop of Alexandria. Jonathan Willis has noted the importance the Church Fathers attached to the singing of psalms, in particular Basil, Ambrose, Augustine and Chrysostom, in *Church Music and Protestantism in Post-Reformation England: Discourses, Sites and Identities* (Aldershot: Ashgate, 2010), pp. 39–44.

[9] The introduction of Geneva-style psalm-singing is dealt with in detail in R. Zim, *English Metrical Psalms: Poetry as Praise and Prayer, 1535–1601* (Cambridge: Cambridge University Press, 1987) and discussed in P. Le Huray, *Music and the Reformation in England 1549–1660* (Cambridge: Cambridge University Press, 1978), pp. 372–6.

for the encrease of virtue: and abolishing of other vayne and triflyng ballades, Collected into English Meter, contained elegant harmonizations in four parts by established composers such as William Parsons, Thomas Caustun and Richard Edwardes.

Allowance for metrical psalms to be included in worship, albeit placed peripherally, was incorporated into Horne's diocesan *Injunctions* of 1571, which required the chanter of the clerks and choristers to have in readiness "books of psalms set forth in English metre to be provided at the costs of the church, and to sing in the body of the church both afore the sermon and after the sermon one of the said psalms to be appointed at the discretion of the said Chanter".[10]

Psalms by alternate sides

The practice of singing the psalms by alternate sides remained a source of contention. That psalms may previously have been sung by sides, Jewel noted, constituted no precedent for them to be sung by priests and clerks alone. It was the whole people who were divided into two parts, the one part "making answer by course to the other".[11] Antiphonal singing of the psalms could be tolerated but only on the condition that the whole congregation was involved. The idea of music being sung by a choir alone was abhorrent and unnervingly redolent of music as an offering made to God by some on behalf of others.

---

[10] "Horne's Injunctions for Winchester Cathedral 1562", Article 18, in W. H. Frere and W. M. Kennedy (eds), *Visitation Articles and Injunctions of the Period of the Reformation, III, 1559–1575* (London: Longmans, Green & Co., 1910), p. 138.

[11] *Works of John Jewel* I, p. 266.

Archbishop Matthew Parker

Throughout his episcopate, Matthew Parker, Archbishop of Canterbury 1559–75, maintained his support for the music appropriate to cathedrals and choral establishments. His long familiarity with this tradition placed him in an advantageous position to appreciate their value. Whilst dean of the College of St John Baptist de Stoke at Stoke-by-Clare in the Diocese of Norwich, a position he held from 1535 until the college's suppression in 1547,[12] Parker was involved in its musical life and consolidated its standing. Originally a Benedictine priory, the college had been secularized in 1415, becoming a collegiate church consisting of a dean and six canons, eight vicars, two greater clerks and five choristers. Parker not only accepted this establishment but raised the number of choristers from five to eight, "then to ten and more".[13] He founded a grammar school for children within the college, the scholars of which were taught "to sing and to play upon the Organs, and other Instruments of Musicke".[14] As a canon of Ely from 1541, Parker may have become familiar with the works of Christopher Tye, who was at Ely from 1541 to 1561.

As well as being immersed in this elaborate style of music, Parker maintained the ceremonies associated with it. During his tenure as dean, articles of accusation against him were sent to Lord Audley, the Lord Chancellor, concerning a procession during the Easter Vigil, probably in 1539. The complaint was that the procession was "but a pageant". The procession was justified, countered Parker, because it was an open proclamation of resurrection faith and a public declaration that "they would henceforth follow Christ in their conversation; that as Christ once died, and died no more, that so would they cease and die to sin, no more to live therein". This liturgical act, he argued, inspired intense devotion as

---

[12] J. Strype, *The Life and Acts of Matthew Parker* (London: printed for John Wyat, 1711), p. 8. 1535 is the date favoured by V. J. K. Brook, *A Life of Archbishop Parker* (Oxford: Clarendon Press, 1962, rev. 1965), p. 16.

[13] Strype, *The Life and Acts of Matthew Parker*, p. 9.

[14] Strype, *The Life and Acts of Matthew Parker*, p. 8. The period spent by Parker at Stoke-by-Clare is discussed fully in Brook, *A Life of Archbishop Parker*, pp. 13–22.

the congregation followed the choir about the church while the antiphon *Christus resurgens*, with the verse commencing *Dicant nunc Iudaei*, was sung.[15] His *Injunctions* of 1570 for Canterbury Cathedral required that the "Chanter, the Mr [Master] of the choristers and Mr Swifte do examine the skill in singing of the vicars and singing men and of the choristers; and thereby to certify my Lord his Grace before Friday next". That the report of the singers' competence was to be submitted to the archbishop indicates Parker's interest in the standard of musicianship in the cathedral and that it be diligently upheld.

Parker's appreciation of the music expected of cathedrals and places where there were choral establishments remained consistent with the monarch's resolve to retain a dignified and richly adorned ceremonial with what was known as skilful music, both choral and instrumental. Parker was aware of Elizabeth's determination to preserve cathedrals and their ecclesiastical and musical establishments which, quite apart from her personal affection for music, she regarded as necessary to give shape and substance to the sovereign's authority as defender of the faith and head of the Church.[16]

---

[15] "Answer to Articles of Accusation sent to the Lord Audley, Lord Chancellor, against M. Parker by Mr G. Colt and other of Clare Town", in J. Bruce and T. T. Perowne (eds), *Correspondence of Matthew Parker, Comprising Letters Written by and to Him, From A.D. 1535 to His Death, A.D. 1575* (Cambridge: Parker Society, 1853, repr. Eugene, OR: Wipf & Stock, 2005), p. 7. *Christus resurgens ex mortuis, iam non moritur, mors illi ultra non dominabitur* (Romans 6:9): "Christ being raised from the dead dies no more; death has no more dominion over him."

[16] C. Haigh, *Why do we have Cathedrals? A Historian's View, or How English Cathedrals Survived the Reformation*, The St George's Cathedral Perth Lecture 1998.

Thomas Whythorne

Parker's support for music was acknowledged in the autobiography of the musician Thomas Whythorne (1528–96), who in 1571 was appointed the Master of Music of Parker's private chapel. Earlier that year he had published a collection of 76 *Songes of three, fower and five partes*. "When all these foresaid circumstances were thus finished about the printing of my music", wrote Whythorne, "there was a motion made unto me to serve Doctor Parker".[17] In a preface to *Of songs for five voyces*, in the tenor book, Whythorne expressed his appreciation of the good work of the zealous few who were committed to restoring music to its former place of honour. In a thinly veiled reference to the iconoclastic enthusiasms of the reformers, he noted that this place of honour held by music had been recently abandoned because of "a lack of virtue achieving the preeminence" [of music]. The welcome renewal of interest in the status of music he attributed to the support of the sovereign and to her more enlightened followers:

> Of Musik, though the chief knowledge hath long time hindered been,
> Because virtue not being maintained, soon ceaseth it is seen,
> Yet through the good zeal of a few, who therein pleasure took,
> No costs nor pains it to preserve of long time they forsook,
> Beside our Prince's charge of late to have it eft renewed,
> With virtuous rulers under her, whose willingness is shewed.[18]

As well as acknowledging the queen for her support, Whythorne's reference to "the virtuous rulers under her" refers logically to Parker as her archbishop, a sentiment supported by his mention of the archbishop at the time of his appointment: "The which service I refused not, because I did know that by his place he was the most honourable man in the realm

---

[17] J. Osborn (ed.), *The Autobiography of Thomas Whythorne* (London: Oxford University Press, 1962), p. 208.

[18] *Of Songs for five voyces, composed and made by Tho. Whythorne* (London, 1571), Tenor book. *Eft*: again.

next unto the Queen."[19] Parker directed Whythorne to provide music for his metrical rendering of Psalm 107. "He willed me", wrote Whythorne, "to make a note and song of four parts to a piece or staff of the 107th Psalm (the which he had translated and turned into English verse) for to be sung in his chapel; the which I did perform."[20]

Parker's support for words to be understood

However, consistent with the new understanding of worship, Parker became a strong advocate for the words which were sung to be understood. On a personal note, this approach may have received some impetus from a curious incident which occurred at the time of Kett's Rebellion in 1549, recorded by his secretary Alexander Neville. Thomas Conyers, vicar of St Martin's Norwich, was saying the Litany under the so-called Oak of Reformation in the rebels' camp at Mousehold Heath, when a moment of prayerful calm was regarded by Parker as a convenient opportunity for the propagation of the gospel, and so he began to preach. The mood of the crowd soon changed from cautious tolerance to simmering hostility and it became apparent that Parker had made an unfortunate error of judgement. As recounted by Neville, "tremendous fear seized him, and he seemed to be in a very dangerous position".[21] A decidedly sinister aspect to Parker's predicament arose when "there was heard a clattering of Weapons under him, so that he looked for present Death".[22] With considerable presence of mind the resourceful Conyers rallied his singers around him and "on purpose to divert the Mischief" fell into singing the *Te Deum*, which stilled the mob and so "gave opportunity to the Preacher to convey himself away".[23] Neville's account of the incident

---

[19] *Autobiography of Thomas Whythorne*, p. 208.

[20] *Autobiography of Thomas Whythorne*, p. 208.

[21] Alexander Neville, *De furoribus Norfolciensium Ketto duce* (London, 1582), p. 23.

[22] Strype, *The Life and Acts of Matthew Parker*, p. 27.

[23] Strype, *The Life and Acts of Matthew Parker*, p. 27.

noted the manner in which the *Te Deum* was sung and the beauty of its effect. Suddenly Conyers

> with three or four sacristans around him, began to sing the *Te Deum* in English to a piece of religious music, and in parts, elegantly distinguished so as to delight the ear. Little by little, their cruel and savage tempers cooled down, soothed by an unaccustomed pleasure (for music was not the usual occurrence) of the singing, filled as it was with sweetness.[24]

That a hostile group of agitators, demonstrating against enclosures which threatened their livelihood and verging on violence, should have been pacified by the singing of a *Te Deum* in English, as well as being sufficiently diverted as to allow an irritating preacher to escape, is remarkable. Whether or not this incident had been enhanced by Neville, the reference to the singing of a *Te Deum* is specific. There are settings of the *Te Deum* in the Wanley books dating from 1547 and 1548[25] and a setting of the *Te Deum* exists in Robert Crowley's *Psalter of David newely translated into Englysh metre* printed in 1549. Whatever setting was used, it clearly engaged the crowd and would have cemented in Parker's mind the material, even life-enhancing, benefits of clearly expressed words in the vernacular with simple harmonies.

By 1562, just three years into his time as archbishop, Parker's sympathy for metrical psalmody became evident in his *Articles* for Merton College Oxford, which enquired as to whether "the warden and more part of the fellows have decreed before Hallowtide last that in the stead of certain superstitious hymns appointed for certain feasts in the hall, English psalms in metre should be sung".[26] By then, the first so-called Sternhold and Hopkins psalter with music had already been printed in Geneva in 1556 and John Day's 1560 edition was also available.

---

[24] Neville, *De furoribus Norfolciensium Ketto duce*, pp. 23–4.
[25] The content of the Wanley books is given and discussed in Le Huray, *Music and the Reformation in England*, pp. 172–5.
[26] "Parker's Articles for Merton College, Oxford, 1562", Article 18, in Frere and Kennedy, *Visitation Articles and Injunctions* Vol. III, p. 121.

In a letter to Cecil on 27 August 1563, Parker gave an account of his visit to the parish church of St Peter's Sandwich, probably occasioned by the presence of Flemish Protestants who since 1560 had been living in Sandwich and had used St Peter's as their church. He wholeheartedly commended the music, which was sung, possibly metrical psalms: "Their Service", he reported, "was sung in good distinct harmony." That the choir was comprised of local villagers, including the mayor, added to Parker's satisfaction.[27] The clarity of the harmonies would have encouraged the discernment of the words and a choir consisting of the general run of parishioners eliminated the spectre of a specialist choir offering music on behalf of the congregation.

On 3 June 1564, Parker informed Cecil of a visit by a French delegation led by Monsieur de Gonour, whose chief purpose was to investigate the "order and using of our religion". He noted much, reported Parker, and was "delighted in our mediocrity [moderation]", charging the Genevans and the Scottish of "going too far in extremities". Parker assured the delegation that in the ministration of the Common Prayer and sacraments "we use such reverent mediocrity, and that we did not expel musick out of our quires, telling them that our musick drowned not the principal regard of our prayer".[28] "Reverent mediocrity" conceded that there was music, but not of an extravagant polyphonic style. "Not expelling music from our Quires" allowed for music sung by choirs. The "principal regard" is stated to be that of edification for which the words had to be clearly delivered and discerned, uncompromised by music. That the words should be distinct was made clear in Parker's final version of the *Book of Advertisements* sent to Cecil on 28 March 1566. They duly appeared as *Advertisements, partly for due order in the publique administration of common prayers and usinge the holy sacramentes, and partly for the apparell of all persons ecclesiasticall*. The first item under "Articles for administration of prayer and sacraments" ordered that

> the common prayer be said or sung decently and distinctly in such place as the Ordinary shall think meet for the largeness

---

[27] *Correspondence of Matthew Parker*, p. 189.

[28] *Correspondence of Matthew Parker*, p. 215.

and straightness of the church and choir, so that the people may be most edified.[29]

Despite his determination to ensure the congregations be edified and therefore the words of worship be presented clearly, Parker resisted attempts to eliminate music described by its detractors as "exquisite singing". He navigated his way adroitly between the edification of the congregation and the preservation of so-called exquisite singing and organs.

Opposition from major reformers

Laurence Humphrey, President of Magdalen College Oxford, and Thomas Sampson, who in 1566 had been deprived of the deanery of Christ Church Oxford, alerted Heinrich Bullinger of 13 blemishes presently corrupting the Church, one of which was "in addition to the exquisite singing in parts, the use of organs is becoming more general in the churches".[30] From Zurich, Bullinger conveyed his horror in a joint letter with Rodolph Gualter to Edmund Grindal and Robert Horne, then bishops of London and Winchester respectively.[31] They had both been signatories to Archbishop Parker's *Advertisements* of 1566, which had failed to discredit or prohibit the liturgical use of exquisite singing, measured chanting and the use of organs.[32] "We have now heard, though we hope the report is false", Bullinger and Gualter tartly observed, "that

---

[29] E. Cardwell (ed.), *Documentary Annals of the Reformed Church of England ... from the year 1546 to the Year 1716*, Vol. I (Oxford, 1844), p. 325.

[30] H. Robinson (ed.), *The Zurich Letters I, A.D.1558–1579* (Cambridge: Parker Society, 1842), p. 164.

[31] Rodolf Gwalter (also Gualter) (1519–86) succeeded Bullinger as Antistes (Head) of the Zurich Church 1575–85.

[32] Cardwell, *Documentary Annals of the Reformed Church of England ... from the year 1546 to the Year 1716*, Vol. I, pp. 321–31; H. Gee and W. J. Hardy, *Documents Illustrative of English Church History* (London: Macmillan, 1896), pp. 467–75.

it is required of ministers, either to subscribe to some new articles, or to relinquish their office. And the articles are said to be; that the measured chanting in churches is to be retained, and in a foreign language, together with the sound of organs."[33] Further dismay was expressed at "music which they call figurative, and ... their musical instruments, all which are contained in a manner in their organs, as they term them".[34] The only possible course of action, they recommended, was "to efface these blemishes from the holy church of Christ which is in England",[35] and to prevent any bishop from dismissing ministers who refused to assent to Parker's *Advertisements*.

In response, Grindal and Horne reassured Bullinger that their personal zeal for the extinction of exquisite singing and organs was undiminished. "We do not assent", they declared, "that the chanting in churches, together with the organ, is to be retained, but we disapprove of it, as we ought to do."[36] This affirmation of reformed orthodoxy has to be tempered by Grindal's communication to Bullinger of six months previously, 27 August 1566, when Grindal conceded that those who are now bishops had "contended long and earnestly for the removal of those things that have occasioned the present dispute; but as we were unable to prevail, either with the queen or the parliament, we judged it best, after a consultation on the subject, not to desert our churches for the sake of a few ceremonies, and those not unlawful in themselves, especially since the pure doctrine of the gospel remained in all its integrity and freedom". This, he added, was a resolution "we do not regret". This was an unsurprising resolution given the queen's determination to maintain the ceremonial and ritual of worship as she saw fit.

Parker's refusal to enforce restrictions on the style of music which was sung fanned the ire of two already disgruntled reformers, George Withers and John Barthelot. In correspondence of August 1567, they complained

---

[33] Cardwell, *Documentary Annals of the Reformed Church of England ... from the year 1546 to the Year 1716*, Vol. I, p. 358.

[34] T. Harding (ed.), *The Decades of Henry Bullinger* (Cambridge: Parker Society, 1849–52), Fifth Decade, Sermon 5, p. 197.

[35] Robinson, *Zurich Letters* I, p. 358.

[36] Robinson, *Zurich Letters* I, p. 178. Dated 6 February 1567.

bitterly to Bullinger and Rodolf Gwalther that despite assurances to the contrary from the bishops of London and Winchester, music persisted to the detriment of true worship. They say, reported Withers and Barthelot, "that they disapprove the chanting of choristers, and the use of organs" but notwithstanding these assurances they all adopt them in their churches. Particular culpability was attributed to Parker, who to their fury had "caused an organ to be erected in his metropolitan church at his own expense".[37]

The content of these *Advertisements* had been a contentious issue with the arch-reformists Humphrey and Sampson from the moment of their submission in draft form to Cecil.[38] Both these reformers, with other dissidents, remained implacable in their hostility to the *Advertisements* and continued to exasperate Parker with their unrelenting complaint. Corresponding with Cecil around Easter 1565, Parker had expressed his wish that Sampson and Humphrey had been "put to the choice, either conformity or depart".[39] He confided to Cecil that "as for the most part of these recusants, I would wish them out of the ministry, as mere ignorant and vain heads".[40]

Parker's version of metrical psalms

Whilst maintaining his endorsement of more complex choral music, Parker's support for metrical psalms remained undiluted, even to the extent of producing his own version with a learned commentary. Whilst the literary quality of Parker's verses is variable, his selection of references which form the Preface to the Psalter unequivocally endorse music's ability to embody the sense of the words. He offered significant ecclesiastical support for the importance of music based on its ability to

---

[37] *Zurich Letters* II, p. 150.
[38] 3 March 1565, *Correspondence of Matthew Parker*, p. 233.
[39] *Correspondence of Matthew Parker*, p. 240.
[40] *Correspondence of Matthew Parker*, p. 272. Parker's use of the word "recusant" refers to those refusing to wear clerical dress rather than Catholics refusing to attend the established services.

represent the meaning of the texts and effectively convey that meaning. His completed work was published in a limited edition in 1567, perhaps 1568, and was entitled *The whole Psalter translated into English Metre, which contayneth an hundredth and fifty Psalmes.*[41]

In his version of Ecclesiasticus 44:4–5, music is praised for replicating human moods and emotions, thereby stimulating a more profound understanding of the Scriptures:

> The fathers olde: both sought and found,
> Sweete musikes moodes full fine:
> The Scripture songes: they did expound,
> Their hartes were all devine.[42]

In the section *Of the vertue of Psalmes*, Parker commends the singing of psalms as a means of acquiring the grace to eschew evil and embrace virtue:

> For who delyghth: them well to sing: [delighteth]
> His mynde shall feele a grace:
> Of sinne both dulde: and cursed sting: [dulled]
> And vertue come in place.

Beautiful music "tuned" the verse and made its reception a joy:

---

[41] Printed by John Day, the Psalter was entered in the registers of the Company of Stationers between 22 July 1567 and 22 July 1568. For discussion of the date, L. Ellinwood, "Tallis's Tunes and Tudor Psalmody", *Musica Disciplina* II (1948), p. 192.

[42] ["Let us now praise famous men, and our fathers in their generations ... There were those ...] leaders of the people in their deliberations and in understanding of learning for the people, wise in their words of instruction; those who composed musical tunes, and set forth verses in writing."

The Psalmes sayth he: in verse he tolde:
And tuned by musike sweete:
The ear to please: of yong and olde:
So David thought it meete.

Parker even acknowledged that the musical settings of the psalms stimulated deeper insights into the human spirit and the heart of humanity than that which could be achieved through the spoken words:

Josephus sayth: and Philo writeth,
That David Metres made:
Quinquemetres: some trimetres,
by musikes tract and trade.[43]

For that that is, commended both
With tune and tyme aright,
It sinkth more sweet: and deeper goth [goeth],
In harte of man's delight.

David's placating of Saul's rage by his performance on the harp affirmed for Parker music's ability to soothe the frenzy of violent emotions:

The Psalmist stayde: with tuned songe,
The rage of myndes agast:
As David did: with harpe among
To Saule in furye cast.

---

[43] Philo Judaeus of Alexandria (20 BC–c. AD 40): Jewish philosopher. *Tract*: attraction; *trade*: course, way, path. "Then they sing hymns which have been composed in honour of God in many metres and tunes, at one time all singing together, and at another moving their hands and dancing in corresponding harmony, and uttering in an inspired manner songs of thanksgiving, and at another time regular odes, and performing all necessary strophes and antistrophes." *De Vita Contemplativa*, in *The Works of Philo*, tr. C. Yonge (Peabody, MA: Hendrickson, 2011), p. 706.

> With golden stringes: such harmonie,
> His harpe so sweete did wrest:
> That he relievd: his phrenesie
> Whom wicked sprites possest.

That music could enhance rather than hinder contemplation of the divine had apostolic endorsement:

> Both Paule and James: in their devise,
> Bid Psalmes with voyce to use:
> In hymnes and songes: sweete exercise,
> To God in hart to muse.[44]

So integral was music to an understanding of the words that Parker judged the work of the musician and the poet to be inseparable:

> The singyng man: and Poete must,
> With grave devine concurre: [divine—priest; theologian]
> As David's skill: all three discust, [musician, poet, theologian]
> When he his harpe did sturre.

In a section entitled *Basilius in Psalmos*, Parker cited several passages from Basil's homilies on the psalms. From the homily on Psalm 1 he referred to Basil's assertion that music was a gift of the Holy Spirit intentionally incorporated by God into that truth of himself which was humanity's destiny to discover. Engagement with the beauty of music enabled the reality of the divine nature to enter the human consciousness unobtrusively and unconsciously:

> What hath he [the Holy Ghost] invented? He hath mixt in his forme of doctrine the delectation of musike, to thintent that the commoditie of the doctrine might secretlye steale into us, while our eares bee touched with the pleasauntnes of the melodie.

---

[44] Paul in Ephesians 5:19 and Colossians 3:16; James in James 5:13.

Also, from this same homily, Parker referred to Basil's statement that whilst music might momentarily claim a love of the sounds for the sounds' sake, this could never be a permanent attitude because the music was so wedded to the text, and so competently enhanced it, that the truth it expressed would in time be appreciated and claim precedence:

> And for this ende be these sweete and harmonious songes devised for us, that such as be children either by age or children by manners, should in deede have their soules wholesomely instructed, though for the time they seme but to sing onely.

Power of music

Perhaps recollecting the incident at Mousehold Heath, Parker extolled the power of music to calm the moods and emotions and prepare the mind for reflection upon the holy, for "certainly though a man were never so furiouslye raging in ire and wrath, yet as soon as he heare the swete tunes of the Psalmes, straight way is he asswaged of his fury, and must depart more quiet in mynd by reason of the melodie".

Parker recalled Basil's observation that David preferred the psalms to be accompanied by the psaltery rather than the harp or lute, because the sweetness of the psaltery, being derived principally from its upper register, was able to direct the worshipper more effectively to the things of heaven. Whilst it was possible that the "sweeteness of the tunes" could stimulate the "sensuall affections and delectations of the fleshe", David's designation of the psaltery, with its concentration on the upper registers, would ensure a proper focus on the divine.

Parker included John Chrysostom's plea that "we have ... muche needs to have Davids harpe to sing to our soule some divine harmony". The sayings of Holy Scripture, in particular the psalms, have a great influence upon the soul and the singing of these psalms is highly valued because it was through singing that "the outwarde voyce maye edifie the inwarde mynde".[45]

Parker included Augustine's oft-quoted musings on the worth of music.[46] Augustine confessed to being stirred to devotion more when the words were set to music than not. Voice and melody conspired together with what Augustine described as a secret familiarity and similitude, diversely to affect, even ravish, the mind. Parker gave a full accounting of Augustine's musical reflections and included passages which credited music with positive attributes, passages omitted by the more strident reformers. So Parker included Augustine's regret that he had resorted to "over much sower gravitie" and had once wished for "all such swete harmonie of delectable singing wherewith Davids Psalter is used to be sung, utterly removed not from mine owne ears only, but banished out of the Church to[o]". Parker also added Augustine's admission that he had advocated such extreme measures because he thought at the time it was only by this means the Church could be protected from abuse. Parker also incorporated the final part of Augustine's admission which the opponents of music conveniently omitted, that when the words are delivered with rich expression and skilful harmony, singing is to be commended. Here Parker gives a true account of Augustine's actual statement and corrects the false impression put about by music's detractors:

> When I cal to minde what teares I wept at the hearings of the songes which thy churche and congregation did use to sing to thee (O Lord) what time I first began to recover my faith unto thee (as me thinke even yet still I feele myself ravished, not yet with the singing, but with the sweete matter which is sung, specially, when it is sung with full expressed voyces and with decent harmonie) then againe I judge this ordinance of singing to be much profitable and expedient.

---

[45] *St. John Chrysostom: Commentary on the Psalms*, Vol. 1, tr. R. Hill (Brookline, MA: Holy Cross Orthodox Press, 1998), Commentary on Psalm 44:12, p. 245.

[46] Cf. Merbecke and Bullinger.

Although Augustine may well have wrestled with his conscience in search of a carefully hedged conclusion, "tost betwixt the danger of vaine delectation and the experience of wholesome edification", he nevertheless ceded to music a facility to convey the word of God in a highly attractive, if sensual, manner. However, this attractiveness, he maintained, could well inspire interest with those for whom the spoken word was not sufficiently inviting. So Augustine found himself "inclined and induced to allowe this custom of singing in the churche... that the weaker sorte of men might by suche delectation of the eare, rise up to godly affection and heavenly devotion". Parker's inclusion of Augustine's complete statement was a powerful rebuttal of those commentators who had misrepresented Augustine's position.

Parker continued with a passage from Flavius Josephus which supported the use of instruments in worship. As well as compose songs and hymns, David had "caused divers instruments to be made, and he taught the Levites how they should in their diversities sing and play hymns on the Sabbath and other festival days".[47] Parker also included Eusebius's account of Philo worshipping in Rome with the early Christians in the reign of the Emperor Claudius. According to Philo these congregations sang hymns "with all kinde of grave numbers and rythmes in a comely honest maner, and with sweete harmonie".[48] The music referred to by Philo was congenial to the learned and virtuous and was to be accepted in worship, whilst music which would deter worthwhile reflection was to be rejected.

---

[47] *The Works of Flavius Josephus*, Vol. I, tr. William Whiston (London: Ward, Lock & Co., 1862), Book 7, Chapter 12, pp. 313–14.

[48] "He [Philo] then goes on to write this about their composing new psalms: 'Thus they not only practise contemplation but also compose songs and hymns to God in all kinds of metres and melodies, setting them, as might be expected, to solemn measures.'" Eusebius, *The History of the Church from Christ to Constantine*, tr. G. Williamson, rev. ed. A. Louth (London: Penguin, 1989), p. 52. Philo, *De Vita Contemplativa*, p. 706.

Parker then reproduced a passage from Basil's address to young men on the right use of Greek literature, *Basilius in concione ad adolescentes*.[49] Here Basil had declared that music could stimulate, incite, compel and calm the very essence of being and gave the example of Timotheus the musician, who "so excelled in that arte and facultie, that he coulde stirre up a mannes mynde to anger by his roughe and sower harmonie, & could asswage and release them agayne by a soft kinde of harmonie at his will and pleasure". Through the moods of his music Timotheus could control Alexander as though he were a puppet. It was Timotheus's singing of the Phrygian harmony which had excited Alexander to run to war. Then, by his most gentle harmony, Timotheus had extinguished Alexander's bellicose attitude and had brought him back sedately to rejoin his guests at supper. Such strength and virtue, affirmed Basil, "is set in the true use of musike".[50]

Not only could music be used to manipulate individuals, Parker noted, it could control crowds, even violent ones. "As Pythagoras once by chance was in co[m]pany among a sort of wanto[n] & drunken folk",

> whereupon he bad the mynstrell to change his song & to rebuke their dissolute wantones with playeng to them the Dorian harmonie, by which musike they were cast so in a shame of the[m] selfe, that they threw from the[m] their garlands, & fled home all confused for their lightnes, where before by the harmonie he played, they raged in fury as men out of their wittes.[51]

---

[49] *Address to Young Men on Reading Greek Literature*, in *Saint Basil, The Letters, And, Address to Young Men on Reading Greek Literature*, Vol. 4, tr. R. Deferrari and M. McGuire (London: William Heinemann Ltd, 1934), p. 411.

[50] Timotheus (c.350–320 BC): an aulos (wind instrument) player from Thebes. He accompanied Alexander III of Macedon (356–323 BC) on his campaigns. Suda, a late Byzantine source, has Timotheus stirring Alexander to prepare for war with a rendition of a battle hymn to Athena. Quoted in Carl Dahlhaus and Ruth Katz (eds), *Source Readings in the Aesthetics of Music*, Vol. 2 (New York: Pendragon Press, 1987), p. 72.

[51] Basil, *Address to Young Men on Reading Greek Literature*, p. 419.

Given music's ability to stir up such a wide range of emotions, Parker urged discretion when selecting a particular style for performance. Vicious songs could precipitate monstrous actions, so it was vital to concentrate on music which would inspire better behaviour. David's selection by which he pacified the mind of Saul when he was in his raging fury was therefore exemplary.

This was an important point that Parker emphasized. The power of music was such that particular harmonies could induce particular moods, including moods conducive to worship. Therefore, music was a valuable, even essential, component of worship.

Method of singing the psalms

The Preface also affirms Parker's support for the singing of psalms by the whole congregation. He quoted Ambrose's effusive description of the "harmonie & singing together of the people" with the sound of singing rushing in and gushing out "as it were waters about all the porches and allies of the temple". The responsories and answers of the psalms billowed out in a great noise "as when there riseth up as it were a concorde rebounde of the waters by the singing of men, women, virgins and children".

On the other hand, Parker also endorsed the practice of psalms being divided into "responsaries and answers", referring to verses sung alternately. Singing the psalms by sides remained a point of incandescence for the reformers. It had been the established practice of monastic communities, as well as cathedral and collegiate choirs, and to the irritation of the reformers, it precluded, at any point, half the congregation from participating. Given the reformed view that the words were best articulated by the whole congregation in order that faith might be legitimately expressed, such a restriction was anathema. Not only was Parker untroubled by this custom, he commended it, citing the Greek Orthodox Patriarch of Constantinople, Nicephorus I, who unreservedly advocated the practice of *alternatim* singing; even the ancient Church from the time of the apostles had sung their songs "by sides and by course".[52] By way of the historians Eusebius and Socrates Scholasticus,[53] Parker unearthed Nicephorus's reference to Ignatius, "the third Bishop in Antioche churche", who when lying in a trance saw in a vision "how that the holy aungels did extol in praise the blessed Trinitie with their songs, by course answering an other". Ignatius is subsequently credited with introducing this form of singing to the church of Antioch and after his example "this custome is spred throughout all churches".

Further, whilst Parker was supportive of the so-called metrical psalms, with the melody for the congregation lying in the tenor and sung by the whole congregation, he was sympathetic to the presence of a choir singing all four parts. Whilst he directed that "the tenor of these parts be for the people when they will sing alone", nevertheless the other parts were "put for greater choirs or to such as will sing or play them privately".

A passage from Bernard of Clairvaux provided Parker's Preface with a fitting summary. It encapsulated his own rationale for the inclusion of music in worship, which was to restore equilibrium to the human spirit and enhance the meaning of the words which were sung:

> If song be had at any tyme, let it be ful of gravitie, that it neither sounde out wantonnes nor rudeness; let it be so sweete that it be not light, let it so delighte the eares, that it move the harts in asswaging heavines, and tempering ire. Let it not deprive the letter of the sense, but rather augment it.

Concluding on a note of caution, Parker affirmed St Bernard's instruction that music should of necessity remain the facilitator of the words, "for it is no light losse of spiritual grace to be caried away from the profitablenes

---

[52] Nicephorus I (c.758–828): Greek Orthodox Patriarch 806–15. Book 13, Chapter 8.
[53] Socrates Scholasticus (380–450). *Historia ecclesiastica. The Ecclesiastical History of Socrates Scholasticus*, rev. A. Zenos (CreateSpace Independent Publishing Platform, 2017), p. 265.

of the sense, with the lightnes of the notes, and to bee more carefull upon the chanting of the voice, than to geve heede to the matter".[54]

Music to enhance the sense of the words

That music should enhance the sense of the words accounted for Parker's inclusion in his Preface of an elementary guide entitled *For the Conjunction of Psalmes and tunes*. First, he directed, "ye ought to conjoyne a sad tune or song with a sad Psalme, and a joyfull tune and songe with a joyfull Psalme, and an indifferent tune and song with a Psalm which goeth indifferently". He then related these three broad categories to the traditionally acknowledged five divisions of the Psalter. His first category, *Psalmes of Joy*, corresponded to the third and fifth divisions; his second category, *sad Psalmes*, to the fourth division; and the third category, *Indifferent*, to the first and second divisions. Psalms could thus be aligned with tunes appropriate to their moods.

Concern that the music accompanying the metrical verses should be of the highest standard is confirmed by Parker's collaboration with Thomas Tallis,[55] who composed nine tunes for Parker's Psalter, one in each of the eight modes with one tune extra, and Parker assigned each of them to one of four categories. Tunes 1 and 8 were Indifferent and marked by the tilde accent; Tunes 2, 3, 6 and 7 were Sad and identified by the grave accent; Tunes 4 and 5 were Joyful and indicated by the sharp accent. This rudimentary allocation was set out by Parker as a table, entitled *The nature of the eyght tunes*:

---

[54] Bernard of Clairvaux (1090–1153): Cistercian abbot and mystic. Bernard, *Epistle 312* to Abbot Guido.
[55] Thomas Tallis (1505/10–85): Gentleman of the Chapel Royal under Henry VIII and Elizabeth.

~ 1. The first is meek: devout to see.
\ 2. The second sad: in majesty.
\ 3. The third doth rage: and roughly brayth.
/ 4. The fourth doth fawne: and flattry playth.
/ 5. The fifth deligth: and laugheth the more.
\ 6. The sixt bewayleth: it weepeth full sore.
\ 7. The seventh tredeth stoute: in froward race.
~ 8. The eyghte goeth milde: in modest pace.

Despite his refusal to condemn the choral polyphony as practised in cathedrals, Parker nevertheless supported the reformed principle of the necessity for the words of worship to be declared unequivocally and rendered comprehensible. This support included a genuine appreciation of the emotional effects able to be stimulated by particular musical intervals and harmonies. It was this awareness which underpinned his conviction that music was able to complement the mood of the text and facilitate a deeper understanding of the faith.

Parker's ecclesiastical standing lent significant authority to his affirmation of the ability of music both to replicate and enhance the sense of the words and to invoke the deepest emotions, thus consolidating the groundwork for music to resume an authentic place in worship.

6

Ceremonial of Worship Affirmed

John Whitgift, Thomas Cartwright, Henry Howard

An attack by Thomas Cartwright (1535–1603), Puritan divine and Fellow of Trinity College Cambridge, on liturgical practices most obviously sympathetic to an embodiment of the divine presence rather than a vehicle for edification was elegantly refuted by John Whitgift (1530–1604), Master of Trinity and Regius Professor of Divinity at Cambridge, and vigorously rebuffed by Lord Henry Howard (1540–1614), a notable Catholic sympathizer.

In their different styles, both argued that such ceremonies, in particular music, as an embodiment of the living presence of the divine, had the capacity to enhance rather than diminish faith, and that those engaged in these liturgical rituals should be affirmed, not denigrated.

Whitgift and Howard framed their responses on attacking the legitimacy of Cartwright's demands for change. If the liturgical changes Cartwright advocated made no sense because their proposed effect was already being observed or could never be achieved, or because their theological or biblical rationale was faulty, then the case for overturning the established practice was lost.

In *A Replye to an Answere made of M. Doctor Whitegifte, against the Admonition to the Parliament* (Hemel Hempstead, 1573), Thomas Cartwright launched a virulent attack on liturgical practices which he understood to undermine the purpose of worship. According to Cartwright, practices affirming worship as an engagement with the divine did nothing but negate edification in the faith and were to be entirely expunged.

John Whitgift responded with *The Defense of the Aunswere to the Admonition, against the Replie of T.C.* (1574).[1]

Liturgical practices not detrimental to faith

Cartwright had argued that whereas the early Church had ministered the sacraments plainly, the Elizabethan Church administered them "pompously, with singing, piping [organ playing], surplice and cope-wearing". Originally the sacraments had been ministered simply as they received it from the Lord; but now, he observed, they are sinfully mixed with man's inventions and devices.[2] These were the ceremonies, with their musical accompaniments, which were not only redolent of the offering of the discredited sacrifice of propitiation but jeopardized the clear expression of faith, thereby denying any possibility of edification.

Whitgift's response was concise: the inclusion of singing, piping, surplice and cope in worship did not of itself constitute proof that the sacrament of the supper was not sincerely ministered. In any case, he added, organ playing was not prescribed for use at the communion "by any rule that I know", so the integrity of the service was logically unrelated to its presence. As for singing, "I am sure you do not disallow, as it is used in all reformed churches and it is an art allowed in Scriptures, and in praising of God by David." Further, "there is no such inventions or devices of man mixed with the supper of the Lord as can make it sinful".[3]

Whitgift also noted that these inventions and devices, so derided by Cartwright, were neither contrary nor disagreeable to the Scriptures and moreover, it was Calvin himself who said that "those things . . . though

---

[1] John Whitgift (1530–1604): Lady Margaret Professor of Divinity at Cambridge 1563; Regius Professor of Divinity at Cambridge 1567; Master of Pembroke College Cambridge 1567; Master of Trinity College Cambridge 1570; Dean of Lincoln 1571; Bishop of Worcester 1577; Archbishop of Canterbury 1583–1604.

[2] John Ayre (ed.), *The Works of John Whitgift, D.D.*, 3 vols (Cambridge: Parker Society, 1851), Vol. III, p. 106.

[3] *The Works of John Whitgift*, Vol. III, p. 106.

they be prescribed by man yet are they God's traditions and not man's".⁴ Based on this comment, argued Whitgift, it was possible for such so-called inventions, devices and practices to embody the divine tradition.

Liturgical practices not compulsory

Whitgift also made the point that "singing, piping (as you call it), surplice and cope-wearing ... these things be free unto Christians", and if they were deemed to be convenient and profitable there was no reason for them to be suppressed. If abused, they could always be omitted. However, since their use was not compulsory, it remained a matter of indifference, and those "things that be indifferent are not repugnant to the word of God".⁵

Alternatim singing defended

Reiterating a persistent theme of the reformers, Cartwright had declared that "in all their order of service there is no edification according to the rule of the apostle, but confusion", typified by the practice of "tossing the psalms like tennis balls".⁶ This method of singing the psalms with verses being sung alternately by opposite sides of the choir or congregation

---

⁴ *The Works of John Whitgift*, Vol. III, pp. 106–7. John Calvin, *Institutes* 4.10.30: "I approve of those human constitutions only which are founded on the authority of God, and derived from Scripture, and are altogether divine. Let us take, for example, the bending of the knee which is made in public prayer. It is asked, whether this is a human tradition, which any one is at liberty to repudiate or neglect? I say, that it is human, and that at the same time it is divine. It is of God, inasmuch as it is a part of that decency, the care and observance of which it is recommended by the apostle; and it is of men, inasmuch as it specially determines what is indicated in general, rather than expounded" (tr. Henry Beveridge).

⁵ *The Works of John Whitgift*, Vol. III, p. 108.

⁶ *The Works of John Whitgift*, Vol. III, p. 384.

had already been defended by Parker. Whitgift's response invoked the principle of historical precedence. "If by 'tossing of psalms' you mean the singing of them *alternatim*," he stated, "then do you disallow that which is both commendable and of great antiquity." He cited an epistle written by Basilius Magnus to the ministers in Neocaesarea, where "he sheweth the self-same order of singing psalms to be then used in the church that we use at this day".[7] If by tossing the psalms like tennis-balls Cartwright was referring to the over-hasty reading or singing of them, then Whitgift granted that this was a habit that was indeed to be disliked. However, since over-hasty reading was not a practice forbidden by the Prayer Book, over-hasty reading could not be a reason for abolishing *alternatim* singing.

A curious, not to say tenuous, argument mounted by Cartwright was that even though singing the psalms side after side had been an ancient custom in the Church, it was its very antiquity which rendered it illegitimate. Attributing its origin to the time of Ignatius and claiming it was a practice derived from heaven with angels singing in this way was, for Cartwright, nothing less than a devilish deceit giving unwarranted status to what was a mere fable "confuted by historiographers".[8] As well, any attempt to prevent the worshippers singing all the verses of the psalms violated the established reformed principle that everyone should be able to sing the praises of God. It was not possible to offer worship when the words of worship were said or sung by others: "It is not meet that they should sing but the one half with their heart and voice, and the other with their heart only. Where they may both with heart and voice sing, there the heart is not enough."[9] Further, claimed Cartwright, when the words are sung by others, as the practice of tossing from side to side made inevitable, it is impossible to comprehend what the other side is singing, which defeats the fundamental principle of worship—edification. For these reasons, he noted, the singing of psalms by sides had been banished in all reformed churches.

---

[7] *The Works of John Whitgift*, Vol. III, p. 385. Basil, *Ad Cler. Neoc. Epist.* ccvii. 3. Tome III, p. 311.

[8] *The Works of John Whitgift*, Vol. III, p. 385.

[9] *The Works of John Whitgift*, Vol. III, p. 386.

Whitgift's rebuttals

Firstly, all the people may sing if they can and will. No one is prevented from singing.

Secondly, singing with the heart only and not the voice is acceptable because the psalms are sung in a tongue that is known and can therefore be understood, whether sung or heard.

Thirdly, there are those who can neither read nor sing and so cannot articulate the words themselves whether they want to or not. They have no option but to listen to those who can read or sing and must join with them in heart only. However, simply because they do not individually articulate those words their worship is not invalid. They participate legitimately by listening.

Fourthly, the prayer of the heart alone is of great force and very effectual, "as the example of Anna in the first of Samuel doth declare".[10] Whilst it is true that "in the public congregation God is to be called upon both in heart and voice", nevertheless

> if a man at some times, either because of the order appointed by the church, or upon some other occasion, do hold his peace, and desire that in heart only, which other sing or pray in voice, no doubt he prayeth effectually.[11]

Fifthly, evidence of the validity of praying with the heart independently of the voice was provided by St Paul, who in his First Epistle to the Corinthians spoke of the worshippers needing to understand what is said in order to register assent to the prayers with the response of "Amen".[12] That "one said the prayers, and the rest of the people joined with him in heart, and therefore said 'Amen' when he had ended his prayers" is evidence that the prayers were not said by all, but by one person only.

---

[10] 1 Samuel 1:13: "Now Hannah, she spake in her heart; only her lips moved, but her voice was not heard."
[11] *The Works of John Whitgift*, Vol. III, p. 387.
[12] 1 Corinthians 14:16.

Sixthly, Calvin had a similar interpretation of this passage: in public worship "he allowed one to pray in heart and voice, and all the rest to pray in heart only".[13] Therefore, "where they may both with heart and voice sing, there to sing with the heart is enough".[14]

Seventhly, as for the necessity for the words to be said by all, "Where learn you this in scripture?" asked Whitgift. "Will you set down general and absolute rules and not tell us upon what authority they be grounded?" To be required to accept propositions unquestionably "is too, too pope-like".[15]

Eighthly, Whitgift noted that Cartwright had been caught in a contradiction of his own making. He had previously criticized the Book of Common Prayer because the people were instructed to repeat certain prayers after the minister. According to Cartwright, it was unacceptable that the people repeated these prayers because "the minister is the only mouth of the people unto the Lord" and it should be the minister alone who delivers the prayers. Yet now, observed Whitgift, Cartwright was complaining because the people were not saying prayers and not singing hymns themselves.[16]

Ninthly, if Cartwright could invoke the principle that it was to preserve the Church's order that the practice of one person saying the prayers and the rest listening were allowed to continue, then it must follow that the same principle should similarly apply now. Singing by sides "hath been of long time the general order of the church ... and therefore may not without disorder be broken, so long as the church doth think it convenient to be kept as a lawful and convenient order".[17]

---

[13] Calvin's *Commentary* on 1 Corinthians 14:16: "Otherwise if you bless in the spirit only, how will the one who fills the place of the ungifted say the 'Amen' at your giving of thanks, since he does not know what you are saying?"

[14] *The Works of John Whitgift*, Vol. III, p. 387.

[15] *The Works of John Whitgift*, Vol. III, p. 387.

[16] "The Order for the Administracion of the Lordes Supper, or Holy Communion" in the 1552 Prayer Book has the instruction, "Then shall the Priest saye the Lordes prayer, the people repeating after him every peticion."

[17] *The Works of John Whitgift*, Vol. III, p. 388.

Tenthly, "the psalms being sung may as well be understood as being said, and better too". "If it be otherwise", Whitgift concluded, "the fault is not in singing, but in the manner of singing, which is the fault of the persons, not of the thing."[18]

Defence of cathedrals

Another grievance of Cartwright's was that music was still permitted to be a part of a liturgy which retained all the trappings of the mediaeval worship. Cathedrals were his prime target. "As for organs and curious singing," he railed, "though they be proper to popish dens, I mean to cathedral churches, yet some others also must have them. The queen's chapel and these churches must be patterns and precedents to the people of all superstitions."[19] Bristling with indignation and in one of his most purple passages, Cartwright decried cathedrals as nothing but

> Dens ... of all loitering lubbers, where Master Dean, Master vice-dean, Master canons, or Master prebendaries the greater, Master petty canons, or canons the lesser, Master chancellor of the church, Master treasurer, or otherwise called Judas the purse-bearer, the chief chaunter, singing men special favourers of religion, squeaking queristers, or organ players, gospellers, pistellers, pensioners, readers, vergers, &c. live in great idleness, and have their abiding.[20]

In case of any question as to how such travesties as cathedrals came into being, Cartwright had the answer. They "came from the pope, as out of the Trojan horse's belly, to the destruction of God's kingdom". They were inauthentic, invalid and worthless: "the church of God never knew them, neither doth any reformed church in the world know them".[21]

---

[18] *The Works of John Whitgift*, Vol. III, p. 388.
[19] *The Works of John Whitgift*, Vol. III, p. 392.
[20] *The Works of John Whitgift*, Vol. III, p. 394.
[21] *The Works of John Whitgift*, Vol. III, p. 394.

Whitgift responded with steely assurance. Contrary to Cartwright's feverish imagination, Whitgift declared cathedrals to be places of godliness, religion and learning and furnished with godly, zealous and learned men. Then, in a rebuke to Cartwright, he added that these zealous and learned men, as much as they may loiter, "may think themselves fit to be compared with such as you are, in any respects".[22] With this flourish, Whitgift labelled Cartwright as just as much a loiterer as any as might be found in cathedrals.

Defence of ornate or figurative singing

As for Cartwright's call for the elimination of that "curious" style of singing which was not only a perversion and distraction but illegitimate, Whitgift responded that "I have heard no reasons yet to improve the manner of singing used in the church of England."[23] If there are no reasons being offered for music's improvement, then logically it does not need improving.

Rites and ceremonies do edify

Cartwright's accusation that music, through its sensuous treatment and obfuscation of the words, prevented a proper understanding of the faith drew one of Whitgift's sharpest rebukes: "You say also that [rites and ceremonies] do not edify ... If you say that they do not edify of themselves, you say truly: for only the holy ghost on this sort doth edify, by the ministry of the word." But if you say that they edify not at all, that is, that "they do not tend to edifying, as other ceremonies and things used in the Church, as pulpit, Church, kneeling, singing, and such like, which be appointed for order and decency, do then speak you that which you are not able by sound judgements to justify."[24]

---

[22] *The Works of John Whitgift*, Vol. III, pp. 394–5.

[23] *The Works of John Whitgift*, Vol. III, p. 108.

[24] *The Works of John Whitgift*, Vol. II, p. 56.

Henry Howard (1540-1614)

Cartwright's *A Replye to an Answere of M. Doctor Whitgifte* provoked a spirited response in support of Whitgift by Lord Henry Howard. Entitled *A Defense of the Ecclesiasticall Regiment in Englande, defaced by T.C. in his Replie against D. Whitgifte* and published in 1574, this work is a vigorous attack on "these newe reformers" who

> thinke their poyson beste bestowed, when it is dispatched into every quarter and corner of the Realme, that beyng conveyed by slanderous libells, as it were by veyns and arteries to the very heart, it mighte breake out at laste with more strong and perillous infection.[25]

Singing in worship

The final section of this work, *Of Singing*, is a robust defence of music in worship. Scriptural evidence in support of singing, urged Howard, was so overwhelming as to be embarrassing: "Touching singing, if a man may quietly debate this matter, why shoulde they so greatly grudge at it, whiche the Prophet David hath so muche commended?" "The Psalmes and bookes of the Kings", he continued, "are so well stored of textes of confirmation for me to travell' in the repetition". Why, he asked, with disarming penetration, should singing be condemned as an ungodly exercise when it was practised extensively by so many godly people? "Surely if this be so ungodly an occupation as we are taught", he demanded, "the 4000 Levites which did nothing else but *canere in organis quae David fecit ad canendum*, 'sing on the instrumentes which David made to sing on' ... spente their tyme unthriftily?"[26] Similarly David would have to be acknowledged as equally culpable, added Howard, for he had

---

[25] Lord Henry Howard, Earl of Northampton, and a Catholic sympathizer. *A Defense*, p. 6.
[26] Howard, *A Defense*, p. 175.

after all his warres were ended, as Josephus witnesseth ... in dyvers kindes of verses made hymnes to the honour of God, and preparing musicall instruments, taught the Levites at the sound of them, to sing prayses unto God, as well on the Sabbath days, as at other feastes.[27]

If the arguments of music's detractors were taken to their logical conclusions, reasoned Howard, then Judith would have been condemned for "persuading men to beginne to sing in cymbals, and other instruments the newe song".[28]

Likewise would Ezekiel have been judged harshly for appointing many singers and musicians with cymbals, viols and harps in the house of God, as did David, Gad the King's Seer and Nathan the prophet, all of whom had commanded music to be used in worship. It was inconceivable for Howard that such eminent people should have been so comprehensively mistaken.

Edification achieved through beauty

Howard chiefly challenged the proposition that musical beauty thwarted edification in the faith. The opposite was true. It was through beauty that music enabled a more profound understanding of the word of God than the text alone could ever achieve. "They saye", he declared, that "our myndes are withdrawne from weighing of the dittie by sweetnesse of

---

[27] Howard, *A Defense*, pp. 175-6. Josephus, *Antiquities of the Jews*, Book 7, Chapter 12, *The Works of Flavius Josephus*, tr. William Whiston (London: Ward, Lock & Co., 1862), Vol. I, pp. 313-14. "And now David being freed from wars and dangers, and enjoying for the future a profound peace, composed songs and hymns to God of several sorts of metre: some of those which he made were trimeters, and some were pentameters: he also made instruments of music, and taught the Levites to sing hymns to God, both on that called the Sabbath-day, and on the other festivals."

[28] Howard, *A Defense*, p. 176. Cf. Judith 16:1-2: "In the presence of all Israel, Judith began this hymn of praise and thanksgiving, which was echoed by the people: 'Strike up a song to my God with tambourines; sing to the Lord with cymbals; raise a psalm of praise to him; honour him and invoke his name.'"

the note—Whereunto I answere that Elisha was of an other judgement, when he thought him selfe to be greatly quickened, and lifted up in his prophecie by the harmonie of a good Musician."[29] Saul also did not find music to be a hindrance, but rather

> by experience found the contrary, the text reporting that when the evil spirit came upon Saul, David took an harp and played with his hand, and Saul was refreshed and was eased, for the evil spirit departed from him.[30]

As well as eradicating the forces of evil, music could also alleviate destructive moods and should therefore be valued in worship rather than excluded. "If Musicke have suche force in daunting evill spirites", Howard argued, "it hath (I doubt not) as great power in suppressing ill affections, and therfore might finde greater favour than to be expelled & thrust out of the Church with so greate extremitie."[31]

Singing as reading opposed

Howard had only contempt for those who advocated singing which was devoid of all musical interest and resembled mere reading. "Of plain and simple singing", he wrote, "though it be to [too] simple for the house of God, M. Cartwright can well enough allowe, [by] marie, of this exquisite and perfect cunning, though it be a special gift of God, he can conceyve no liking."[32]

With relish Howard continued to confound the reformers' abhorrence of sophisticated music. He ridiculed their rejection of so-called cunning

---

[29] Howard, *A Defense*, p. 176. Cf. 2 Kings 3:15: "But now bring me a minstrel. And it came to pass, when the minstrel played, that the hand of the Lord came upon him." Not 1 Kings 3 as stated in the *Defense*.

[30] Howard, *A Defense*, pp. 176–7. Cf. 1 Samuel 16:23: "And it came to pass, when the evil spirit from God was upon Saul, that David took an harp, and played with his hand: so Saul was refreshed, and was well, and the evil spirit departed from him."

[31] Howard, *A Defense*, p. 177.

[32] Howard, *A Defense*, p. 177.

singing, given that they commended cunning saying. Those who allowed the spoken word but disallowed the sung word were trapped in a contradiction of their own making, for "cunning saying, and cunning singing are al one in effect". If Aaron were commended for his use of cunning saying, cunning singing should be equally commended. If God were pleased with that which was cunning, then, concluded Howard, it matters not whether it be reading or singing.

Music appropriate in worship

As well, Howard pointed out that there was no evidence from either the life of Christ or the lives of the early Fathers which indicated that music was appropriate for human enjoyment but inappropriate for the worship of God, and he challenged anyone to contradict him: "If any answer that this skill of music is more tolerable in any other place than in the Church, whensoever they shall prove that either Christ or any of the ancient fathers were of this judgement, I will subscribe to their opinion."[33]

Edification not compromised by lack of clarity of words

Howard was uncompromising in his belief that the current, voguish demand for music to ensure that the words be heard and their meaning understood was an illogical limitation and an unnecessary obstacle. Texts which were difficult to understand would not be sung, and in the case of any obscurity this would be of no consequence, as the words, drawn from the Scriptures and the psalms, would be known to the congregation anyway. "Nothing is usually sung in the Church, but what the people hath by rote", he declared, "& therefore neede we the lesse to feare their wante of edification, so long as the scriptures are distinctly read, and the Psalmes treateably & in good order sounded."[34]

Treatment of singers

It was also faulty logic, insisted Howard, to despise singers on the grounds that they provided music for worship. It was mischievous for Cartwright and others to treat these conveyors of a gift of God so mercilessly and

---

[33] Howard, *A Defense*, pp. 177–8.
[34] Howard, *A Defense*, p. 178.

despicably: "They rayle on them, & slander them in the most opprobrious & contemptuous maner that possibly can be devised." Howard pointed out that Ezechias [Hezekiah], far from despising singers, welcomed them, and "spake comfortably to as many as had knowledge to sing unto the Lord".[35] In any case, to maintain a belligerent and obstructive attitude towards singers contravened the injunction stated in the book *Ecclesiasticus*: *Musicam non impedies*, "thou shalt not hinder Musick".[36]

Legitimacy of liturgical practices
As to the argument that music, with its exquisite and cunning singing, should be disallowed in worship because it had never been authorized by Christ, this was another foolish statement, argued Howard, for on those grounds much of the liturgical practice since the earliest times would be invalidated. Cartwright and his followers had maintained that "this pricksong is not verbally or litterally comanded in the Gospell, & therefore may not be allowed".[37] However, if this rule were to apply, retorted Howard, many devout practices that had emerged as a result of private devotion rather than scriptural command would stand condemned: the building of altars and offering of sacrifices of Abel, Noah, Abraham and Moses; the Jewish practice of abstinence from eating meat; the building of an altar of twelve stones by Elias in remembrance of the twelve children of Jacob; the offering of gold, incense and myrrh by the three Wise Men; the anointing of Christ's feet by Mary Magdalen; and the spreading of garments in the path of Christ's entry to Jerusalem, among others.[38]

---

[35] Howard, *A Defense*, p. 178. Cf. 2 Chronicles 30:21-22: "Hezekiah spake comfortably unto all the Levites that taught the good knowledge of the Lord (v. 22); and the Levites and the priests praised the Lord day by day, singing with loud instruments unto the Lord (v. 21)."

[36] Howard, *A Defense*, p. 178. Cf. Ecclesiasticus 32:3. This reference in Ecclesiasticus actually refers to social etiquette at a banquet at which conversing during musical items was deemed unacceptable.

[37] Howard, *A Defense*, pp. 178-9.

[38] Howard, *A Defense*, pp. 179ff.

7

Participation in Christ's offering

Richard Hooker

Richard Hooker (1554–1600) was appointed Master of the Temple in 1585 and during his first year delivered *A Learned Discourse of Justification, Works, and how the Foundation of Faith is Overthrown*, first published in 1612. Here he broadened the perspective of the offering of worship previously held by the reformers—the so-called sacrifice of praise and thanksgiving—and then made the case for works of beauty to be accepted as part of that offering.

Salvation by Christ

Hooker begins from the same position as the reformers: "Salvation only by Christ is the true foundation whereupon indeed Christianity standeth."[1] It was through this perfect sacrifice that humanity had been forgiven, accepted and justified. This being so, there was no place for works to be offered to God with the intent of effecting such justification, for this had already been accomplished. It was the prerogative of Christ. Salvation by Christ, and by Christ alone, was the foundation of Christianity. As a result, nothing within human ability could appease God's wrath, compensate for the gravity of sin or induce rewards either in heaven or earth. It was a blatant fault of the Church of Rome, Hooker

---

[1] Richard Hooker, *Of the Laws of Ecclesiastical Polity*, Vol. 1 (London: Everyman's Library, 1954), p. 57. Also in *Tractates and Sermons*, ed. W. Speed Hill (Cambridge, MA: Harvard University Press, 1990), pp. 149–50.

asserted, that "she attributeth unto works a power of satisfying God for sin; and a virtue to merit both grace here, and in heaven glory".[2] On this basis Hooker deemed works to be irrelevant.

Acceptance of works

Yet, in a major break from the reformers, he declared works to be irrelevant only in the sense that they were impotent to effect justification. Whilst it was Christ's perfect sacrifice alone that remained the indisputable foundation of salvation, Hooker insisted it was never intended that the offering of works should be precluded from worship. Rather than negating or even compromising the authority of Christ's offering, works were an acceptable addition to the foundation of salvation, for it was a foundation "not subverted by every kind of addition". Whilst Christ came to effect salvation, he came "not to abrogate and to take away good works".[3] The proposition that "our salvation is by Christ alone, therefore howsoever, or whatsoever, we add unto Christ in the matter of salvation, we overthrow Christe" was untenable. "Our case were very hard", said Hooker, "if this argument so universally meant as it is proposed were sound and good."[4] In a check to the reformers' manifesto, Hooker declared that "we ourselves do not teach Christe alone, excluding our own faith, unto justification; Christ alone, excluding our own works, unto sanctification; Christ alone, excluding the one or the other as unnecessary unto salvation". It remained true that faith alone justifies, yet this precept was "never meant to exclude ... works from being added as necessary duties, required at the hands of every justified man".[5] Faith was not invalidated by the presence of

---

[2] Hooker, *Of the Laws of Ecclesiastical Polity*, Everyman's Library, p. 61; *Tractates and Sermons*, p. 153.

[3] Hooker, *Of the Laws of Ecclesiastical Polity*, Everyman's Library, p. 58; *Tractates and Sermons*, p. 150.

[4] Hooker, *Of the Laws of Ecclesiastical Polity*, Everyman's Library, p. 59; *Tractates and Sermons*, p. 151.

[5] Hooker, *Of the Laws of Ecclesiastical Polity*, Everyman's Library, p. 5; *Tractates and Sermons*, p. 151.

works. They were neither an impediment nor an irrelevance to worship and were not to be undervalued or rejected. Rather the opposite. They constituted a crucial element of the human response. Hooker's positive appreciation of works marked a clear break from those for whom works were not only irrelevant but anathema to the divine–human relationship.

Participation in Christ's offering

In the fifth book of his *Of the Laws of Ecclesiastical Polity*, first published in 1597,[6] Hooker reiterated that satisfaction for sin had been fully accomplished by the one, perfect sacrifice offered to God by Jesus Christ. However, in another major rebuttal of the reformers' position, he maintained that the effect of this sacrifice could not be restricted to a simple, even simplistic, acknowledgement of a life offered, sin forgiven, salvation granted and acceptance assured. Christ's offering of himself did not create a final, static divine–human situation from which no development was possible. Whilst decisive as a declaration of the extent of God's love for his people, Christ's sacrifice was not a terminus in divine–human dealings; it was an action which inaugurated an ever-deepening relationship between God and humanity. "There is no stint", Hooker maintained, "which can be set to the value or merit of the sacrificed body of Christ, it has no measured certainty of limits, bounds of efficacy to life it knows none, but is also itself infinite in possibility of application."[7] The result of this "possibility of application" was the creation of a new relationship by which humanity was brought into living contact with the substance of the divine life. So pervasive was this participation in

---

[6] The first four books of *Of the Laws of Ecclesiastical Polity* were first published in 1593. The sixth and eighth books were published in 1648, the seventh book in 1662. The date of the first edition of the preface and Books I–IV is discussed in R. Hooker, *Of the Laws of Ecclesiastical Polity*, ed. Georges Edelen (Cambridge, MA: Harvard University Press, 1977), I, p. xxix.

[7] Richard Hooker, *Of the Laws of Ecclesiastical Polity*, Book V, Chapter 55, ed. A. S. McGrade (A Critical Edition with Modern Spelling, Oxford: Oxford University Press, 2013), Vol. 2, p. 157.

the divine nature that Hooker maintained it were as though Christ and man possessed each other: "Participation is that mutual inward hold which Christ has of us and we of him, in such sort that each possesses the other by way of special interest property and inherent copulation."[8] As a result, Christ and the believer "mutually participate in one another through an asymmetric pattern of salvific transformation", and by virtue of this participation human nature is restored and fulfilled in (re)union with God.[9]

The ancient Fathers' references to the "mixture of [Christ's] flesh with ours" implied for Hooker no contamination of Christ's offering. Such a mixture was not "to mingle wine with puddle, heaven with earth, things polluted with the sanctified blood of Christ".[10] What may have been the puddle, earth and pollution of man's nature is transformed by virtue of unity with Christ, for "we all receive of his fullness, because he is in us as a moving and working cause; from which many blessed effects are really found to ensue".[11] Christ's crucified body and blood shed for the life of the world comprised the "true elements of that heavenly being which makes us such as himself is of whom we come".[12] This is an extraordinary

---

[8] Hooker, *Of the Laws of Ecclesiastical Polity*, Book V, Chapter 55, OUP 2013, Vol. 2, p. 157.

[9] Paul Anthony Dominiak, *Richard Hooker: The Architecture of Participation*, Studies in English Theology (London: T&T Clark, 2020), Introduction. Dominiak gives a detailed account of Hooker's doctrine of participation with special attention to the biblical idioms of "abiding" and "inward fellowship" in which Hooker's perceptions of participation are grounded.

[10] Hooker, *Of the Laws of Ecclesiastical Polity*, Everyman's Library, p. 57; Vol. 1, *Tractates and Sermons*, p. 149.

[11] Hooker, *Of the Laws of Ecclesiastical Polity*, Book V, Chapter 55, OUP 2013, Vol. 2, p. 162.

[12] Hooker, *Of the Laws of Ecclesiastical Polity*, Book V, Chapter 56, OUP 2013, Vol. 2, p. 160. This passage is also dealt with in Peter Lake, *Anglicans and Puritans? Presbyterianism and English Conformist Thought from Whitgift to Hooker* (London: Unwin Hyman, 1988), p. 174. In this work (pp. 145–97), Lake gives an analysis of Hooker's Christology and his theology of the Church, the sacraments and worship.

statement. To declare that humanity is made "such as himself" and further, that as a result of being made as himself, "it pleases him in mercy to account himself incomplete and maimed without us",[13] flies in the face of reformed orthodoxy. Hooker goes further. Thus integrated into the nature of Christ, humanity's offering of worship became thoroughly integrated into Christ's offering. Here is a radical departure from the reformed understanding that in worship there is no possibility of any unity between the human and divine offerings, and certainly no human co-existence in the sacrifice offered by Christ.

This understanding of the inter-penetration of the divine and human natures made it possible for Hooker to declare that it was the divine will to have all people saved, not just a few. If Christ accounted himself incomplete and maimed without us, then Christ must have offered himself not just for a few selected souls who currently believe, but for all, and this "all" included those whose belief was at present embryonic, even non-existent. Christ was a "forcible means to procure the conversion of all such as are not yet acquainted with the mysteries of that truth which must save their souls".[14]

It was doubtless true, he held, that the one who believes is already a child of God. That was never in doubt. However, it did not follow that the one who does not currently believe will never be a child of God and is consequently condemned irrevocably to perdition. "He which believes not as yet may be the child of God", Hooker insisted, and therefore "it becomes not us during life altogether to condemn any man seeing that (for anything we know) there is hope of every man's forgiveness, the possibility of whose repentance is not yet cut off by death". The charity which "hopes all things, prayeth also for all men", not just some.[15] As a warning to those who delighted in judging and excluding others, Hooker declared that no one has the right to disperse wrath or mercy on the basis

---

[13] Hooker, *Of the Laws of Ecclesiastical Polity*, Book V, Chapter 56, OUP 2013, Vol. 2, p. 162.

[14] Hooker, *Of the Laws of Ecclesiastical Polity*, Book V, Chapter 49, OUP 2013, Vol. 2, p. 135.

[15] Hooker, *Of the Laws of Ecclesiastical Polity*, Book V, Chapter 49, OUP 2013, Vol. 2, p. 136.

of their knowledge of others, for that knowledge is personal and therefore incomplete, even skewed. No one can presume to see others as God sees them, and just as no one is beyond redemption, so no works which are offered are unacceptable.

Human and divine united in the worship of the Church

For Hooker, the body of Christ was manifested supremely in the body of the Church. It was "out of the very flesh, the very wounded and bleeding side of the Son of man" that the Church was formed. To participate in the body of the Church was therefore to participate in the body of Christ and, conversely, to participate in Christ it was necessary to participate in the body of the Church. The Church is in Christ as Eve was in Adam, argued Hooker, therefore incorporation into Christ involved adoption into the body of the Church: "Yea by grace we are every one of us in Christ and in his Church as by nature we are in those our first parents.."[16]

Being incorporated into the Church was crucial, for it ensured that humanity became so closely united with the divine nature it were as though there existed a common flesh and blood. "For in him", Hooker declared,

> we actually are by our actual incorporation into that society which has him for their head and does make together with him one body ... for which cause, by virtue of this mystical conjunction, we are of him and in him even as though our very flesh and bones should be made continuate with his. We are in Christ because he knows and loves us even as parts of himself.[17]

---

[16] Hooker, *Of the Laws of Ecclesiastical Polity*, Book V, Chapter 56, OUP 2013, Vol. 2, p. 160.
[17] Hooker, *Of the Laws of Ecclesiastical Polity*, Book V, Chapter 56, OUP 2013, Vol. 2, p. 160.

Offering of worship united with Christ's offering

This mystical conjunction between the human and the divine in the life of the Church found for Hooker its most poignant expression in worship, which became a work shared by both the triumphant and militant Church, "a work common to men with Angels". To participate in prayer was to participate in both the celestial and divine,[18] and, thus united with the worship of the Church in heaven, the worship of the Church on earth assumed the same character and authority of the worship of heaven. Further, in an observation guaranteed to induce in the reformers a state of incandescence, Hooker declared that this offering of worship was empowered to share in the propitiatory character of Christ's sacrifice. Our prayers are therefore

> those most gracious and sweet odors; those rich presents and gifts which being carried up into heaven do best testify our dutiful affection, and are for the purchasing of all favour at the hands of God the most undoubted means we can use.[19]

Heavenly worship incorporated into earthly worship

There was a further development. The unity of earthly worship with heavenly worship allowed the characteristics of heavenly worship to become incorporate in earthly worship, and as the essence of heavenly worship consisted in all that was beautiful, glorious and majestic, therefore earthly worship had also to incorporate these beautiful, glorious and majestic qualities. This position of Hooker's was a decisive counter to the arguments so vehemently expressed by the reformers.

---

[18] Hooker, *Of the Laws of Ecclesiastical Polity*, Book V, Chapter 23, OUP 2013, Vol. 2, p. 74.

[19] Hooker, *Of the Laws of Ecclesiastical Polity*, Book V, Chapter 23, OUP 2013, Vol. 2, p. 73.

United with Christ's offering, human offering inspires divine forgiveness

Hooker pressed further. He affirmed that what was offered in worship was so incorporate in Christ's body and therefore so incorporate in Christ's offering that it could inspire divine forgiveness and acceptance. Whilst this human offering lacked the decisive authority of Christ's unique offering, yet Hooker believed the influence of the human offering to be a critical factor in the establishment of divine-human unity. This is what made it possible for Hooker to affirm that neither baptism nor the eucharist were "bare *resemblances* or memorials of things absent, neither for *naked signs* and testimonies assuring us of grace received before, but ... means effectual whereby God, when we take the sacraments, delivers into our hands that grace available to eternal life, which grace the sacraments represent or signify".[20]

Worship of heaven and earth joined

What has been described as Hooker's exalted image of the sacrament can be attributed to his fundamental conviction that it was possible for the reality of what was offered on earth to become united with the reality of the offering of Christ.[21] This being so, all the characteristics of earthly worship had of necessity to embody the characteristics of the worship of heaven. This included buildings, vestments, ceremonial, prayers and music. That the worship of the Church embodies the worship of heaven explains Hooker's advocacy of the beauty, even sumptuousness, of the places where worship was held. Touching God himself, he remarked, "hath he anywhere revealed that it is his delight to dwell beggarly? And that he takes no pleasure to be worshipped saving only in poor

---

[20] Hooker, *Of the Laws of Ecclesiastical Polity*, Book V, Chapter 57, OUP 2013, Vol. 2, p. 166. Quoted by Lake, *Anglicans and Puritans?*, p. 174.
[21] Lake, *Anglicans and Puritans?*, p. 164.

cottages?"[22] It was through the beauty of churches that the extent of human love and respect for God could be revealed, for "we do thereby give to God a testimony of our cheerful affection which thinks nothing too dear to be bestowed about the furniture of his service". As worship revealed the characteristics of heaven, so it became the expression of the full glory of God. The furniture of his service, maintained Hooker, "serves to the world for a witness of his almightiness, whom we outwardly honour with the chiefest of outward things, as being of all things himself incomparably the greatest".[23]

Hooker waved off criticisms of the cost of achieving such beauty as would make places of worship consistent with the beauty of heaven. He conceded that St Jerome condemned what he judged to be irresponsibly lavish elaboration and decoration of churches with huge expenditure on timber and stone. However, the cause of Jerome's condemnation, he noted, was the fact that the decoration and expenditure had supplanted relief for the poor.[24] Charity and almsgiving were Christian duties, indispensable to the fulfilling of the Christian life, but their observance was never intended to disqualify the honourable work of providing the most beautiful of settings for worship.[25]

---

[22] Hooker, *Of the Laws of Ecclesiastical Polity*, Book V, Chapter 15, OUP 2013, Vol. 2, p. 37.

[23] Hooker, *Of the Laws of Ecclesiastical Polity*, Book V, Chapter 15, OUP 2013, Vol. 2, p. 39.

[24] Hooker, *Of the Laws of Ecclesiastical Polity*, Book V, Chapter 15, OUP 2013, Vol. 2, p. 39. Hooker's reference to Jerome is derived from "Ad Nepotian. de vita Cleric", in *Omnium Operum Divi Eusebii Hieronymi* (Basle, 1516), Tom. X. It is: *Multi aedificant parietes, et columnas Ecclesiae substruunt; marmora nitent, auro splendent laquearia, gemmis altare distinguitur; et ministrorum Christi nulla electio est.* Hooker's translation is: "The walls of the church there are enough contented to build and to underset it with goodly pillars, the marbles are polished, the roofs shine with gold, the altar hath precious stones to adorn it; and of Christ's ministers no choice at all.".

[25] Hooker, *Of the Laws of Ecclesiastical Polity*, Book V, Chapter 15, OUP 2013, Vol. 2, p. 39.

The expense necessary to erect and adorn a church was in any case justified because of the purpose of the work. "Churches receive as everything else their chief perfection from the end whereto they serve," said Hooker, "which end being the public worship of God, they are in this consideration houses of greater dignity than any provided for meaner purposes."[26] The very majesty and holiness of the place where God is worshipped "has *in regard of us* great virtue, force, and efficacy, for that it serves as a sensible help to stir up devotion". So integral was this majesty and holiness to the building in which worship was held that it was impossible for Hooker to contemplate the liturgy occurring outside it: "We think not any place *so good* as the Church, neither any exhortation so fit as that of David, *O worship the Lorde in the beauty of holiness*."[27]

The vestments of those participating in the liturgy were similarly to be of the finest quality. Ecclesiastical officiants should not be denied a beauty of attire which was unquestionably granted to officiants at other, non-ecclesiastical occasions: "To solemn actions of royalty and justice their suitable ornaments are a beauty. Are they only in religion a stain?"[28] Hooker affirmed Jerome's proposition that "divine religion ... has one kind of habit wherein to minister before the Lord, another for ordinary uses belonging to common life".[29] Opposing Pelagius, who found the glory of clothes and ornaments a thing contrary to God and godliness, Hooker cited Jerome's ridiculing of those who likened beauty to ungodliness. "Is it enmity with God", asked Jerome,

---

[26] Hooker, *Of the Laws of Ecclesiastical Polity*, Book V, Chapter 16, OUP 2013, Vol. 2, p. 40.

[27] Hooker, *Of the Laws of Ecclesiastical Polity*, Book V, Chapter 16, OUP 2013, Vol. 2, p. 40. This passage is discussed by Lake, *Anglicans and Puritans?*, p. 167.

[28] Hooker, *Of the Laws of Ecclesiastical Polity*, Book V, Chapter 29, OUP 2013, Vol. 2, p. 82.

[29] Hooker, *Of the Laws of Ecclesiastical Polity*, Book V, Chapter 29, OUP 2013, Vol. 2, p. 82. Hooker is referring to the passage, "*Porro religio divina alterum habitum habet in ministerio, alterum in usu vitaque communi in Ezechielem Prophetam*", Ca. LXIIII, in *Omnium Operum Divi Eusebii Hieronymi* (Basle, 1516), Tom. V, f. 257r.

if I wear my coat somewhat handsome? If a Bishop, a Priest, a Deacon and the rest of the ecclesiastical order come to administer the usual sacrifice in a white garment, are they hereby God's adversaries? Clarks, Monkes, Widowes, Virgins, take heed, it is dangerous for you to be otherwise seen then in foul and ragged clothes.[30]

God derived pleasure from the beauty of ecclesiastical vestments, argued Hooker, for such beauty represented both the joy with which God was praised by saints on earth and the glory of the worship of the saints in heaven. Moreover, it was by means of such beauty that angels both revealed the glory of God to humanity and also made intercession to God on humanity's behalf. Beauty, therefore, was a common characteristic which spanned the divine–human experience. So Hooker commended the beauty of vestments which

> suits so fitly with that lightsome affection of joy, wherein God delights when his Saints praise him; and so lively resembles the glory of the Saints in heaven, together with the beauty wherein Angels have appeared to men, that they which are to appear for men in the presence of God as Angels, if they were left to their own choice and would choose any, could not easily devise a garment of more decency for such a service.[31]

---

[30] Hooker, *Of the Laws of Ecclesiastical Polity*, Book V, Chapter 29, OUP 2013, Vol. 2, p. 82. The passage to which Hooker refers is: "*Adjungis, gloriam vestium et ornamentorum deo esse contrarium. Quae sunt, rogo, inimicitiae contra deum, si tunicam habuero mundiorem: si episcopus, presbyter et diaconus et reliquus ordo ecclesiasticus in administratione sacrificiorum candida veste processerint? Cavete clerici, cavete monachi, viduae et virgines: periclitamini, nisi sordidas vos atque pannosas vulgus aspexerit. Taceo de hominibus saeculi, quibis aperte bellum indicitur, et inimicitiae contra deum, si preciosis atque nitentibus utantur exuviis.*" *Dialogorum Hierony. Adversus Pelagium*, Liber I, in Jerome, *Omnium Divi Eusebii Hieronymi* (Basle, 1516), Tom. II, f. 124v.

[31] Hooker, *Of the Laws of Ecclesiastical Polity*, Book V, Chapter 29, OUP 2013, Vol. 2, p. 85.

Ceremonial of earthly worship to be consistent with heavenly worship

The unity of the divine and human in the offering of worship also implied the conjoining of the ceremonial of heaven and earth. The gestures of earthly worship are therefore to be in sympathy with the gestures of heavenly worship. In consequence, worship was to be offered with all dignity, grace and beauty, for it was being offered as at one with the offering of Christ, "as before his sight whom we fear, and whose presence to offend with any the least unseemliness we would be surely as loath as they who most reprehend or deride that we do".[32]

The house of prayer therefore became "a court beautified with the presence of celestial powers", in which "we stand, we pray, we sound forth hymns to God, having his Angels intermingled as our associates".[33] The beauty and majesty of the place of worship was able to inspire the richness of devotion appropriate to being joined to the praise of the angels. How can we come to this house of prayer, asked Hooker, and not be moved with the very glory of the place itself, "so to frame our affections praying, as does best beseem them, whose suits the almighty does there sit to hear, and his Angels attend to further?"[34]

Music engages the whole of humanity

Of these elements of worship, Hooker attributed special significance to music because it was music, he believed, which has most affinity with "that part of man which is most divine". "Touching musical harmony whether by instrument or by voice", he said,

---

[32] Hooker, *Of the Laws of Ecclesiastical Polity*, Book V, Chapter 30, OUP 2013, Vol. 2, p. 88.

[33] Hooker, *Of the Laws of Ecclesiastical Polity*, Book V, Chapter 25, OUP 2013, Vol. 2, p. 76.

[34] Hooker, *Of the Laws of Ecclesiastical Polity*, Book V, Chapter 25, OUP 2013, Vol. 2, p. 76.

> it being but of high and low in sounds a due proportionable disposition, such notwithstanding is the force thereof and so pleasing effects it has even in that very part of man which is most divine, that some have been thereby induced to think that the soul itself by nature is, or has in it harmony.[35]

Hooker reinforced the position affirmed by Archbishop Parker and others that the power of music was such that it could embody the widest range of emotions and temper those emotions for good. Music was a thing which "delighteth all ages and beseemeth all states". It was "a thinge as seasonable in griefe as in joy; as decent beinge added unto actions of greatest waight and solemnitie, as beinge used when men most sequester them selves from action". This breadth of emotion was representative of the whole of humanity and so it became an expression of the whole of humanity being united to God in worship. So Hooker commended

> the admirable facility which music has to express and represent to the mind more inwardly than any other sensible means the very standing rising and falling, the very steps and inflections every way, the turns and varieties of all passions whereto the mind is subject.[36]

He also observed that music portrayed the range of human emotion with such realism that by engaging with the various sounds it was possible to discern the priorities for Christian living. "In harmony the very image and character even of virtue and vice is perceived," he noted, "the mind delighted with their resemblances, and brought by having them often iterated into a love of the things them selves."[37] Not only Christian

---

[35] Hooker, *Of the Laws of Ecclesiastical Polity*, Book V, Chapter 38, OUP 2013, Vol. 2, p. 101.

[36] Hooker, *Of the Laws of Ecclesiastical Polity*, Book V, Chapter 38, OUP 2013, Vol. 2, p. 101.

[37] Hooker, *Of the Laws of Ecclesiastical Polity*, Book V, Chapter 38, OUP 2013, Vol. 2, p. 101.

living but also the essential elements of the spiritual life were able to be represented. "We are", he explained,

> at the hearing of some [harmony] more inclined to sorrow and heaviness; of some, more mollified and softened in mind; one kind apter to stay and settle us, another to move and stir our affections; there is that draws to a marvellous grave and sober mediocrity, there is also that carries as it were into ecstasies, filling the mind with an heavenly joy and for the time in a manner severing it from the body.[38]

Music transcends words

In a further severing from the priorities of the reformers, Hooker declared that the effectiveness of music was not to be dependent on the meaning of the words being made explicit. It was by virtue of the sound itself that the effect was achieved. "We lay altogether aside", he insisted, "the consideration of ditty or matter, the very harmony of sounds being framed in due sort and carried from the ear to the spiritual faculties of our souls." It was by the "native puissance and efficacy" of the sound alone that music could represent the human condition, bringing to a perfect temper "whatsoever is there troubled",

> apt as well to quicken the spirits as to allay that which is too eager, sovereign against melancholy and despair, forcible to draw forth tears of devotion if the mind be such as can yield them, able both to move and to moderate all affections.[39]

Hooker noted that although David was proficient in the composition of poetry and appreciative of its value in conveying a sense of the divine

---

[38] Hooker, *Of the Laws of Ecclesiastical Polity*, Book V, Chapter 38, OUP 2013, Vol. 2, pp. 101–2.

[39] Hooker, *Of the Laws of Ecclesiastical Polity*, Book V, Chapter 38, OUP 2013, Vol. 2, p. 102.

presence, he did not rest content with the words only. He added music, both vocal and instrumental. Not only was the meaning of the words enhanced by being sung, the use of instruments, of themselves delivering no texts, contributed to the profitable reception of the poetic lines. So David

> having therefore singular knowledge not in poetry alone but in musique also, judged them both to be things most necessary for the house of God, left behind him to that purpose a number of divinely indited poems, and was farther the author of adding unto poetry melody in public prayer, melody both vocal and instrumental for the raising up of men's hearts and the sweetening of their affections towards god.[40]

From these considerations Hooker concluded that "the Church of Christ does likewise at this present day retain music as an ornament to God's service, and an help to our own devotion".[41]

Further, the inclusion of instrumental music was eminently logical for it was a nonsense to forbid instrumental music whilst at the same time permitting vocal music to remain. "They which under pretence of the law ceremonial abrogated", he stated, "require the abrogation of instrumental music approving nevertheless the use of vocal melody to remain, must show some reason wherefore the one should be thought a legal ceremony and not the other."[42]

Nevertheless, to be effective, music had to be of a quality appropriate to the gravity and beauty of the heavenly worship it purported to embody. Light, inconsequential music which appealed only to the superficial aspects of human nature was to be steadfastly rejected:

---

[40] Hooker, *Of the Laws of Ecclesiastical Polity*, Book V, Chapter 38, OUP 2013, Vol. 2, p. 102. Ecclus. xlvii: 8–9.

[41] Hooker, *Of the Laws of Ecclesiastical Polity*, Book V, Chapter 38, OUP 2013, Vol. 2, p. 102.

[42] Hooker, *Of the Laws of Ecclesiastical Polity*, Book V, Chapter 38, OUP 2013, Vol. 2, p. 102.

> In Church music curiosity and ostentation of art, wanton or light or unsuitable harmony, such as only pleases the ear and doth not naturally serve to the very kind and degree of those impressions which the matter that goes with it leaves or is apt to leave in men's minds, doth rather blemish and disgrace that we do than add either beauty or furtherance to it.[43]

Music's ability to edify

These faults avoided, however, the value of music in worship was undeniable, for even though it was unable to edify by dialectical presentation, it would edify by stimulating an appreciation and love of the divine. "The force and efficacy of the thing itself" [musical harmony], Hooker continued,

> when it drowns not utterly, but fitly suits with matter altogether sounding to the praise of God, is in truth most admirable, and does much edify if not the understanding because it teaches not, yet surely the affection because therein it works much.[44]

Hooker's attack on the reformed position continued unabated. Given that the sheer beauty of the sound itself was able to convey a profound awareness of the divine presence over and above the expression of words, Hooker despaired of those for whom music made no impression, even the simple music of the metrical psalms. "They must have hearts very dry and tough", he lamented, "from whom the melody of psalms does not sometimes draw that wherein a mind religiously affected delights."[45]

---

[43] Hooker, *Of the Laws of Ecclesiastical Polity*, Book V, Chapter 38, OUP 2013, Vol. 2, p. 102.

[44] Hooker, *Of the Laws of Ecclesiastical Polity*, Book V, Chapter 38, OUP 2013, Vol. 2, p. 102.

[45] Hooker, *Of the Laws of Ecclesiastical Polity*, Book V, Chapter 38, OUP 2013, Vol. 2, p. 102.

Hooker was careful to distinguish between two avenues by which music could stimulate faith. In simple, unadorned music the words could be presented clearly, thereby allowing faith to be directly proclaimed. This was the preferred option for those who were prepared to tolerate a basic form of music in worship. With more stylistically developed music, however, where the words could not be so readily distinguished, Hooker believed that faith was still able to be conveyed, but by means of the impact it could make on the emotions. The benefit of this more elaborate style was that it could make an impression on those for whom mere words were not compelling. For support he referred to the Frankish Benedictine monk and archbishop of Mainz, Rabanus Maurus Magnentius. "Be it as Rabanus Maurus observes",

> that at the first the Church in this exercise was more simple and plain than we are, that their singing was little more than only a melodious kind of pronunciation, that the custom which we now use was not instituted so much for their cause which are spiritual, as to the end that into grosser and heavier minds whom bare words do not easily move, the sweetness of melody might make some entrance for good things.[46]

Hooker also cited an argument put forward by Basil of Caesarea in his homily on Psalm 1 that humans were not easily drawn to virtue but were attracted to whatever gave them pleasure. Astutely, observed Basil, the Holy Spirit recognized music as one of those objects of pleasure with which people instinctively became engaged and, if used in this way, it could convey divine truth unobtrusively. Paraphrasing Basil, Hooker wrote that

---

[46] Hooker, *Of the Laws of Ecclesiastical Polity*, Book V, Chapter 38, OUP 2013, Vol. 2, p. 102. Rabanus Maurus Magnentius (*c*.780–4 February 856): Archbishop of Mainz (848–56). "*Primitiva Ecclesia ita psallebat, ut modico flexu vocis faceret resonare psallentem: ita ut pronuncianti vicinior esset quam canenti. Propter carnales autem in Ecclesia non propter spiritualis consuetudo cantandi est instituta: ut, quia verbis non compunguntur, suavitate modulaminis moveantur.*" (*De institutione clericorum* II, 48.)

whereas the Holy Spirit saw that mankind is to virtue hardly drawn, and that righteousness is the less accounted of by reason of the proneness of our affections to that which delights, it pleased the wisdom of the same spirit to borrow from melody that pleasure, which mingled with heavenly mysteries, causes the smoothness and softness of that which touches the ear, to convey as it were by stealth the treasure of good things into man's mind.[47]

For Hooker, the metrical psalms were valuable for they offered the opportunity of coming to faith by both words and music. The words which were sung offered a clear statement of faith; yet should their meaning prove elusive, the beauty of the music, independently of the words, would convey a sense of the divine. "To this purpose were those harmonious tunes of psalms devised for us", said Hooker, again drawing from Basil, "that they which are either in years but young, or touching perfection of virtue as yet not grown to ripeness, might when they think they singe, learn." Further, that music was a thing of beauty was not a reason for it to be banished from worship, concluded Hooker, again from Basil, for thankfully the heavenly Teacher has found a way whereby "doing those things wherein we delight, we may also learn that whereby we profit".[48]

---

[47] Hooker, *Of the Laws of Ecclesiastical Polity*, Book V, Chapter 38, OUP 2013, Vol. 2, pp. 102–3. Saint Basil, *Exegetic Homilies*, Homily 10 (On Psalm One), in *The Fathers of the Church*, tr. A. C. Way (Washington D.C.: The Catholic University of America Press, 1963), p. 151. "When the Holy Spirit saw that the human race was guided only with difficulty towards virtue, and that, because of our inclination towards pleasure, we were neglectful of an upright life, what did He do? The delight of melody he mingled with the doctrines so that by pleasantness and softness of the sound heard we might receive without perceiving it the benefit of the words."

[48] Hooker, *Of the Laws of Ecclesiastical Polity*, Book V, Chapter 38, OUP 2013, Vol. 2, p. 103. Basil. *In Psalmum* I, p. 125. "Oh! The wise invention of the teacher who contrived that while we were singing we should at the same time learn something useful; by this means, too, the teachings are in a certain way

Singing psalms by sides

Complaints concerning the singing of psalms by sides were dismissed by Hooker with disarming elegance. He acknowledged that it was not lawful for the people jointly to praise God in the singing of psalms, and that it was permissible to sing the psalms with the heart, the voice remaining quiet, but took issue with the proposition that the words which were sung cannot be understood when the psalms are sung side by side'. The first two allegations are true, stated Hooker, "but lack strength to accomplish their desire". The third allegation might have been strong enough to persuade "if the truth thereof were not doubtful".[49] Moreover, Hooker found it incomprehensible that this way of singing psalms, which had been accepted by churches throughout the world, ratified by councils and laws over many ages, which was "never found to have any inconvenience" in it, which the best men and wisest governors of God's people did think they could never commend enough, which strengthened the meditation of the holy words and raised up the hearts of men, should ever be questioned, let alone suppressed. This was a practice, he insisted,

> which edified souls . . . filled minds with comfort and heavenly delight . . . stirred up desires and affections according to the meaning of the words . . . allayed base and earthly cogitations . . . banished evil secret suggestions, waters the heart that it may fructify . . . makes the virtuous in trouble full of magnanimity and courage . . . [and which] serves as a most approved remedy against all doleful and heavy accidents which befall men in this present life.[50]

---

impressed more deeply on our minds." *Saint Basil, Exegetic Homilies*, Homily 10 (On Psalm One), p. 153.

[49] Hooker, *Of the Laws of Ecclesiastical Polity*, Book V, Chapter 39, OUP 2013, Vol. 2, p. 105.

[50] Hooker, *Of the Laws of Ecclesiastical Polity*, Book V, Chapter 38, OUP 2013, Vol. 2, p. 106.

To finish, Hooker took a verse so beloved of the reformers in their inexorable attempts to censure singing in favour of the spoken word and used it to prove the opposite. Singing by sides, he declared, was a practice which "fitly accordeth with the Apostle's own exhortation, 'Speak to yourselves in psalms and hymns and spiritual songs, making melody, and singing to the Lord in your hearts'". Surely, he concluded, regarding this practice of singing the psalms, "there is more cause to fear lest the want thereof be a maim, than the use a blemish to the service of God". So Hooker's theological insights made possible a staunch advocacy for music that rendered it acceptable in worship on account of its inherent beauty, its facility in representing the emotions, and its ability to enhance the meaning of the words.

Unity with the Divine

Hooker's support for the uniting of the worship of the Church with the worship of heaven gave force to the view that in worship it was possible to become united with the divine. In consequence, worship was not to be a simple remembrance of Christ's offering but a means of partaking in the fullness of the divine presence and thus to engage with a transcendent reality, a sublime mystery which transcended rational definition and propositional assertions. The ceremonial of earthly worship had therefore to signify the essence of the divine, which lay beyond the power of words fully to express. Hence music was valued because it invoked a presence not constrained by any verbal framework. It testified to conceptions, feelings and experiences far deeper than the mere words of worship could convey.

8

Turning Earth into Heaven

That worship was the enactment of the unity of the human with the divine and therefore the means of participating in the divine nature was argued strongly by Lancelot Andrewes and John Buckeridge.

Lancelot Andrewes

Lancelot Andrewes (1555–1626) was Chaplain to Queen Elizabeth, St Giles's Cripplegate, Prebendary of Westminster (1597), Dean of Westminster (1601), Bishop of Chichester (1605), Bishop of Ely (1609), Dean of the Chapel Royal (1618) and Bishop of Winchester (1619).

Divine mercy prevails

Lancelot Andrewes levelled a formidable counter to the reformers' position that humanity, irrevocably corrupt, was destined forever to live in the mire of divine condemnation and that any unity between the offering of Christ and the offering of humanity was impossible. Andrewes argued that divine mercy comprehensively prevailed over divine condemnation and therefore there was no impediment to the human offering becoming united with the divine offering. As a result, works were to be accepted as a legitimate aspect of the offering of worship. Not just works but works of beauty. Incorporate in Christ's offering, they became pleasing to God and were accepted by God.

This rebuttal was expressed clearly by Andrewes in a sermon of 30 March 1593 preached before the court at St James's Palace on the text Mark 14:4–6:

... some disdained among themselves, and said, To what end is this waste of ointment? For it might have been sold for more than three hundred pence, and been given to the poor. And they grudged against her. But Jesus said, Let her alone, why trouble ye her? She hath wrought a good work on Me.[1]

Andrewes highlighted the precious quality of the ointment. It was nard, the finest of all ointments, and contained *pistice*, the finest of all nards. Drawn from the spike rather than the leaf, it was ointment of the highest quality. Yet despite such pedigree and value, this gift was offered neither sparingly nor grudgingly. It was poured out in its entirety, the container being shattered in the process of offering.[2] This was an act which was "well taken of Christ". As a result, the woman was not to be dissuaded but encouraged. Consisting of the finest it was possible to produce, such offerings were to be accepted without hindrance:

> *Sinite illam*, saith Christ. Not as they hoped, *sistite illam*, "stay her" indeed it is but a waste work she is about; but *sinite illam*, "let her alone, the work is good", suffer her to proceed. His meaning is: Such acts as this was, are to be let alone, and they that so disposed, not to be troubled.[3]

Because of its beauty and expense, Christ predicted the inevitable condemnation. He noted there would always be those who would begrudge such offerings. Yet Christ's words, Andrewes noted, were

---

[1] L. Andrewes, *Ninety-Six Sermons*, ed. J. Wilson and J. Bliss, 5 vols (Oxford: Parker Society, 1841–3), Vol. II, p. 37. Andrewes's sermons were originally included in the folio *XCVI Sermons* edited by William Laud and John Buckeridge (1629). The extent of Andrewes's preaching at court is discussed in P. McCullough, *Sermons at Court: Politics and Religion in Elizabethan and Jacobean Preaching* (Cambridge: Cambridge University Press, 2011), pp. 135–6.

[2] Andrewes, *Ninety-Six Sermons*, Vol. II, p. 38.

[3] Andrewes, *Ninety-Six Sermons*, Vol. II, p. 49. *Sinite illam*: allow her; *Sistite illam*: stop her.

intended to counter such criticisms, and to counter them in perpetuity: "To this day, they will not let her alone, but disquiet her still. He hath therefore left in His Gospel these words, as a fit answer, to stay their hands, and stop their mouths, for ever."[4]

The work offered by the woman was not just allowable, but commendable, and not just to be tolerated, but to be welcomed. Christ "tells the very work itself is good" and so pleads and justifies it, not as sufferable only, but worthy of praise, for this is the meaning of *"bonum opus operata est"* [She did a good work].[5] It was a work which was accepted by God because it was offered in Christ:

> And a reason of *bonum opus est*; for His "in Me" is warrant sufficient, why the work is to be reckoned good. Yea, in saying it is not only good done, but done to him, He giveth it a dignity, and lifteth up this work above.[6]

In Christ the offering is made acceptable

Being offered in Christ, the offering was made worthy and accepted. Being in Christ the gift was transformed. Christ bestowed upon it a dignity and lifted it up just as he would continue to dignify and lift up all offerings made in him, whether they be as costly as Mary Magdalene's ointment or as modest as the widow's mite. All works thus offered to God in Christ's name, whatever their quality, would be dignified above their limitations. Such offerings could therefore never be dismissed as irrelevant, wasteful or presumptuous, for they were made acceptable to God by being united with Christ's own offering. Not only acceptable to God, but in the case of the offering of works of beauty, pleasurable.

Works of beauty being included in the offering of worship was particularly despised by the reformers, for it assumed that whilst God was unresponsive to humanity's ordinary works, he was susceptible to works that were above the ordinary—that is, works of beauty. To counteract the idea that God should be denied such offerings of beauty, Andrewes

---

[4] Andrewes, *Ninety-Six Sermons*, Vol. II, p. 49.
[5] Andrewes, *Ninety-Six Sermons*, Vol. II, p. 50.
[6] Andrewes, *Ninety-Six Sermons*, Vol. II, p. 50.

asked why, if such treasures were freely available for human use, should they be withheld from God? Were human treasures reserved for the use of humans only and often wicked people at that? Why should it be Christ who was excluded from the gifts which were being offered? Was Christ actually unworthy that he should not be offered the finest and most exquisite gifts at mankind's disposal? "Do bees make honey, and *nardus* bear ointment, for wicked men only?" Why is this honey made available for any who desire it and yet denied to Christ? Is He unworthy?[7]

It was also true, remarked Andrewes, that not only had Christ made provision against human nakedness and emptiness, but he had also accommodated human comeliness and daintiness. Just as humanity received the gift of life, so humanity received the gift of the adornment of life:

> But as He, without any bar or *ut quid* [exception], alloweth us not only *indumenta* [garments] for nakedness, but *ornamenta* for comeliness; not only *alimenta* [nutrition] for emptiness, but *oblectamenta* [delights] for daintiness.[8]

After all, he continued, if ointment could be spent on Aaron's head under the law, seeing Christ is greater than Aaron, why should it not be bestowed on Christ as well?

Andrewes related a passage from the First Book of the Chronicles [17:1] where David remarked to the prophet Nathan that while he, David, lived in a well-appointed house of cedars, the Lord lived inauspiciously in a tent. David was troubled by the lack of dignity afforded the Lord and was contemplating rehousing the Ark of the Covenant with more appropriate magnificence. Andrewes drew a parallel between those who opposed the building of the temple with costly cedar and those who thought the offering of the *nardus* too expensive for Christ. The woman's desire to anoint Christ with an ointment of great beauty and expense was as legitimate as David's desire to honour the Lord with a temple of similar

---

[7] Andrewes, *Ninety-six Sermons*, Vol. II, p. 54.
[8] Andrewes, *Ninety-six Sermons*, Vol. II, p. 54.

beauty and expense. Both offerings were equally received by God with satisfaction and delight.[9]

Moreover, said Andrewes, those who during their time of exile in Egypt had experienced the simple, unadorned, portable tent used to house the Ark of the Covenant expressed no desire to have this tent reinstated, even when faced with the burden of carrying around such an elaborate and cumbersome Tabernacle. Their silence was evidence enough for Andrewes of their preference for the more beautiful structure despite its inconvenience, and in the absence of any criticism of the splendour and beauty of the completed Solomon's Temple, Andrewes found Judas's criticism of the woman inexplicable. Christ had instructed the woman to proceed and described her offering as a good work. His condemnation of Judas remains relevant for all time: it is a condemnation which embraces all those who would seek either to eliminate or even reduce offerings of beauty to God.

Andrewes also invited reflection on humanity's offering in comparison with Christ's offering. When considered in relation to Christ's offering of his blood and life, the offering of the *nardus* could never be thought of as excessive. In consequence, the offering to God of such gifts of beauty was not inappropriate: "If toward us neither blood nor life were too dear on His part, shall on ours any *nardus* be too dear, or any cost too much, that is on Him bestowed?"[10]

After all, noted Andrewes, not only had God created the beauty of the world for pleasure as well as utility, God had also so enriched humanity with such prosperity, plenty and peace that humanity was able to bestow this beauty on others, even on God himself. Far from being an affront or indignity to God, this offering of beauty represented only a meagre part of all that should rightly be offered. It was the least that could be done. Double, even ten times the present offering to God would be more appropriate and so vital was this offering to the divine–human relationship that it needed to be the finest, most sophisticated possible.

Andrewes noted that the woman's critics, in their abhorrence of the so-called lavish offering bestowed on Christ, labelled it "extraordinary".

---

[9] Andrewes, *Ninety-six Sermons*, Vol. II, pp. 54–5.
[10] Andrewes, *Ninety-six Sermons*, Vol. II, p. 55.

Extraordinary offerings were, however, precisely what were required in response to God's extraordinary consideration for humanity. It was, in fact, an extraordinary conceit to label as extraordinary anything one did not wish to do. By this argument, it would be possible to absolve oneself from any religious activity considered distasteful, especially the activity of offering, for of all human actions this was the one which most needed to be extraordinary. An ordinary, common offering was patently inadequate. God was deserving of the most precious gifts and treasures.[11]

Andrewes was aware of the implacable determination of those opposed to physical as distinct from spiritual offerings, particularly offerings of works of beauty. Even the most modest offering was reckoned by them to be as wasteful and inappropriate as Mary Magdalene's extravagant ointment. Despite Christ reckoning this offering to be well done, it was nevertheless maligned and Andrewes anticipated no end of complaints disallowing works of beauty as acceptable offerings to God: "For this her act that was well done, if Christ knew what it was to do well, yet we see it is disdained, grudged at, and she molested for it." "Whence we learn," he wrote, "Be a thing done to never so good purpose, yet some Judas will mutter and malign, and come forth with his *Ut quid*?" [to what purpose?], and "some Judas will cast his dead fly into Mary Magdalene's box of ointment".[12]

Andrewes noted that such criticisms of the principle of offering were not confined to Mary Magdalene. Nehemiah and David were both vilified for the offerings they made to God.[13] In the face of such criticism, "when things well done be evil taken", Andrewes deemed it imperative to persist in doing exactly what Mary Magdalene did; "not once, or twice, but three

---

[11] Andrewes, *Ninety-six Sermons*, Vol. II, pp. 56–7. Lake identifies Andrewes's understanding of works as including charity, piety and worship as distinct from "those merely formal marks of apparent zeal, devised by hypocrites like pharisees and the puritans". P. Lake, "Lancelot Andrewes, John Buckeridge, and Avant-Garde Conformity at the Court of James I", in L. L. Peck (ed.), *The Mental World of the Jacobean Court* (Cambridge: Cambridge University Press, 1991), p. 116.

[12] Andrewes, *Ninety-six Sermons*, Vol. II, pp. 57–8.

[13] Cf. Nehemiah 6:3–6; 2 Samuel 16:7–8.

several times, one after another; neither to hold our hand or shut our box, nor spare our ointment".[14] Neither the quality nor frequency of offering were to be diminished. Inevitable criticisms were to be withstood. Offerings were to be made to God with vigour and determination for they had as their authority the example of Christ himself. It was therefore critical "to look not to Judas on earth, who disliketh, but to Christ in Heaven Who approveth it", and it was he, not Judas, who "made answer for Mary Magdalene against Martha, Simon, and Judas, and all her accusers".[15] The so-called divinity of Judas is *perditio*, whereas the divinity of Christ is *bonum opus*.[16]

Liturgical implications

This understanding of offering informed Andrewes's liturgical priorities. Andrewes's "Notes on the Book of Common Prayer"[17] make a strong declaration of divine mercy prevailing over divine condemnation. Sentences selected for Morning and Evening Prayer in the 1552 Prayer Book succinctly conveyed the unacceptability of human wickedness, the devastating consequences of the divine displeasure and the urgent need for repentance. In stark contrast, the scriptural passages chosen by Andrewes abandon the condemnatory approach and contain an assurance of divine mercy. They include such comforting phrases as, "But God, being full of compassion, forgave their iniquity, and destroyed them not: yea, many a time turned he his anger away, and did not stir up all his wrath" (Psalm 78:38), and "I will not cause my anger to fall upon you: for I am merciful, saith the Lord, and I will not keep anger for ever" (Jeremiah 3:12). Another reference is listed simply as "Heb. 4", and it could well have been verse 16 that Andrewes had in mind: "Let

---

[14] Andrewes, *Ninety-six Sermons*, Vol. II, p. 59.
[15] Andrewes, *Ninety-six Sermons*, Vol. II, p. 59.
[16] P. McCullough, "Absent Presence: Lancelot Andrewes and 1662", in S. Platten and C. Woods (eds), *Comfortable Words: Polity and Piety and the Book of Common Prayer* (London: SCM Press, 2012), pp. 54–5.
[17] First printed in *Comment on the Book of Common Prayer*, William Nicholls, 1710. These *"Notes"* are discussed fully by P. McCullough in "Absent Presence", pp. 49–68.

us therefore come boldly unto the throne of grace, that we may obtain mercy, and find grace to help in time of need."[18]

Of the six verses printed in full as the introduction to Morning Prayer, Andrewes has retained only one of those stipulated in the 1552 Prayer Book, that referring to the return of the Prodigal Son to the forgiving father (Luke 15:18). To others he has added the theme of God's mercy and forgiveness: "He that covereth his sins shall not prosper: but whoso confesseth and forsaketh them shall have mercy" (Proverbs 28:13) and "O my God, incline thine ear, and hear; open thine eyes, and behold our desolations, and the city which is called by thy name: for we do not present our supplications before thee for our righteousnesses, but for thy great mercies" (Daniel 9:18).

Offertory more significant
This promise of forgiveness and restoration to God's favour enabled Andrewes to invest the Offertory with greater significance. The sentences appointed to be read in the communion services of 1549 and 1552 had diverted attention away from the offering of gifts, concentrating instead on the collection of alms for the poor. However, in his newly devised set of Offertory Sentences, entitled *Peculiar Sentences for the Offertory*, Andrewes affirmed the principle of an offering of gifts being gratefully received by God, and that in consequence God looked favourably on the offerers:

> In process of time it came to pass, that Cain brought of the fruit of the ground an offering unto the Lord. And Abel brought also of the firstlings of his flock, and of the fat thereof. And the Lord had respect unto Abel and his offering. Gen.iv, 3, 4.

God so welcomed the gifts that he promised to respond with an offering of his own: "Speak unto the children of Israel, that they bring me an offering: of every one that giveth it willingly with his heart they shall

---

[18] Peter McCullough suggests verses 8 or 10, in "Absent Presence", p. 56.

take my offering. Exod.xxv.2."[19] The gifts constituted a commendation to God, inviting entrance into the divine presence: "Give unto the Lord, ye families of the people, give unto the Lord glory and power. Give unto the Lord the glory of his Name; bring an offering, and enter into his courts. Psal.xcvi.7, 8."[20]

To maintain the integrity of the offering Andrewes moved almsgiving away from a position following the sermon. In the 1559 service, the churchwardens were instructed at this point to collect alms from members of the congregation individually and place them in the poor men's box. Andrewes derided this practice as wandering about in a disorderly manner, after the Genevan practice.[21] His liturgical solution was to remove almsgiving from the offering of the bread and wine and also to relocate the Offertory Sentences to a place after the Gloria and before the Blessing. It was at this point, in returning to their seats "having made their adoration", that the congregation was instructed to "put a small piece of silver into the poor men's box" (*cippus pauperum*).[22] This relegation of the giving of alms to the end of the service allowed for an undistracted focus on the offering of the bread and wine as representative of the sacrifice offered by Christ on behalf of all humanity.[23]

---

[19] L. Andrewes, "Notes on the Book of Common Prayer", in *Two Answers to Cardinal Perron, and other Miscellaneous Works of Lancelot Andrewes* (Oxford: John Henry Parker, 1854), pp. 153–4.

[20] Andrewes, "Notes on the Book of Common Prayer", p. 154.

[21] "*Sapit haec collectio per capita Genevensem illum per Ecclesias tumultuaria forma discurrendi morem.*"

[22] Andrewes, "Notes on the Book of Common Prayer", p. 158. McCullough, "Absent Presence", p. 65.

[23] Andrewes's instruction that where there are two priests at the eucharist, they should stand at the north and south ends of the altar, representing the two cherubim at the mercy-seat, suggests to McCullough Andrewes's indebtedness to Eastern Orthodoxy, with the clergy likened to cherubs hovering over the body and blood that is the new covenant's mercy-seat. McCullough, "Absent Presence", p. 59.

Acknowledgement of the Divine Presence

It was crucial for Andrewes that the divine presence experienced in worship receive proper recognition, such as the keeping of holy days and kneeling during significant moments of the eucharist, especially at the reception of communion.[24]

Place of sermons

In contrast to the reformers, whose interpretation of offering as the sacrifice of praise and thanksgiving gave prominence to edification, Andrewes did not consider a sermon to be an indispensable component of worship: "At the end of the Litany. Here the Minister riseth, and if there be a sermon an Introit is sung; and after the sermon they ascend with three adorations towards the Altar."[25] Where a sermon was to be included, Andrewes deliberately placed it after the Litany which followed Morning Prayer. This manoeuvre provided a practical solution to the necessity for the sermon to coincide with the presence of the monarch, whose arrival and departure could be haphazard.[26] The more substantial liturgical reason, however, was that it excised the sermon from the eucharist, thus avoiding any disruption to the sacramental impetus.

Reverence for the place of worship

Such ritual requirements were for Andrewes critical aspects of an offering whose purpose was to unite the human with the divine. This purpose also embraced the place where worship was offered. The building—its architectural design and ornamental detail—was to affirm the correspondence between human and divine. So Andrewes praised King David for his maintenance of the Ark and his reverence for the

---

[24] Andrewes, *Sermon Preached... the Fift of November Last, 1617*, and *A Sermon Preached before his Maiestie at Whitehall, on Easter Day Last* (1618), referred to by McCullough, *Sermons at Court*, p. 138.

[25] Andrewes, "Notes on the Book of Common Prayer", p. 156. Lake, "Lancelot Andrewes, John Buckeridge, and Avant-Garde Conformity".

[26] *Works of Lancelot Andrewes, sometime Bishop of Winchester* (Oxford: J. H. Parker, 1841–54), Vol. III, pp. 318–19, quoted by McCullough, *Sermons at Court*, p. 162.

Temple. He included this reference to David in a sermon before the queen, which would have affirmed her support for the beautification of places of worship, and also for the ceremonial with which the services were conducted.[27]

Music in worship

Of the works offered in worship, music for Andrewes was crucial. He made this plain in a sermon preached before Queen Elizabeth at Greenwich on 11 March 1589. It was based on Psalm 75:3, for which he used the translation, "The earth and all the inhabitants thereof are dissolved: but I will establish the pillars of it." By possessing a force able to move the human mind, music was able to exert an influence for good or ill and therefore had a critical role to play in the setting up of these pillars. It was a role established by Moses with divine authority. Referring to Deuteronomy 31:19, Andrewes claimed it was Moses who, by special direction from God, first began "to make music the conveyer of men's duties into their minds",[28] a skill perfected by David in his settings of the psalms.[29] When put to a holy and heavenly use, music could set the human condition in tune, individually and corporately. The resulting harmony would be the inspiration for the pillars of the new order promised by God. So by means of the holy and heavenly use of his harp and through his tunes of music, did David

> teach men how to set themselves in tune. How not only to tune themselves, but how to tune their households. And not only there, but here in this Psalm, how to preserve harmony, or, as he termeth it, how to sing *ne perdas*, to a commonwealth.[30]

Music was therefore a divinely appointed means for the achieving of an inner harmony of emotion and spirit, as a result of which the human

---

[27] McCullough, *Sermons at Court*, pp. 32, 98.
[28] Andrewes, *Ninety-six Sermons*, Vol. II, p. 3.
[29] Andrewes, *Ninety-six Sermons*, Vol. II, p. 3.
[30] Andrewes, *Ninety-six Sermons*, Vol. II, p. 3. *Ne perdas*: destroy not—the opening words of verse 9 of Psalm 75 (Vulgate).

could be united with the divine. The condition of an entire nation could therefore be discerned according to the quality and mood of its music. Untuneful and weak music created untuneful and weak people. Their music was all out of tune, and "affecteth the inhabitants with fear".[31] A more pleasant music inspired a stronger city, more able to demonstrate the salvation of God.[32] Not only had music the capacity to instil a sense of new life into the dispirited inhabitants of the city; it unnerved the enemy and restored the confidence of those outside the city. "This music hath life in it", affirmed Andrewes, and "hearteneth the inhabitant afresh; quaileth the enemy and resolveth the neighbour to say, 'Thine are we, O David, and on thy side, thou son of Jesse.'"[33] Music of this calibre could inspire personal equilibrium and create new hope and resolution. It embodied the blessings of God and was therefore of itself blessed.[34]

Andrewes's appointment as Dean of the Chapel Royal in 1618 gave him the opportunity to introduce these reforms, which gave liturgical shape to his theological understandings. What has been described as "sacrament-filled ritualism"[35] is none other than the liturgical manifestation of a doctrine of grace that regards the offering of worship as instrumental in effecting participation in the divine nature. It is testimony to a belief that the offering of worship and all that is associated with it, its ceremony, architecture and music, can assume the numinous character of the divine.

John Buckeridge

John Buckeridge was President of St John's College Oxford 1605, Canon of Windsor 1606, Bishop of Rochester 1611 and Bishop of Ely 1628.

---

[31] Andrewes, *Ninety-six Sermons*, Vol. II, p. 4.
[32] Andrewes, *Ninety-six Sermons*, Vol. II, p. 5. Cf. Isaiah 26:1.
[33] Andrewes, *Ninety-six Sermons*, Vol. II, p. 5. Cf. 1 Chronicles 12:18.
[34] Andrewes, *Ninety-six Sermons*, Vol. II, p. 5.
[35] Lake, "Lancelot Andrewes, John Buckeridge, and Avant-Garde Conformity", and quoted by McCullough, *Sermons at Court*, p. 151.

On 22 March 1617, John Buckeridge, then Bishop of Rochester, preached before King James [I and VI] at Whitehall.[36] First, he conceded the reformed principle that the sacrifice offered to God in the eucharist was not that offered by Christ on the cross. It was inconceivable, he argued, that the action of Christ's sacrifice on the cross and of the priests with the host are one and the same. This was logically impossible, for if Christ's original sacrifice "be divers and many in number, then Christ must be offered, and so suffer often, which is directly against the Apostle".[37] So the sacrifice offered by the Church was not a physical repetition of Christ's sacrifice but a spiritual offering made through Christ. The sacrifices offered by the Church are, according to St Peter, "Hostiae Spirituales, spiritual sacrifices, acceptable unto God by Jesus Christ".[38] The sacrifice which the Church offers is not "Jesum", but *"per Jesum Christum"*. It is through Jesus Christ, the only High Priest, that the offering is presented to and accepted by God.[39]

Human and Divine united

This said, however, Buckeridge attributed a richer significance to the offering of this sacrifice than the reformers had allowed and went so far as to identify the human offering with the divine. By virtue of its consecration, he argued, the sacrifice became not merely a remembrance but a representation or commemoration of Christ's offering. The sacrifice then assumed, if not an identification, at least a compelling affinity with the sacrifice of Christ. This in turn endowed it with a persuasive character in commending humanity to God. So this sacrament of the Lord's Supper, he insisted, "which contains a commemoration of Christ's one and only all-sufficient Sacrifice,

---

[36] John Buckeridge, *A Sermon Preached before his Majesty at Whitehall, March 22, 1617, being Passion Sunday, Touching Prostration, and Kneeling in the Worship of God* (London, 1618).

[37] Buckeridge, *Touching Prostration, and Kneeling*, p. 3.

[38] Cf. 1 Peter 2:5.

[39] Buckeridge, *Touching Prostration, and Kneeling*, p. 51.

consummated upon the Cross, and never more to be reiterated by any man, hath the same double respect in it; and therefore it is represented to God by our consecration, so it may well be called "Sacrificium repraesentatium," or "commemoratium", a representative, or commemorative Sacrifice.[40]

Divine-human unity allows for worship to be a sacrament of Christ's offering

As a sacrifice that applied the force of Christ's sacrifice, it could also be called *sacrificium communicatium*, a communicative sacrifice, or the communication or application of that sacrifice that was offered for us on the cross. As a representation of Christ's original sacrifice, this offering is united to Christ's offering and can plead before God with the force of that original sacrifice. The daily offering of worship therefore becomes a sacrament of Christ's offering. "Our Saviour Christ in the forme of God, receiveth Sacrifice with his Father, with whom he is one God", declared Buckeridge,

> yet in the form of a servant he chose rather to be a Sacrifice, then [than] receive sacrifice ... By this, he is the Priest, he is the offerer, and he is the oblation ... Of which (his Sacrifice) he would have the daily Sacrifice of the Church to be a Sacrament: which Church, being the body of the head himself, doth learn to offer herself, by him.[41]

In fact, every prayer ending *"Per Jesum Christum Dominum nostrum*, through Jesus Christ our Lord, doth represent and offer Christ crucified to God, and entreats remission and grace, through his death and passion".[42]

---

[40] Buckeridge, *Touching Prostration, and Kneeling*, p. 52.
[41] Buckeridge, *Touching Prostration, and Kneeling*, p. 60. St Augustine of Hippo, *The City of God against the Pagans,* Book 10:20, tr. G. E. McCracken (Cambridge, MA: Harvard University Press, 2011), p. 291.
[42] Buckeridge, *Touching Prostration, and Kneeling*, p. 52.

Human offering identified with Christ's mystical body, not natural body

Buckeridge emphasized that what is offered by the Church is not the natural body of Christ, but Christ's mystical, spiritual body.[43] However, because the sacrifice being offered was spiritual did not mean it should be invisible, without physical substance, for the physical nature of the offering was the necessary expression of the spiritual offering. Visible offerings, he insisted, are the signs of invisible offerings, as words are the signs of things. In worship, therefore, the spiritual was necessarily inseparable from the physical and so the offering of the heart must have its physical expression. "Come, let us go together to God's worship", he urged, for

> here is *Latria*, divine Adoration: *Adoremus*, Let us worship with the inward devotion, and sacrifice of the heart. Here's *Servitus*, Service or, outward worship of the body: *Procidamus*, let us prostrate our bodies together with the inward intention of our Souls.[44]

Necessity of physical as well as spiritual offering

An outward and physical offering was required to give expression to the inner, spiritual offering. "Come, let us pay him the Rent of Sacrifice and adoration," he exhorted: "He that bends the knees of his soul ought likewise to stoop and bend the knees of his body."[45] In fact, the outward offering was as crucial as the inner, spiritual offering of the heart and mind. The one could not be divorced from the other. They were undivided companions: "Inward adoration in the devotion of the heart; Outward worship in the prostration & kneeling of the body, and sighs and tears in the compunction of the soul must ever be tendered at the Altar of the Lord our Maker."[46] In short, maintained Buckeridge,

---

[43] Buckeridge, *Touching Prostration, and Kneeling*, pp. 60–1.
[44] Buckeridge, *Touching Prostration, and Kneeling*, p. 2.
[45] Buckeridge, *Touching Prostration, and Kneeling*, p. 3.
[46] Buckeridge, *Touching Prostration, and Kneeling*, p. 3. Peter Lake discusses Buckeridge's advocacy of kneeling in "Lancelot Andrewes, John Buckeridge,

"the whole man must be offered up as a living sacrifice to God, 'ut totus hic sit, & totus in Caelo offeratur' in order that the whole man being in the Temple may at the same instant be presented to God in Heaven".[47] Whilst the inward devotion and sacrifice of the heart in prayer and praise is always required—"God cares not for the outward, nay, he loathes it, if the inward be wanting"[48]—yet the inner offering of the sacrifice of the heart and soul could not be experienced in isolation. There existed an inherent interdependence between that which Buckeridge described as *excitatio mutua*—mutual excitation.[49]

Without the offering of the body the sacrifice would be incomplete, for "I have two mites, a body, and a soul" and both should be offered.[50] The worship of the disciples themselves consisted of the offering of both body and soul: "The Apostles did adore Christ at his ascension with external, singular, and visible worship, Luke 24:52, for with internal devotion they did always adore him. But this special worshipping must be understood both of soul and body."[51]

Buckeridge professed himself unaware of any restriction that required the Church's offering to be exclusively spiritual.[52] In the presence of God, physical, bodily devotion is as necessary as spiritual devotion. When we stand in the sight of God, he quoted from Cyprian of Carthage,

> *Placendum est divinis oculis, & habitu corporis, & modo vocis,* We must please the eyes of God with the habit of our body, and the tune of our voice....

---

and Avant-Garde Conformity", p. 118.

[47] Buckeridge, *Touching Prostration, and Kneeling*, p. 7.
[48] Buckeridge, *Touching Prostration, and Kneeling*, p. 12. *In sacrificus externis semper desiderantur interna*: In external sacrifices, the internal things are always desired.
[49] Buckeridge, *Touching Prostration, and Kneeling*, p. 19.
[50] Buckeridge, *Touching Prostration, and Kneeling*, p. 96.
[51] Buckeridge, *Touching Prostration, and Kneeling*, p. 185.
[52] Buckeridge, *Touching Prostration, and Kneeling*, p. 192.

> Devotion is sometimes the inward Adoration of the heart, but in God's solemn worship, outward Adoration is required with it.[53]

So it was evident for Buckeridge that the offering of worship could not be restricted to the spiritual sacrifice of the heart and mind as the sole commemoration of Christ's own offering. It had to encompass the offering of the whole person, physical and spiritual. Buckeridge summoned Eusebius who "joineth both these; that is, the commemorative sacrifice, and the sacrifice of ourselves together, with other sacrifices concurring in that action".[54]

This broadened understanding of sacrifice allowed for the inclusion in worship of works of beauty which could be received and appreciated by God in terms of physical pleasure. Buckeridge drew again from Eusebius:

> we burn that prophetical sweet odour in every place, and we offer to him that sweet smelling fruit of divinity, abounding with all virtue, doing this with prayers directed to him; which another Prophet teacheth also who saith, Let my prayer be as incense in thy sight, therefore we do but sacrifice and offer incense ... sometimes celebrating the memory of that great sacrifice ... and giving thanks for our salvation, and offering to him religious hymns and sacred prayers.[55]

---

[53] Buckeridge, *Touching Prostration, and Kneeling*, p. 181. Cyprianus Carthaginensis, *Liber de Oratione Dominica*, Treatise IV, "On the Lord's Prayer": "Let us consider we are standing in God's sight. We must please the divine eyes both with the habit of body and with the measure of voice", in Philip Schaff (ed.), *The Early Church Fathers—Ante Nicene Fathers Vol. 5: Fathers of the Third Century: Hippolytus, Cyprian, Caius, Novatian*, (Edinburgh: T&T Clark, 1990), p. 784.

[54] Buckeridge, *Touching Prostration, and Kneeling*, p. 66. Eusebius, *The proof of the Gospel: being the Demonstratio Evangelica of Eusebius of Caesarea*, ed. W. J. Ferrar, Vol. I (London: SPCK, 1920), p. 62.

[55] Buckeridge, *Touching Prostration, and Kneeling*, pp. 66-7. Eusebius of Caesarea, *Demonstratio Evangelica*, Vol. I, p. 62.

Far from distorting or compromising the spiritual integrity of the offering, the outward, physical aspect enhanced it.[56]

Original purpose of reformation

Buckeridge recalled the original purpose of the reformation of the liturgy in 1549, 1552 and then in 1559. It had been initiated by the Prince and Prelates of this Church who had "proceeded to the reformation of superstitions and abuses, crept into the worship of God by the corruptions of Popery". In the pursuit of this aim, they had "endeavoured to take away the multitude of idle, and superfluous Ceremonies that made the state of Christianity more intolerable than the state of the Jews was". Buckeridge pointed out that the reformers had been bound to exercise discretion and restraint, for "their meaning was not to make a new Church but to reform according to the first, and primitive, and Apostolical institution".[57] Such an obligation, however, had not been honoured and Buckeridge condemned the immoderate lengths to which the reformers had gone. Their drive to eliminate superstition from the liturgy had become so indiscriminate that the effect was not one of purity but of profanity. Their purpose should not have been "to take the crooked staff, and bow it so far from one extreme to the other, that from superstition, they would presently decline to profaneness".[58] As a solution he advocated "the golden mean": "neither retaining all Ceremonies, lest Religion might seem to be nothing else but external pomp, and gesticulation; neither rejecting all, lest Religion having lost all external majesty, might appear naked, and soon decay at the heart".[59]

Buckeridge's views on the offering of worship constitute a powerful counterblast to the immoderate reactions so avidly promoted by the mid-sixteenth-century reformers.

---

[56] Buckeridge, *Touching Prostration, and Kneeling*, pp. 205–6.
[57] Buckeridge, *Touching Prostration, and Kneeling*, p. 241.
[58] Buckeridge, *Touching Prostration, and Kneeling*, pp. 241–2.
[59] Buckeridge, *Touching Prostration, and Kneeling*, p. 242.

Offering valid through Christ's offering

Preaching at the funeral of Lancelot Andrewes on 11 November 1626, Buckeridge reiterated the principle that the one, perfect and true sacrifice was the sacrifice of Jesus Christ, and that it was without question the only legitimate sacrifice effective for salvation.[60] "One in itself, and once only offered", it was Christ's sacrifice alone which had power to appease God's wrath and make all other sacrificers and sacrifices acceptable.[61] Nevertheless, he insisted, the sacrifice offered in worship was an authentic sacrifice because it was a "representation or commemoration of the true sacrifice of Christ",[62] and being offered in, by and through the sacrifice of Christ the sacrifice was valid.[63] This sacrifice was the "sacrifice of the soul and spirit ... which God ever accepted in the sacrifice of His Son Christ",[64] and without this inward aspect of sacrifice the external offering would become hollow.

Offering to be both physical and spiritual

However, it was a sacrifice which should not be exclusively spiritual. As the sacrifice offered in worship was the sacrifice of the whole Church, the whole person had to be offered and this whole person was comprised of both body and soul. As stated in the prayer of the Holy Communion, the offering was one of "ourselves, our souls, and bodies [as] a living sacrifice, holy and acceptable to God, which is our reasonable service of him".[65]

---

[60] John Buckeridge, "A Sermon preached at the Funeral of the Right Reverend Father in God, Lancelot, late Lord Bishop of Winchester", in Andrewes, *Ninety-six Sermons*, Vol. V, p. 259.

[61] Buckeridge, "A Sermon preached at the Funeral of the Right Reverend Father in God, Lancelot, late Lord Bishop of Winchester", p. 260.

[62] Buckeridge, "A Sermon preached at the Funeral of the Right Reverend Father in God, Lancelot, late Lord Bishop of Winchester", p. 261.

[63] Buckeridge, "A Sermon preached at the Funeral of the Right Reverend Father in God, Lancelot, late Lord Bishop of Winchester", p. 262.

[64] Buckeridge, "A Sermon preached at the Funeral of the Right Reverend Father in God, Lancelot, late Lord Bishop of Winchester", p. 280.

[65] Buckeridge, "A Sermon preached at the Funeral of the Right Reverend Father in God, Lancelot, late Lord Bishop of Winchester", p. 266.

A purely spiritual offering was therefore incomplete without its external, bodily counterpart, for "true religion is no way a gargleism only, to wash the tongue and mouth, to speak good words; it must root in the heart and then fructify in the hand, else it will not cleanse the whole man".[66] It was necessary that the whole person, body as well as soul, be that which was represented. To say, as did the reformers, that the offering of worship had of necessity to be a spiritual offering of the heart and mind alone was insufficient, for there were other elements involved that were pleasing to God. There was the sacrifice "representative or memorial of Christ's sacrifice, the Eucharist, which is truly the sacrifice of praise", and there is the "daily sacrifice of ourselves, our souls and bodies, in devotion and adoration to God. And the sacrifice of mercy and alms . . . these be the sacrifices . . . that please God".[67]

Works that were once maligned and dismissed as having no place in worship were now commended. However insignificant or worthless these works may previously have appeared, they were not despised but rather welcomed by God. They are "*sacrificia sunt, et talia sunt*, they are sacrifices, and sacrifices of much price". Though they be but crumbs of bread or drops of water, they are so much the more precious because they express gratitude to God.[68]

Offering of works persuasive

Whilst they achieved no propitiatory effect these works were nevertheless persuasive in stimulating God's affection. With the offering of works, said Buckeridge, "*Delectatu*, or *placatur Deus*, 'God is pacified,' or 'God is well pleased'; and all the world is well given to appease and pacify His wrath, and gain His favour". Works were therefore not to be despised

---

[66] Buckeridge, "A Sermon preached at the Funeral of the Right Reverend Father in God, Lancelot, late Lord Bishop of Winchester", p. 269. Referred to by Lake in "Lancelot Andrewes, John Buckeridge, and Avant-Garde Conformity", p. 115.

[67] Buckeridge, "A Sermon preached at the Funeral of the Right Reverend Father in God, Lancelot, late Lord Bishop of Winchester", p. 280.

[68] Buckeridge, "A Sermon preached at the Funeral of the Right Reverend Father in God, Lancelot, late Lord Bishop of Winchester", p. 269.

and banished as unworthy of being offered to God. "God cannot forget them, if we do remember and perform them", he declared, "nay God holds them at a great rate, He accepts them as sacrifices, and such sacrifices as both pacify and please him: *Talibus sacrificiis*, with such sacrifices God is pleased."[69]

Whilst not eliciting divine forgiveness, this offering nevertheless interceded with a force which surpassed mere words. "It will appear", he said, "that the voice of a few good works, done for Christ's sake, will speak louder, and plead harder and more effectually for us, than all our glorious words and professions."[70] Works were not to be afforded the status of merits, but then, no part of the sacrifice which was offered could claim the right to a divine reward. However, this was no reason for them to be dismissed from the offering of worship, for with them God was pacified, reconciled, pleased, delighted and cheered:

> *Placatur* or *conciliatur*, "God is pacified" or "reconciled", as some read; *Delectatur*, "God is pleased", or "delighted". *Hilarescit*, or *pulchrescit*, "God is cheered", or "looks upon us with a serene or pleasant countenance"; but the Vulgar will have it, *Promeretur Deus*, "God is pro-merited", in favour of merits.[71]

Buckeridge expressed caution regarding this last association of works with merit and stated his preference for a translation of *promeretur* which would eliminate any idea of merit. Yet, he insisted, whilst works may not deserve merit, they were accepted by God. Man was an unprofitable servant, his best works were imperfect and inconsequential in securing forgiveness and acceptance, and God was not bound to bestow any reward for these impoverished efforts. Yet God responded positively to offerings made with sincerity and conviction: "Though God be not

---

[69] Buckeridge, "A Sermon preached at the Funeral of the Right Reverend Father in God, Lancelot, late Lord Bishop of Winchester", p. 269.

[70] Buckeridge, "A Sermon preached at the Funeral of the Right Reverend Father in God, Lancelot, late Lord Bishop of Winchester", pp. 272–3.

[71] Buckeridge, "A Sermon preached at the Funeral of the Right Reverend Father in God, Lancelot, late Lord Bishop of Winchester", p. 282.

bound, and man merits not, yet God never failed any man that did do any good work, but he was sure of his reward."[72]

Appropriate offerings constituted a force of such significance as God could not ignore, and when joined to the perfect offering of Christ they became the "viaticum or viands to carry us to heaven: for though *non hic coelum* 'heaven be not here' in this life, yet *hic quaeritur coelum*, 'here in this life heaven is to be sought and here it is either found or lost'".[73] Works might not be able to achieve the ultimate allaying of God's anger or the forgiveness of sin, yet they could initiate a revelation of the divine glory, and when offered as part of the sacrifice of praise and thanksgiving would constitute "the art of turning earth into heaven".[74] It would be possible for the offering of worship to encapsulate the unity of the human with the divine and for the reality of the divine presence to be experienced.

---

[72] Buckeridge, "A Sermon preached at the Funeral of the Right Reverend Father in God, Lancelot, late Lord Bishop of Winchester", p. 283.

[73] Buckeridge, "A Sermon preached at the Funeral of the Right Reverend Father in God, Lancelot, late Lord Bishop of Winchester", p. 272. *Non hic coelum*—heaven is not here; *Hic quaeritur coelum*—heaven is sought here. Lake discusses the acceptance of works when offered in Christ in "Lancelot Andrewes, John Buckeridge, and Avant-Garde Conformity", p. 122.

[74] Buckeridge, "A Sermon preached at the Funeral of the Right Reverend Father in God, Lancelot, late Lord Bishop of Winchester", p. 279.

9

The Experience of Transcendence

John Donne

Celebrated as a preacher and writer, John Donne (1572–1631), Dean of St Paul's London (1621) and Vicar of St Dunstan's in the West (1624), made a forceful contribution to the reversal of the concept of worship as propounded by the Book of Common Prayer. A bedrock of Donne's theology was his keen appreciation of the authority and efficacy of divine forgiveness which comprehensively demolished the immoveable tenet of the reformers that humanity was so hopelessly corrupted as to be incapable of offering any work to God.

Human sin and corruption

Donne acknowledged the force of this corruption and of humanity's predilection for sin and expressed it eloquently and with considerable poetic force. It was inherent in the human condition: "Our will is poysoned in the fountaine", he declared, and in consequence we are "willing to sin as soone as we can, and sorry we can sin no sooner, and sorry no longer".[1] Notwithstanding that in the very first minute of life the image of God is imprinted in the soul, sin is present as soon as that image is there. The image of God and the image of Adam enter in one

---

[1] E. M. S. Simpson and G. R. Potter (eds), *The Sermons of John Donne*, 10 vols (Berkeley, CA: University of California Press, 1953 ff.), Vol. 7: Sermon 8, p. 4. *Preached upon Whitsunday [28 May 1626]*.

and the same act.² This inclination to sin is planted at birth and is so encrusted in human nature that mankind is willing to sin even before the Devil is willing, and willing after the Devil is weary. Worse, occasions of temptation are sought even when the Devil presents none. Our bodies contribute to such foulness, harbour it and retain it. It is an unquenchable fire and a brand of hell itself.³ This original weakness, Donne asserted, "hath banished me out of my self; It is no more I that do any thing, but sin that dwelleth in me" and this sin "doth not only dwell, but reign in these mortall bodies; not only reign, but tyrannize, and lead us captive under the law of sin".⁴

Moreover, attempts to avoid culpability on the grounds that sin is inherent in human nature, beyond human choice and *peccatum involuntarium*, a sin "without any elicite act of the Will, and so properly no sin" were futile. The reason, Donne argued, is that we are all partakers of Adam. All humanity is in Adam, our wills and actions are irrevocably caught up in Adam and so Adam's sin has invaded every particular man.⁵ Further, it was impossible to argue that because Adam's original sin had been contracted without human consent it was irrelevant to the human condition. Adam's sin may well have been Adam's sin in particular, but it had been propagated by mankind. Therefore, humanity is equally complicit, equally culpable and equally subject to the penalty.⁶

---

2   Donne, *Sermons*, Vol. 2: Sermon 1, p. 11. *Preached at Lincolns Inne, 1618*.
3   Donne, *Sermons*, Vol. 7: Sermon 8, p. 4.
4   Donne, *Sermons*, Vol. 6: Sermon 5, p. 4. *Preached upon Whitsunday [1624?]*.
5   Donne, *Sermons*, Vol. 6: Sermon 5, p. 4.
6   Donne, *Sermons*, Vol. 2: Sermon 3, p. 11. "Donne's discussion of the tension between Adam's sin and original righteousness is grounded in 1 Corinthians 15, 2 Corinthians 12 and Romans 5:12–21.

The potency of Divine forgiveness

That said, however, Donne embarked on a comprehensive and meticulous demolition of the concept of Original Sin. It was inconceivable, he insisted, that God would ever place a curse on mankind at birth. In any case, no sin could ever be greater than the mercy of God. Divine mercy prevailed in every circumstance. With the exception of the blasphemy against the Holy Ghost which shall not be forgiven, the assurance that God shall forgive all manner of sin and blasphemy was inviolable. Moreover, if God, who is almighty, is unable to exercise this forgiveness, He is not almighty. The affirmation that "his mercy endures for ever" is invalidated if that mercy is restricted: "His mercy endures not for ever, if he doe not forgive all."[7] This ought not to come as a surprise, he added, because mercy is the pre-eminent of all the divine qualities:

> If we could think of more degrees of goodnesse in God, of an exaltation of God himself in God, of more God in God, of a Superlative in God, we must necessarily turn upon his mercy, for that *Mercie* must be the *Superlative*.[8]

God's first thought and action towards humanity was therefore mercy. "Mercy was the first-born, and first-mover in all,"[9] so much so that God was prepared to "emprison himselfe in me" and forgive my sins, "not only against my neighbour, but against myself".[10] God's mercy was never expressed in the Scriptures in terms of restriction, caution or grudging compliance but of largeness and excessive generosity: "God hath no way towards man but goodnesse" and so "God glorifies himselfe in nothing upon man, but in his owne goodnesse."[11]

---

[7] Donne, *Sermons*, Vol. 2: Sermon 3, p. 11.
[8] Donne, *Sermons*, Vol. 7: Sermon 14, pp. 4–5. *Preached to the King, at White-Hall, the first Sunday in Lent* [Probably 11 February 1626/7].
[9] Donne, *Sermons*, Vol. 7: Sermon 14, p. 5.
[10] Donne, *Sermons*, Vol. 5: Sermon 3, p. 5.
[11] Donne, *Sermons*, Vol. 9: Sermon 5, pp. 10–11. *Preached upon Christmas day* [?1629].

Moreover, God's instinct is not to destroy what he has created. Instead, God "seems to summone himself, to assemble himselfe, to muster himselfe, all himselfe, all the persons of the Trinity, to doe what he could in the favour of man".[12] As a result, mankind is "armed with consolation" for "how low so ever God be pleased to cast you, Though it be to the earth, yet he does not so much cast you downe ... as bring you home".[13]

It was consequently inconceivable for Donne that God could ever taint humanity with a curse at birth. It was unimaginable that God would regard humanity as a competitor or even an adversary and impose a handicap at the outset to improve God's chances of victory, especially before anything had been done to warrant it. "Imagine God *Ludere in humanis*, to play but a *game at Chesse* with this world", he proposed; "Imagine God to be but at play with us, but a gamester", having sport "making little things great, and great things nothing". A gamester might well deliver a curse after losing, but not before losing or before there is even any danger of losing. Why, then, should God apply a curse before there was a loss, before any sin had been committed? So for Donne Original Sin was not a penalty imposed by God. Insofar as there was anything original about it, it was "the sinne that my Parents cast upon me ... and the sinnes that I cast upon my children" by way of "an ill example".[14]

Concept of Original Sin inconceivable

Just as it was inconceivable that God would deliberately blight humanity by imposing an indelible defect at birth, it was equally inconceivable that, if indeed imposed, this original sin could ever be a permanent impediment. God's mercy would prevail over all human actions and conditions and continually temper God's judgement. "*Water* is a frequent emblem of *Affliction* in the Scriptures; and so is *oyl* of *Mercy*", and if at

---

[12] Donne, *Sermons*, Vol. 5: Sermon 14, p. 12. Preached at S. Pauls [1615–30].

[13] Donne, *Sermons*, Vol. 6: Sermon 10, p. 9. Preached at S. Pauls, The Sunday after the Conversion of S. Paul [1624/5].

[14] Donne, *Sermons*, Vol. 7: Sermon 14, p. 13.

any time, he noted, "in any place of Scripture, God seemed to begin with water, with a judgement, yet the oyle will get to the top". "In that very judgement", he added, "you may see that God had first a mercifull purpose in inflicting that medicinall judgement; for his mercy is his first-born."[15]

God's mercy available to all

In a formidable counter to the reformed position and guaranteed to ignite the fury of the extreme Protestants, Donne insisted that God's mercy was not limited to the righteous: "God finds weaknesse, wickednesse in us, yet hee *came to call, not the righteous, but sinners to repentance*." As a consequence, no repentant sinners can be shut out or denied their part in the resurrection.[16] Christ "feeds not one Parish, nor one Diocese, but *humanum genus*, all Mankinde, the whole world".[17] God's mercy is boundless and embraces all. "Some men will continue kinde, where they finde a thankfull receiver", he maintained, "but *God is kinde to the unthankfull*, says Christ himself." Moreover, "There may be found a man that will dye for his friend ... But God dyed for his enemies."[18]

If the idea of God being kind to the unthankful was a sure-fire certainty to invoke the wrath of those true to the reformed position, his assertion that God's kindness extended even to those who did not believe would have been enough to provoke apoplexy. Especially irritating was the cool logic of his argument. Firstly, he stated that God's intention that all shall be saved would be thwarted if those presently declaring themselves to be non-believers were excluded. Secondly, there was always the possibility that self-professed non-believers might ultimately come to believe. So to the question "How can all be saved since all do not beleeve?", Donne simply introduced a counter-question: "Because actually they do not

---

[15] Donne, *Sermons*, Vol. 7: Sermon 14, p. 7.
[16] Donne, *Sermons*, Vol. 8: Sermon 16, p. 18. *Preached upon Easter-day, 1629.*
[17] Donne, *Sermons*, Vol. 9: Sermon 5, p. 3.
[18] Donne, *Sermons*, Vol. 9: Sermon 5, p. 8.

believe, is it therefore impossible they should beleeve?"[19] With a few deft strokes, the argument was won.

Christ died for all, so all are pardoned

In any case, he added, in dying for all Christ has effected a general pardon for all and, by instituting the Church, Christ established the means for that general pardon to be made particular to each individual. Rejoice, therefore, that Christ has died for all, because this has brought about "Gods general forgiving of Transgressions", and "multiply thy joy" because "Christ hath instituted a Church in which that general pardon is made thine in particular".

> Then there will be cause to exalt thy joy because God, not imputing any iniquity, shall receive thee, at thy last houre, in thy last Bath, the sweat of death, as lovingly, as acceptably, as innocently, as he received thee, from thy first Bath, the laver of Regeneration, the font in Baptisme.[20]

By virtue of this act of baptism, "we are washed from original, and from actuall sins".[21] "Is thy sinne Actuall sinne?" asked Donne. Then "knowest thou not that there is a Lamb bleeding before upon the Altar, to expiate that?" Or if there is sin which is attributed to what is inherent and original in the human condition, then that sting is also blunted by baptism.[22] So it was by baptism and the eucharist—the water of baptism and the blood of Christ—that God's forgiveness obliterated all sin, both original and actual.

The ultimate assurance of this divine forgiveness was the faithfulness of God. The Lord is a faithful God, whom St Paul referred to as "*Fidelem*

---

[19] Donne, *Sermons*, Vol. 9: Sermon 5, p. 9.
[20] Donne, *Sermons*, Vol. 9: Sermon 13, p. 24. *Preached upon the Penitentiall Psalmes.*
[21] Donne, *Sermons*, Vol. 9: Sermon 13, p. 24.
[22] Donne, *Sermons*, Vol. 7: Sermon 14, p. 8.

Creatorem, A *faithfull* Creator". "God had gracious purposes upon me, when he created me", said Donne, and consequently he will be faithful to those purposes. God's faithfulness to his purposes at creation is so unshakeable that it seemed to Donne as though God must be "faithfull to some contract, to some promise that hee hath made. And that promise is my evidence".[23]

The efficacy and thoroughness of divine forgiveness was vitally important for Donne because it facilitated what he called "the *putting on of* Christ", which in turn formed his view of the present reality of Christ in the offering of worship. Forgiven, we can be made partakers of Christ's act of offering and so become incorporate in the divine nature:

> for we are not to put on Christ onely as a Livery, to be distinguished by externall marks of Christianity; but so, as the sonne puts on his father; that we may be of the same nature and substance as he.[24]

God and man become one person

This incorporation of the divine and human was for Donne neither peripheral nor transitory. God is in man in every way to the same degree that God is in Christ. So we put on a two-fold clothing: we put on Christ as a garment so that we shall be his; we put on Christ as a person so that we shall be He.[25] We put on Christ as a livery to show we belong to him, but we put on Christ as the Son puts on his Father so that we may be participants in the divine nature and substance: "We shall not onely put on Christ as a *garment*, but we shall put on his *person* and we shall stand

---

[23] Donne, *Sermons*, Vol. 8: Sermon 2, p. 12. *A Sermon of Commemoration of the Lady Danvers, late Wife of Sir John Danvers. Preach'd at Chilsey, where she was lately buried. By John Donne Dean of St. Pauls, London. 1 July 1627.*

[24] Donne, *Sermons*, Vol. 5: Sermon 7, p. 8. Preached at a Christning [? 1615–30]. Donne's reference to the 'putting on' of Christ is reminiscent of Colossians 3:10–15.

[25] Donne, *Sermons*, Vol. 5: Sermon 7, p. 8.

before his Father with the confidence and assurance of bearing his person and the dignity of his innocence."[26] God's promise is that He will be with us, not only as He has been from the dawn of time, but "hereafter as he was never yet, he would be *Immanuel, God with us,* as that God and man should be one person".[27]

Whole of human nature involved

Crucially for Donne, this incorporation into Christ involved the whole of human nature, not just a part. All of humanity is incorporate in Christ, not merely a select few who imagine themselves to be the elect. Just as "when God seems to have held a consultation about the making of Man, man put on all the Trinity, *all* God", so "in the redemption God put on *all Man*; not onely all the nature of Mankind in general, but in particular, *every Man*".[28] As a result, man is to "so inwrap himselfe in Christ, and in his Merits, as to make the whole nature of Christ his own: 'He that puts on Christ, must put him on *all*'". This degree of intimacy was possible because "Christ hath dyed, not onely that he hath died for *him*, but that he also hath died *in* Christ, and that whatsoever Christ suffered, *he* suffered *in* Christ".[29] That is, so complete is this indwelling of mankind in Christ that when Christ suffered, mankind, in Christ, also suffered, and when Christ died, mankind, in Christ, also died.

The theme of God's mercy in Christ negating the force of sin and thereby making possible incorporation into the person of Christ became dominant throughout Donne's sermons, and he regularly elaborated on the nature and extent of this incorporation. God will have a co-operation, a concurrence of persons, he insisted.[30] God has stamped his Image upon

---

[26] Donne, *Sermons*, Vol. 5: Sermon 7, p. 17.
[27] Donne, *Sermons*, Vol. 9: Sermon 5, p. 14.
[28] Donne, *Sermons*, Vol. 5: Sermon 7, p. 7.
[29] Donne, *Sermons*, Vol. 5: Sermon 7, p. 7.
[30] Donne, *Sermons*, Vol. 4: Sermon 7, p. 8. *A Sermon upon the XX. Verse of the V. Chapter of the Booke of Judges. Wherein occasion was justly taken for the Publication of some Reasons, which his Sacred Majestie had been pleased*

us, "and so God is our *Statuarius*, our Minter, our Statuary".[31] The soul is precious because "thine Image is stampt, and imprinted upon it",[32] and so there is "such a cooperation as should put God and man in Commission together", making "grace and nature Collegues in the worke":[33]

> Wee are that *Semen Dei*, that Malachie speakes of, the seed of God, which hee hath sow'd in his Church; and by that extraction, we are *Consortes divinae Naturae*, Partakers of the divine Nature it selfe; And so grow to bee *Filij Dei*, The Sonnes of God; And by that title, *Cohaeredes Christi*, Joint-heires with Christ; And so to bee *Christi ipsi*, Christs our selves; as God calls all his faithfull, his Anointed, his Christs.[34]

Partakers of the divine nature

So Donne declared that "God hath made all good men *partakers of the Divine Nature*". "They are *the sons of God*, the *seed of God*",[35] and as such it is possible "to grow to that height, to be of the *Quorum*, in that Commission ... and not onely *Gods* by *Representation*, but *Idem Spiritus cum Domino*; So become the same *Spirit* with the *Lord*":[36]

> We shall grow up to that perfection as that we shall *Induere personam*, put on *him*, his person; that is, we shall so appeare

---

to give, of those Directions for Preachers, which hee had formerly sent forth. Preached at the Crosse the 15th of September 1622. By John Donne, Doctor of Divinitie, and Deane of Saint Pauls, London.

[31] Donne, *Sermons*, Vol. 9: Sermon 5, p. 2.
[32] Donne, *Sermons*, Vol. 8: Sermon 2, p. 1.
[33] Donne, *Sermons*, Vol. 8: Sermon 16, p. 15.
[34] Donne, *Sermons*, Vol. 8: Sermon 2, p. 10. Malachi 2:15.
[35] Donne, *Sermons*, Vol. 8: Sermon 5, p. 5.
[36] Donne, *Sermons*, Vol. 8: Sermon 2, p. 10.

before the Father, as that he shall take us for his owne Christ; we shall beare his name and person.[37]

In so doing "we put on his righteousnesse, and his innocency, by imitation, and conforming ourselves to him".[38] In that "we have received his Absolution, his Remission, his Pardon", we are "restored to the innocency of his Baptisme, nay to the integrity which Adam had before the fall, nay to the righteousnesse of Christ Jesus himself".[39]

Offering of worship has a propitiatory quality

Thus granted a righteousness equivalent to that of Christ and as a partaker of the divine nature, appearing before the Father as if he were Christ himself, Donne believed it possible for the offering of worship which, incorporate in the offering of Christ and inspired by the Holy Spirit, assumed the efficacy of that original offering. This was a momentous statement from Donne. It acknowledged a propitiatory element to the offering of worship. "As ye were baptized in the holy Ghost", he said, "and as your bodies are Temples of the holy Ghost, so your soules may be Priests of the holy Ghost, and you, altogether a lively and reasonable sacrifice to God, in the holy Ghost."[40] As a result humanity becomes the Temple of the Holy Ghost, "so when we pray, it is the Holy Ghost who is praying; it is the Giver who is the Asker, as the Asker becomes the Giver".[41] If the prayers of worship are actually those of the Holy Ghost and it is the Holy Ghost who is receiving those prayers, then logically they cannot be denied, because the Holy Ghost would never reject his own supplications: "What can be denied where the Asker gives?"

---

[37] Donne, *Sermons*, Vol. 5: Sermon 7, p. 9.
[38] Donne, *Sermons*, Vol. 5: Sermon 7, p. 9.
[39] Donne, *Sermons*, Vol. 7: Sermon 8, p. 17.
[40] Donne, *Sermons*, Vol. 8: Sermon 11, p. 16. *Preached at S. Pauls upon Whitsunday, 1628.*
[41] Donne, *Sermons*, Vol. 5: Sermon 12, p. 3. *Preached to the Nobility.*

As the sacrifice offered by Christ was a propitiatory sacrifice effective for reconciliation, so Donne understood the sacrifice offered in the sacramental and ceremonial worship to be possessed of a corresponding propitiatory significance. The sacrifice of prayer and praise, and the offering of Christ in the sacrament of the eucharist, was not only a commemorative sacrifice but a real sacrifice,

> in which the Priest doth that which none but he does; that is, really to offer up Christ Jesus crucified to Almighty God for the sins of the people, so, as that that very body of Christ, which offered himself for a propitiatory sacrifice upon the cross, once for all, that body, and all that that body suffered, is offered again, and presented to the Father.

By means of this sacrifice, "the Father is intreated, that for the merits of that person, so presented and offered unto him, and in contemplation thereof, he will be merciful to that congregation, and applie those merits of his, to their particular souls".[42]

Not transubstantiated but transformed

Donne carefully distinguished between a propitiatory sacrifice and transubstantiation of the elements of the eucharist. "In the blessed, and glorious, and mysterious Sacrament of the Body and Blood of Christ Jesus", he stated, "thou seest *Christum Domini*, the Lords Salvation, and thy Salvation, and that, thus far with bodily eyes." However

> That Bread which thou seest after the Consecration is not the same bread which was presented before; not that it is Transubstantiated to another substance, for it is bread still (which is the hereticall

---

[42] Donne, *Sermons*, Vol. 2: Sermon 12, p. 7. *To the Prince and Princess Palatine, the Lady Elizabeth at Heydelberg, when I was commanded by the King to wait upon my L. of Doncaster in his Embassage to Germany. First Sermon as we went out, June 16, 1619.*

Riddle of the Roman Church, and Satan's sophistry...) but that it is severed, and appropriated by God... to another use.[43]

Whilst not being transubstantiated, the bread is nevertheless transformed. This was a transformation which "cannot be intended of the outward form and fashion, for that is not changed; but be it of that internall form, which is the very essence and nature of the bread". The bread is transformed in that it has "received a new form, a new essence, a new nature, because whereas the nature of bread is but to nourish the body, the nature of this bread now is to nourish the soule".[44] The sacramental bread is therefore the body of Christ. This is because "God hath shed his Ordinance upon it and made it of another nature in the use, though not in the substance. By the words of Consecration in the Sacrament", Donne affirmed, "we make the naturall body of Christ Jesus applicable to our soules".[45]

For Donne, the true transubstantiation occurs when "it becomes my very soule; that is, My soule growes up into a better state, and habitude by it, and I have the more soule for it, the more sanctified, the more deified soule by that Sacrament".[46] Thus it follows that independently of what we see, "that which we receive, is to be adored; for we receive Christ. He is *Res Sacramenti*, The forme, the Essence, the substance, the soule of the Sacrament".[47]

How the body and blood of Christ becomes present, Donne conjectured, is a riddle to be understood in God's good time and in the light of faith. Regarding the manner of "how the Body and Bloud of Christ is there", we are to "wait his leisure, if he have not yet manifested that to thee". That God has not made clear to the Church either the way or the manner of his presence in the sacrament is not a matter for our

---

[43] Donne, *Sermons*, Vol. 7: Sermon 11, p. 16. *Preached at S. Pauls upon Christmas day, 1626*.
[44] Donne, *Sermons*, Vol. 7: Sermon 11, p. 17.
[45] Donne, *Sermons*, Vol. 7: Sermon 11, p. 18.
[46] Donne, *Sermons*, Vol. 7: Sermon 12, p. 22. *The fourth of my Prebend Sermons upon my five Psalmes: Preached at S. Pauls, 28 January 1626 [1626/7]*.
[47] Donne, *Sermons*, Vol. 7: Sermon 12, p. 21.

concern: "Grieve not at that, wonder not at that, presse not for that" for like Simeon the prophet we are "patiently to attend Gods time". For the present, "exercise thy faith onely . . . and leave thy passion at home, and referre thy reason, and disputation to the Schoole".[48] Nevertheless there was no doubt that "this Sacrament, whilst it is ministered to us is nothing but a sacrament, but when it is offered to God, it is a Sacrifice, and this is a fearful, a terrible thing.[49] If the sacrifices of the Law, the blood of goats and rams, were deemed to be both fearful and terrible, then "how reverentiall a thing is the blood of this immaculate Lambe, the Sonne of God?"[50]

The offering of this sacrifice was therefore neither illegitimate nor presumptuous. "God goes low, and accepts small Sacrifices",[51] and regardless of the quality it will be acceptable. Even if the sacrifice is deemed to be indifferent, if "it were offered to God for any honest calling, is acceptable to God, if Gods glory be intended in it".[52]

Offering of worship both physical and spiritual

What was offered was not a reiteration of Christ's death but a representation of his whole life, and since it was the whole body of Christ's actions and passions which was offered to God, so it had to be the whole of humanity which was united to that offering, not just the spirit.[53] And just as it was flesh as well as spirit—all the faculties of the soul and all the organs of the body—which became united and reconciled in Christ, so it must be that it is with both physical and spiritual offerings that God is glorified in this world. The worship which is offered is therefore a foretaste of the heavenly existence, where

---

[48] Donne, *Sermons*, Vol. 7: Sermon 11, pp. 12–13.
[49] Donne, *Sermons*, Vol. 7: Sermon 12, p. 22.
[50] Donne, *Sermons*, Vol. 7: Sermon 12, p. 22.
[51] Donne, *Sermons*, Vol. 4: Sermon 7, p. 9.
[52] Donne, *Sermons*, Vol. 7: Sermon 11, p. 5.
[53] Donne, *Sermons*, Vol. 7: Sermon 17, p. 17. *Preached at Saint Pauls Crosse 6 May, 1627.*

in the next world wee shall be glorified by him, and with him, in soule, and in body too, where we shall bee thoroughly reconciled to one another, no suits, no controversies; and thoroughly to the Angels.[54]

Obviously, this offering could not be limited to a spiritual offering. After all, Donne observed, "a spirituall man is not all spirit, he is a man still".[55] Man is not made all soul but is a composed creature of both body and soul.[56] Whilst the body is at once "obsequious and serviceable" to the soul, the soul has nevertheless been granted a body to work in as "an Organ to praise God upon". Soul and body must therefore serve God "joyntly together because God having joined them, man may not separate them".[57]

Complementarity of faith and works

It was the complementary relationship between soul and body which Donne insisted was the basis for a similar co-dependency between faith and works. Of themselves, "good works are no cause of our justification", he declared, but neither is faith alone. "Faith it selfe is no cause; no such cause, as that I can merit Heaven, by faith", for faith "is but one of those things which in severall senses are said to justifie us". However, he insisted, we are simultaneously justified by our works, for only they can "assure thy conscience, and the World, that thou art justified".[58]

---

[54] Donne, *Sermons*, Vol. 4: Sermon 11, p. 19. *Preached at St. Pauls, upon Christmas day, 1622*.

[55] Donne, *Sermons*, Vol. 4: Sermon 11, p. 19.

[56] Donne, *Sermons*, Vol. 1: Sermon 3, p. 25. *A Sermon Preached at Pauls Cross to the Lords of the Council, and other Honorable Persons, 24 Mart. 1616 [1616/17]. It being the Anniversary of the Kings coming to the Crown, and his Majesty being then gone into Scotland.*

[57] Donne, *Sermons*, Vol. 7: Sermon 3, pp. 14–15. *The first Sermon upon this Text, Preached at S. Pauls, in the Evening, upon Easter-day, 1626.*

[58] Donne, *Sermons*, Vol. 7: Sermon 8, p. 14.

The interdependence of faith and works was exemplified in Christ. The death of Christ would do no good without what Donne called instrumental justification, that is, apprehension by faith; neither would it do any good without declaratory justification, which belongs to works. Neither of these can justify alone. Our justification consists of a chain of contributing factors, and it is impossible to be justified by any one link of that chain. So we cannot be justified by God without Christ, by Christ without faith, or by faith without works.[59] God was all spirit, yet "put on bodily lineaments, Head, and Hands, and Feet, yea and Garments too, in many places of Scripture ... to manifest himself to us".

Here was the authority for Donne to argue that when we appear before God, we are to "put on lineaments and apparel upon our Devotions and digest the Meditations of the heart into words of the mouth".[60] God came to us in the word and the word was made flesh. Therefore "it is with the words of the mouth as well as the meditations of the heart that God is to be praised. God loves the service of Prayer or he would never have built a house for Prayer; And therefore we justly call Publique prayer, the Liturgy, Service."[61] Indeed, God has "laide up a Record for their glorie, who expressed their faith in *Workes*, and assisted his service".[62]

Donne was scathing in his condemnation of those who had condemned and banished previously accepted works from worship, such as rites and ceremonies. In a robust denunciation of the earlier reformers, Donne declared that "the Sacraments have fallen into the hands of flatterers and robbers ... some have attributed too much to them, some detracted. Some have painted them, some have withdrawn their naturall complexion". Also, the preaching of the word had been made "a servant of ambitions, and a shop of many mens new-fangled wares".[63]

---

[59] Donne, *Sermons*, Vol. 7: Sermon 8, p. 14.
[60] Donne, *Sermons*, Vol. 8: Sermon 5, p. 4.
[61] Donne, *Sermons*, Vol. 8: Sermon 5, pp. 4–5.
[62] Donne, *Sermons*, Vol. 4: Sermon 7, p. 9.
[63] Donne, *Sermons*, Vol. 5: Sermon 12, p. 2.

Liturgical reality of Christ's presence

Donne unleashed a devastating criticism of the indiscriminate censoring by the reformers of words such as sacrifice, merit, penance and altar. "It is a miserable impotency", he railed, "to be afraid of *words*." That these subjects may have become distorted in the past was no reason for them to be rejected in the present, especially in the sense "in which those blessed men, who used those words first, at first used them".[64] "Certainly the Christian Church is not to be *without Sacrifice*," he insisted, and that sacrifice was to include an offering made specifically by the priest on behalf of the people: "The *Communion Table* is an *Altar;* and in the *Sacrament* there is a *Sacrifice*... not only a Sacrifice of *Thanksgiving*, common to all the Congregation, but a *Sacrifice peculiar to the Priest, though for the People.*"[65]

Donne reiterated that the sacrifice which he regarded as authentic was not a re-enactment of Christ's original sacrifice:

> We doe not (as at Rome) first invest the power of God, and make ourselves able to *make* a Christ, and then invest the malice of the Jews, and *kill that Christ*, whom we have made; for, Sacrifice, Immolation (taken so properly, and literally as they take it) is a killing.[66]

Nevertheless, Donne confidently attributed a strong propitiatory status to the sacrifice now offered in worship. The priest, he declared,

> *offers up* to God the Father (that is, to the remembrance, to the contemplation of God the Father) the whole body of the merits of Christ Jesus, and begges of him, that in contemplation of that Sacrifice so offered, of that Body of his merits, he would vouchsafe to return, and to apply those merits to that Congregation.[67]

---

[64] Donne, *Sermons*, Vol. 7: Sermon 17, p. 16.
[65] Donne, *Sermons*, Vol. 7: Sermon 17, p. 16.
[66] Donne, *Sermons*, Vol. 7: Sermon 17, pp. 16–17. Italics in the original.
[67] Donne, *Sermons*, Vol. 7: Sermon 17, p. 16.

The mystery of the Divine

This offering of worship constituted engagement with a sacred dimension, an otherness, a reality, a holiness that was beyond the immediate understanding and which was difficult, even impossible, to describe. "Great is the mystery of Godliness", he quoted of Paul in the apostle's First Letter to Timothy 3:16.[68] Godliness is a mystery, "a Secret". It is "not present, not obvious, not discernible with every eye; it is a Mystery, and a great Mystery". The divine is "a Mystery, a Secret; not that I cannot see it, but that I cannot see it with any eyes that I can bring".[69]

Appreciation of the divine was experienced in the worship of the Church. "I see not this mystery", he stated, "by the eye of Nature, of Learning, of State, of mine own private sence; but I see it by the eye of the Church; by the light of Faith, that's true; but yet organically, instrumentally, by the eye of the Church."[70] He recalled that the sacrifices of the Old Testament were full of "mysterie, and horror, and reservation" and that God answered them. Similarly, whilst the "Schedules, the Codicils of men beggar us",[71] the substance of the divine, "the matter of Doctrine", was "delivered mysteriously, and with much reservation, and un-intelligibleness".[72]

Whilst the joy and glory of heaven were not easily understood by "their temporall abundances of Milke, and Honey, and Oyle, and Wine", yet it was in these "and scarce any other way" that heaven was made evident to the people by Moses. Just as the reality of God became known through the mystery and darkness of the sacrifices which were then offered, so it was through the mystery of Christ's sacrifice that this divine reality was experienced in the Church. Even by shedding his blood for the world, Christ was not easily discerned as Messiah and Saviour in their Types and Sacrifices; yet there was scarcely any other way that Christ was revealed to

---

[68] Donne, *Sermons*, Vol. 3: Sermon 9, p. 1. *A Lent-Sermon Preached before the King, at White-Hall, February 16, 1620* [1620/21].
[69] Donne, *Sermons*, Vol. 3: Sermon 9, p. 2.
[70] Donne, *Sermons*, Vol. 3: Sermon 9, p. 5.
[71] Donne, *Sermons*, Vol. 3: Sermon 9, p. 3.
[72] Donne, *Sermons*, Vol. 7: Sermon 12, p. 16.

them. Moreover, it was God who said, "*I have multiplied visions, and used similitudes, by the ministry of the Prophets*", and so "they were Visions, they were Similitudes, not plaine and evident things, obvious to every understanding, that God led his people by".[73]

Authenticity of parables and dark sayings

The experience of the divine in the context of mystery, visions and similitudes was endorsed by an order of doctors amongst the Jews, Donne noted, who taught by means of "Parables and darke sayings", and these "were the powerfullest Teachers amongst them". They had a power, he declared,

> a dominion over the affections of their Disciples, because by teaching them by an obscure way, they created an admiration and a reverence in their hearers, and laid a necessity upon them, of returning againe to them, for the interpretation and signification of these darke Parables.[74]

This was the way of teaching in which Christ abounded and excelled. "Of Christ it is said, Without a Parable spake he not",[75] and he continually astonished his hearers by his interpretation of "these reserved and darke sayings". In fact, it was this very darkness, the "darke way", which increased their desire to penetrate the mystery of God.[76] Undoubtedly the saints of God saw God better in the dark than they did in the light. Their tribulation "hath brought them to a nearer distance to God, and God to a clearer manifestation to them".[77] Darkness does not signify the absence

---

[73] Donne, *Sermons*, Vol. 7: Sermon 12, p. 16. Italics in the original.
[74] Donne, *Sermons*, Vol. 7: Sermon 12, p. 16.
[75] Donne, *Sermons*, Vol. 7: Sermon 12, p. 17.
[76] Donne, *Sermons*, Vol. 7: Sermon 12, p. 16.
[77] Donne, *Sermons*, Vol. 8: Sermon 1, p. 17. *Preached at S. Dunstanes upon Trinity-Sunday, 1627.*

of God for "God hath made darknesse his secret place".[78] Moreover, the shadows in which the presence of God is to be discerned are nothing but a thicker light. Shadows presume light: "Shadowes could not be, except there were light."[79] The darkness is enhanced by contrast with the brightness, or "made all the more perceptible by contrast by some last vestige of brightness, which it is, as it were, on the point of extinguishing". And it is with this semi-darkness that the mystical effect begins.[80]

So Donne affirmed that the God of our salvation, working within the Christian Church, "calls us to Holinesse, to Righteousnesse, by Terrible things; not Terrible, in the way and nature of revenge; but Terrible, that is, stupendious, reverend, mysterious".[81] Both in the Old Testament and through Christ in the New Testament, God has

> conditioned his Doctrine, and his Religion (that is, his outward worship) so as that evermore there should be preserved a Majesty, and a reverentiall feare, and an awfull discrimination of Divine things from Civill.[82]

In summary, "all our Religious affections are reduced to that one, To a reverentiall feare",[83] and worship was therefore to be imbued with this sense whereby the mystery of God could be contemplated and the divine presence experienced.

---

[78] Donne, *Sermons*, Vol. 8: Sermon 1, p. 18.
[79] Donne, *Sermons*, Vol. 7: Sermon 14, p. 12.
[80] Rudolf Otto, *The Idea of the Holy: An Inquiry into the Non-Rational Factor in the Idea of the Divine and Its Relation to the Rational*, tr. John W. Harvey, 2nd edn (Oxford: Oxford University Press, 1958), p. 68.
[81] Donne, *Sermons*, Vol. 7: Sermon 12, p. 15.
[82] Donne, *Sermons*, Vol. 7: Sermon 12, p. 17.
[83] Donne, *Sermons*, Vol. 7: Sermon 12, pp. 17–18.

Not reformation but destruction

Donne's views were in stark contrast to those of the reformers, of whom he was mercilessly critical. David had observed, he noted, that "The fool hath said it in his heart: There is no God" (Psalm 14:1). Fools were to be found in abundance: in the Court, the Cloister and in Councils. But there were also enemies, who in Religion and outward worship ... "deny God his House".[84] On the one hand, he claimed, it was the papists who "deny us any Church, any Sacrament, any Priesthood, any Salvation", and on the other it was the "non-Conformitans" who "deny Gods house any furniture, any stuffe, any beauty, any ornament, any order". The text "Beware of dogs, beware of evil workers, beware of the concision" (Philippians 3:2) gave Donne the opportunity of delivering one of his most vehement attacks: "Their end is not Circumcision, but Concision: they pretend Reformation, but they intend Destruction, a tearing, a renting, a wounding the body, and frame, and peace of the Church." This destruction, he believed, had come about in three distinct ways: First, "*Concisionem corporis*, the shredding of the *body* of Christ into fragments, by unnecessary wrangling in Doctrinall points." Second, "*Concisionem vestis*, the shredding of the *garment* of Christ into rags, by unnecessary wrangling in matter of *Discipline, and ceremoniall points*." Third, "*Concisionem spiritus*, the concision of thine owne spirit, and heart, and minde, and *soule*, and *conscience*, into perplexities, and into sandy and incoherent doubts, and scruples, and jealousies, and suspitions of *Gods purpose* upon thee."[85]

It was on the second point of destruction, the concision of the garment, that Donne most berated the reformers. At the beginning of the Reformation, this circumcision involved paring away ceremonies that were superstitious or superfluous, "of an ill use or of no use", and this, he conceded, was legitimate and necessary. It was an acceptable circumcision. However, what was illegitimate and unnecessary were

---

[84] Donne, *Sermons*, Vol. 3: Sermon 12, pp. 1-2. *Psalm 14. Preached upon Trinity-Sunday.*

[85] Donne, *Sermons*, Vol. 3: Sermon 12, p. 2. *Psalm 14. Preached upon Trinity-Sunday.*

the actions of those who began with a *Concision* of the *garment* yet proceeded, not just to a diminishing but an extinction of worship and its ceremonies as the means of experiencing the reality of the divine presence. This destruction provided neither for the life of the Church as a whole, nor "for the exaltation of *Devotion in the Church*". In fact, the suppression of the ceremonies of worship ignored the tradition inherited from the Old Testament, where it was the ceremonial aspect which was the greater part. Whilst ceremonies were "not of the revenue of Religion", yet they were "of the *subsidy* of Religion".

Though they were not "the *soule* of the Church yet are they those *Spirits* that unite soule and body together".[86] Donne deplored how reform had become indiscriminate and much that was valuable and necessary to worship had been needlessly destroyed. The laudable example of Hanun had sadly been ignored. Hanun did but *"shave the beards* of *Davids* servants, he did not cut off their heads".[87]

Ceremonies as shadows

Donne likened ceremonies to shadows. Of themselves they were nothing, but as shadows they were shadows of something. They testified to a reality beyond themselves. If there is no shadow, there is no body either.[88] So whilst ceremonies may ultimately be nothing of themselves, nevertheless "where there are no Ceremonies, order, and uniformity, and obedience ... Religion it selfe will vanish". "When thou hast lost thy hold of all those handles which God reaches out to thee, in the Ministry of his Church", Donne warned, and "thou hast no meanes to apply the promises of God in Christ to thy soule ... Thou wilt soon sinke into an irrecoverable desperation, which is the fearfullest concision of all".

---

[86] Donne, *Sermons*, Vol. 3: Sermon 12, p. 14. *Psalm 14. Preached upon Trinity-Sunday.*

[87] Donne, *Sermons*, Vol. 3: Sermon 12, p. 14. *Psalm 14. Preached upon Trinity-Sunday.* II Samuel 10:4.

[88] Donne, *Sermons*, Vol. 3: Sermon 12, p. 14.

"*Videte*", he concluded, "beware of this concision."[89] Donne deemed a proper valuing of such ceremonies to be vital because ceremonies gave form to the worship which embraced the mystery of the divine and facilitated entry into the time, the place, the spiritual reality beyond the immediate apprehension. That being established, it was crucial for Donne that the offering of worship should be of the highest standard and be comprised of the offering of works of the utmost beauty. This offering included the buildings in which worship was held, the ritual and ceremony of the services, the art works which adorned the churches and the music which was played and sung.

Music heightens the impact of words

Of particular concern to Donne in the offering of works of beauty in worship was music. He understood the sweetness and beauty of its sound possessed the capacity to heighten the impact of the words. Whilst "all the words of *God* are always sweete in themselves", he said, they are sweeter when received by means of the natural gifts or learned insights of certain prophets and apostles. However, these words are sweetest of all "where the Holy Ghost hath beene pleased to set the word of *God* to Musique, and to convay it into a Song".[90] The words of God are most powerfully received when set to music.

Music unites earth and heaven

Further, music was instrumental in enabling the divine-human relationship, a role it had assumed since the creation of the world. The first world began with a song, for "assoone as Adams sinne was forgiven him, he expressed ... *Sabbatum suum*, his Sabboth, his peace of conscience, in a Song". The next world also began with a song "if wee count the beginning of that (as it is a good computation to doe so) from

---

[89] Donne, *Sermons*, Vol. 3: Sermon 12, p. 15.
[90] Donne, *Sermons*, Vol. 4: Sermon 7, p. 2. Italics in the original.

the coming of Christ Jesus". This coming of Christ was expressed on earth in different songs, which included "the blessed *Virgins* Magnificat; *My soule doth magnifie the Lord*", "*Zacharies* Benedictus; *Blessed be the Lord God of Israel*", and "Simeons Nunc dimittis; *Lord, now lettest thou thy servant depart in peace*".[91]

Donne was convinced that music was a means whereby earthly worship could become at one with heavenly worship. Through music the worship of the Church militant and the worship of the heavenly Church are united. When both worlds join, he said, "and make up one world without end", the music of earthly worship "shall continue so in heaven, in that Song of the *Lamb*, Great and marveilous are thy works, Lord God Almighty, just and true are thy ways, thou King of Saints".

As the means by which God could establish such an intimate relationship with humanity, music enabled the divine will authentically to be communicated and faithfully to be received. "God speaks in his musique, in the harmonious promises of the Gospel, and in our musique, in the temporall blessings of peace, and plenty",[92] and "nothing is more properly the word of God to us than that which God himself speakes in those Organs and Instruments".[93] As a result the soul "is ever tun'd toward God", no matter what "string be stricken in her, base or treble, her high or her low estate".[94]

Music benefits the human experience

Thus incorporate in heavenly worship, music was able to give an order, serenity and balance to human life. It can "Tune us, to Compose and give us a Harmonie and Concord of affections, in all perturbations and passions, and discords in the passages of this life".[95] Music had the ability to restore human equilibrium in the face of every disquieting

---

[91] Donne, *Sermons*, Vol. 4: Sermon 7, p. 3. Italics in the original.
[92] Donne, *Sermons*, Vol. 6: Sermon 10, p. 13.
[93] Donne, *Sermons*, Vol. 5: Sermon 12, p. 1.
[94] Donne, *Sermons*, Vol. 4: Sermon 12, p. 8.
[95] Donne, *Sermons*, Vol. 4: Sermon 7, p. 3.

and threatening circumstance. This is evident, Donne pointed out, in the Song of Moses at the Red Sea, in the Psalms of David, and especially in the Song of Deborah, which was more than enough "to slumber any storme, to becalme any tempest, to rectifie any scruple of Gods slacknesse in the defence of his cause".[96] For the comforting and allaying of every temptation and tribulation there is a "*Canticle*, a *love-song*, an *Epithalamion*, a *mariage song* of God, to our souls, wrapped up, if wee would open it, and read it, and learn that new tune, that musique of God".[97]

Music's ability to represent God's deliverance from the tragedies which beset the human experience was evidence that God, in his "administration and providence" uses "natural means and instruments", such as music, to achieve his purposes. For Donne, this was proof enough that "there is some kind of creation in us, some knowledge of God imprinted, *sine sermone*, without any relation to his word".[98]

So it was that Donne regarded music as an instrument of God's healing and compassion. God is a God neither of punishment nor destruction and will not destroy what he has made. Where there is a falling away, a disobedience or a disunity, God will always repair that which is broken or out of alignment, for "God is a God of harmony and consent, and in a musicall instrument, if some strings be out of tune, wee doe not presently breake all the strings, but reduce and tune those which are out of tune".[99] The human framework and constitution is as it were "an excellent song, an admirable piece of musick and harmony", and God will restore it and renovate it rather than allow it to disintegrate. The Holy Ghost "sets this Instrument in tune, and makes all that is musique and harmony in the faculties of this natural man".[100] The effect of the work of the Spirit in setting mankind in tune is that "God's whole Quire is in tune", there is

---

[96] Donne, *Sermons*, Vol. 4: Sermon 7, p. 3. Song of Deborah, Judges 5.
[97] Donne, *Sermons*, Vol. 2: Sermon 1, p. 20.
[98] Donne, *Sermons*, Vol. 1: Sermon 8, p. 6. *A Sermon Preached at White-Hall. April 19, 1618.*
[99] Donne, *Sermons*, Vol. 3: Sermon 5, p. 15. *Preached at Lincolns Inne upon Trinity-Sunday, 1620.*
[100] Donne, *Sermons*, Vol. 7: Sermon 8, p. 8.

peace in Sion and the music thus created is "the musick of the Sphears", the spheres being all the churches, and the "Stars in those Sphears" being all the "Expositours in all Churches".[101]

Music encompasses God's mercy and accommodation for all

As part of the worship of heaven, music is also the embodiment of God's welcoming of all, the wideness of his mercy and forgiveness and the assurance of his acceptance of whatever offering is made. All are included, all are forgiven and therefore all are able to play their part. "Howsoever God deale with thee", said Donne, "be not thou weary of bearing thy part, in his Quire here in the Militant Church", for "God will have low voyces as well as high; God will be glorified *De profundis* as well as *In excelsis*; God will have his tribute of praise, out of our adversity, as well as out of our prosperity".[102] The world is a great and harmonious organ, he declared, "where all parts are play'd, and all play parts". Therefore no one must sit idle, simply listen to this music and make no offering to God within the life of the Church.[103]

Music embodied the doctrines of the Creation, Fall, Incarnation, Original Sin and Salvation. Concerning the Creation, "God made this whole world in such a uniformity, such a correspondency, such a concinnity of parts, as that it was an Instrument, perfectly in tune."[104] As for the Fall, "we may say, the trebles, the highest strings were disordered first", and then "the best understandings, Angels and Men, put this instrument out of tune". In response, God "rectified all again, by putting in a new string, *semen mulieris*, the seed of the woman". Christ is born, and it is "by sounding that string in your ears, become we *musicum carmen*, true musick, true harmony, true peace to you".[105]

---

[101] Donne, *Sermons*, Vol. 7: Sermon 14, p. 1.
[102] Donne, *Sermons*, Vol. 8: Sermon 1, p. 17.
[103] Donne, *Sermons*, Vol. 1: Sermon 3, p. 25.
[104] Donne, *Sermons*, Vol. 1: Sermon 3, p. 7.
[105] Donne, *Sermons*, Vol. 1: Sermon 3, p. 7.

Strings represent Divine mercy, not condemnation

Donne continued with the analogy of the strings of an instrument to cement his earlier attack on the doctrine of Original Sin. "If we shall say", he posited, "that Gods first string in this instrument was Reprobation, that Gods first intention was, for his glory, to damn man", and further, that God added another string, of creating man so that he might have someone to damn, and then another string for "enforcing him to sin, so that he might have a just cause to damn him", and yet another string of "disabling him to lay hold upon any means of recovery", then, declared Donne, "there's no musick in all this, no harmony, no peace in such preaching".[106] On the other hand,

> if we take this instrument, when Gods hand tun'd it the second time, in the promise of a *Messias*, and offer of the love and mercy of God to all that will receive it in him; then we are truly *musicum carmen*, as a love-song, when we present the love of God to you, and raise you to the love of God in Christ Jesus.

This is the authentic gospel, he insisted, and it is a gospel of mercy and hope, not of condemnation and despair. It is the "musick of the Sphears", and although we can neither hear this ultimate music of heaven within our own limited experience, nor see the decrees of God in heaven, yet "our musick is onely that salvation which is declared in the Gospel to all them, and to them onely, who take God by the right hand, as he delivers himself in Christ".

---

[106] Donne, *Sermons*, Vol. 1: Sermon 3, p. 7.

The worship of the earthly Church is united with the worship of heaven

Donne's belief that it was possible to be united with Christ and therefore become participants in the divine nature led him to the conviction that that which is of heaven can be experienced on earth. "I cannot put off mortality", he insisted, "but I can looke upon immortality; I cannot depart from this earth, but I can looke into Heaven."[107] Given that "I cannot possesse that final and accomplished joy here", it is possible to put off the "manifold and miserable encumbrances of this world" and enter into the holy joy of heaven. The new heavens and the new earth, the heavenly Church, will constitute an experience so unique as to defy human definition.

Between Christ and the Church there is a mutual complacency, he said, whereby that which is treasured on earth finds its ultimate satisfaction and fulfilment in heaven. Those who delight in music are promised "continuall singing, and every minute, a new song",[108] and in the beauty of this music can be discerned the beauty of heaven. "Howling is the noyse of hell", he observed, "singing the voice of heaven."

For the moment, however, the experience of the new heavens and the new earth is contained within the experience of the present, militant Church, which is sustained by the Holy Ghost's promise of glorifying or "improving" the "naturall affections of men". In this present life, the Holy Ghost proceeds "by *improvement* of things which wee *have*, and *love* here".[109] Offered in worship, that which is of this world is transformed by the Spirit of God in anticipation of the New Jerusalem. "To those that are affected with *beauty*, hee promises an everlasting association with that beautifull Couple", Christ and the Church, and their "mutual complacencie", and "To those which delight in *Musicke*, hee promises continuall *singing*, and every minute, a *new song*."[110]

---

[107] Donne, *Sermons*, Vol. 5: Sermon 14, p. 20.
[108] Donne, *Sermons*, Vol. 8: Sermon 2, p. 23.
[109] Donne, *Sermons*, Vol. 8: Sermon 2, p. 23. Italics in the original.
[110] Donne, *Sermons*, Vol. 8: Sermon 2, pp. 22-3. Italics in the original.

Necessity of singing psalms

Donne retained a special affection for the singing of psalms. It was a practice common amongst members of the early Church. Even in a time of persecution, when meetings were held at night without candles for fear of discovery, psalms were sung. Later, when vigils and night-meetings were discontinued, "their singing of Psalmes, when they did meet, they never discontinued, though that, many times, exposed them to dangers, and to death it selfe".[111] So essential were the psalms to the worship of the early Christians, he recalled, that admission to the priesthood was forbidden to those "as were not perfect in the Psalmes". In Bethlehem, those who could not sing psalms were compelled to remain silent, because there was nothing to be heard but psalms. Farmers that plough, sow, reap and gather all sing psalms as they labour; lovers make themselves attractive to each other by singing psalms; shepherds, labourers, children and servants all have no other songs but psalms.[112] The psalms, said Donne, catechize children, edify congregations, convert Gentiles, and convince heretics.[113]

Calvin's mention of singing in churches, Donne claimed, could only have been referring to the singing of psalms, for the churches of the West followed the tradition of the Eastern churches that had been introduced to the Church in Milan. This style, said Donne, comprised "the modulation and singing of *Versicles* and *Antiphons* and the like" and, according to Calvin, was in use amongst the *apostles* themselves.[114]

---

[111] Donne, *Sermons*, Vol. 5: Sermon 14, p. 21.
[112] Donne, *Sermons*, Vol. 5: Sermon 14, p. 21.
[113] Donne, *Sermons*, Vol. 5: Sermon 14, p. 22.
[114] Donne, *Sermons*, Vol. 4: Sermon 15, p. 12.

Appreciation of metrical psalms

In a sermon "Preached upon the Penitentiall Psalmes" in 1623, Donne commends metrical psalms as faithfully representing the form of the psalter whereby the final phrase enforces the core message. Being left to the end of the psalm, the essential meaning makes the best impression. "And therefore it is easie to observe", he says, "that in all Metricall compositions, of which kinde the booke of Psalmes is, the force of the whole piece, is for the most part left to the shutting up." It is as though "the whole frame of the Poem is a beating out of a piece of gold, but the last clause is as the impression of the stamp, and that is it that makes it currant".[115]

To God the Father

Donne's first biographer, Izaak Walton, mentions that Donne "caused" his hymn *To God the Father* "to be set to a most grave and solemn tune and to be often sung to the organ by the choiristers of St Paul's Church, in his own hearing; especially at the Evening Service". According to Walton, at his return from services, Donne would remark that

> the words of this hymn have restored to me the same thoughts of joy that possessed my soul in my sickness, when I composed it. And, O the power of church music! that harmony added to this hymn has raised the affections of my heart, and quickened my graces of zeal and gratitude; and I observe that I always return

---

[115] Donne, *Sermons*, Vol. 6: Sermon 1, p. 3. The organist throughout the time of Donne's deanship at St Paul's was John Tomkins, half-brother of the illustrious Thomas. Succeeding Orlando Gibbons as organist of King's College Cambridge in 1606, John Tomkins was appointed organist of St Paul's in 1619 and remained in post throughout Donne's tenure of 1621-31. With Thomas, John contributed settings to Thomas Ravenscroft's *The Whole Booke of Psalmes* of 1621, an expanded version of the Sternhold and Hopkins psalter, and was himself responsible for Psalms 10, 48 and 143.

from paying this public duty of prayer and praise to God, with an unexpressible tranquillity of mind, and a willingness to leave the world.[116]

Donne's understanding that it was possible for humanity to participate in the nature of Christ meant that the offering of worship could become united with the offering of Christ. Earthly worship would then embody the worship of heaven. In the offering of worship, two worlds co-inhabit, or in Donne's words, share a mutual relationship which is the equivalent of the relationship between Christ and the Church. In worship, that which is of heaven can be experienced on earth, which had made it possible for Donne to observe that whilst he could not put off mortality, he could look upon immortality; and whilst he could not depart from this earth, yet he could look into heaven.[117]

---

[116] Izaak Walton, *The Life of Dr John Donne, Late Dean of St Paul's Church, London*, in *The Lives of Dr John Donne, Sir Henry Wotton, Mr Richard Hooker, Mr George Herbert, and Dr Robert Sanderson*, ed. C. Dick (London: Walter Scott, Ltd, Paternoster Square, 1899), pp. 43–4. "To God the Father" was also set by Pelham Humfrey (1647–74). It is possible that the setting to which Donne refers is that of John Hilton the younger (c.1599–1657), organist of St Margaret's Westminster from 1628.

[117] Donne, *Sermons*, Vol. 5: Sermon 14, p. 20.

10

Worship united with Christ's offering

Arthur Lake, William Laud, Foulke Robarts

The revising of the understanding of divine forgiveness, forcefully advocated by John Donne, was replicated by other theologians, thus continuing a trend fundamental to the investing of the concept of offering with implications well beyond the original intentions of the reformers.

As Donne had eloquently articulated, if divine forgiveness were to prevail over the force of human sin and thereby extinguish its debilitating consequences, then it was possible for the offering of worship to be united with the offering of Christ. This being so, then it became possible once more for works to be accepted as a legitimate constituent of worship.

Arthur Lake

Arthur Lake (1569–1626) was Master of St Cross Hospital Winchester 1603, Archdeacon of Surrey 1607, Dean of Worcester 1608, Warden of New College Oxford 1613, Vice-Chancellor of Oxford 1616 and Bishop of Bath and Wells 1616.

Lake continued to wrest the concept of divine forgiveness away from the claustrophobic interpretation to which the reformers were so beholden. Using the imagery of the landlord's merciful treatment of the tenant, Lake examined how it was possible for humanity to be restored to favour with God. "God's Covenant is like a lease that hath a clause of re-entry", he maintained, "but leaveth a power in the Land-lord to use extremity or deal mercifully with his Tenant." He likened God to a kind landlord dealing with bad tenants: "He doth not take forfeits as often as we make them, he doth not re-enter upon our Tenement, not strip us of our salvation." "We are often damnable", he concluded, "yet we are not damned."[1]

Original Righteousness
Lake believed it possible for humanity to resort to its earlier endowment from God, which he described as "Original Righteousness". The basic human stamp, he argued, was one of righteousness, not of sin, and in Christ it was possible to be restored to that original and authentic state of righteousness. Even though sin could be described as "original" in the sense that it was deeply ingrained in the human substance, yet not being of the fundamental essence of the substance it could be cured by regeneration. The return to Original Righteousness was comparable to other natural restorative processes—the sun's light after the moon's eclipse, daylight after darkness, spring after winter and health after sickness.

Acceptance of Original Righteousness meant that works were no longer debarred from the offering of worship. Instead, they were to be offered with all the enthusiasm of King David himself, who when he offered, offered to God with all his strength, and with all his strength danced before the Ark.[2] David's example should inspire all to employ whatever abilities and gifts they have to the best advancement of the love of God.[3] In essence, Lake believed that the impediment of sin could be overcome by the mercy of God, thereby allowing works to be included in a sacrifice made possible by its identification with Christ's perfect sacrifice.

Nevertheless, Lake cautioned, the critical difference between Christ's offering and ours was always to be observed, for "his Righteousness is perfect, ours is but imperfect; we cannot exceed the measure of our

---

[1] Arthur Lake, "An Exposition of the one and Fiftieth Psalm. Psalm 51 Verse 12: *Restore unto me the joy of thy salvation, and stablish me with a free spirit*", in *Sermons with some Religious and Divine Meditations* (London, 1629), p. 172.
[2] Lake, *Sermons*, pp. 152-3.
[3] Lake, *Sermons*, pp. 332-3.

Regeneration, and therefore we may not ascribe unto it more worth than it hath in it". The only sacrifice which ultimately obtained with God was that offered by Christ, for it was in him that the Righteousness of the offerer and the Righteousness of the offering were most absolute. This is the reason Christ is a priest for ever and King of Righteousness after the order of Melchisedek.[4]

Human offering made righteous by participation in Christ's offering
However, with this caution, and having been released from the stultifying impediment of Original Sin, and justified by the perfect offering of Christ, humanity was able to participate in the grace of Christ. As a result, Lake concluded, our devotion "may also pass for a most absolute Sacrifice of Righteousness", for through this participation in Christ both our persons and our gifts become righteous, even as he is righteous.[5] United with Christ's offering, humanity became priests with Christ and so the sacrifice was able to be offered both by priest and people. "The Priest must not post over Devotion to the people", stated Lake, "nor the people to the Priest, both must make their presents."[6] All our services must therefore be sacrifices:

> We must present them at God's Altar, and must offer them with the fire of heaven; for therefore doth God separate his Church from the world, that he may devote it unto himself; neither would God ever do us the honour to make us kings, except he did expect honour from us as we are his Priests.[7]

Sacrifice of Righteousness
This unity is possible, claimed Lake, because the Sacrifice of Righteousness is a double righteousness, consisting of the offerer and of

---

[4] Lake, *Sermons*, p. 234.
[5] Lake, *Sermons*, p. 235.
[6] Lake, *Sermons*, pp. 235–6.
[7] Lake, *Sermons*, p. 225.

the offering.⁸ Whilst the righteousness of the offerer, consisting of faith and repentance, is always variable and inadequate, the righteousness of the offering, consisting of purity of devotion with understanding and affection, untainted by hypocrisy, vain-glory or unrighteousness, will always be acceptable to God, not least "because God will never refuse what [he] himself commanded".⁹

Unity of the divine and human at creation
The fundamental principle of human participation in the divine, Lake maintained, had its origin in the unique relationship between God and humanity at creation. Humanity had been created in the image of God and in consequence had been endowed with the likeness of God. Here was a fundamental bond between the divine and human natures.¹⁰

A more profound unity
However, this unity established at creation had been surpassed by a more profound unity, as a result of which human nature took full receipt of the divine nature and the divine now dwelt completely within the human. For even though the life of God had been implanted in humanity at creation, and so "God's image is found in us by Nature, for we were made according to his Image",¹¹ God had become "much more mine in the Redemption". Through the offering of Jesus Christ, mankind experienced a second creation which re-established him in that image from which he had fallen. This is our regeneration, "wherein we are reformed unto that Image according to which God at first created us".¹²

---

⁸ Lake, *Sermons*, p. 234. *Then shall they be pleased with the sacrifices of Righteousness with burnt offerings, and whole burnt offerings: then shall they offer bullocks upon thine Altar* (Psalm 51:19).
⁹ Lake, *Sermons*, p. 238.
¹⁰ "Nine Sermons on the two and twentieth Chapter of the Gospel according to St Matthew; The fourth Sermon. Matthew 22 Verse 27 'The Lord thy God'", in Lake, *Sermons*, p. 303.
¹¹ "Nine Sermons on the two and twentieth Chapter of the Gospel according to St Matthew; The seventh Sermon", in Lake, *Sermons*, p. 331.
¹² Lake, *Sermons*, p. 331.

That God had bestowed such a dignity upon humanity Lake found to be indeed remarkable. It was bewildering that God, who had angels, archangels, cherubim and seraphim to love him, should stoop so low as to engage humanity in such an intimate relationship. Nevertheless, this is precisely what God has done. He has stooped to the meanest of our abilities and raised this abject human condition to a divine stature. "He commands our Dust and Ashes, this worm's meat our vile selves, to Love him", said Lake, "that is, to be as it were consorts with him; for *amor nescit inequalitatem* [love knows not inequality] therefore God doth (as it were) deify that which he doth so far honour."[13]

Offering not restricted to the spiritual

This raising of humanity to a divine stature cemented the understanding that works could be accepted in worship for, being thus incorporate in the life of God, human works partook of the merit of the divine works: "My nature hath possession of his person, and is admitted into an association in his works."[14] These presents, these services, these devotions, as Lake had it, were to embrace the physical as well as the spiritual, the body as well as the soul. Psalm 72 and Isaiah 49 and 60 were evidence for Lake that the sacrifice being offered was not to be restricted to the spiritual. These passages clearly included "literal" works, as he described them, involving all kinds of "choice things" being received by God as acceptable offerings:

> The Psalm touching the Munificency, saith, that the Kings of Tharsis and of the Isles should bring presents, the Kings of Seba and Sheba should give gifts. The Prophet Esay, cap. 49 & 60. doth particularize the Gold, the Silver, the Jewels, the Plants, the Beasts, all kind of choice things that were to be tendered unto Christ: And the Story of the Church shows that this was accomplished not only mystically, but even literally.[15]

---

[13] Lake, *Sermons*, p. 308. *Love knows not inequality.*
[14] Lake, *Sermons*, p. 303.
[15] "Sundry Sermons de Tempore: Sixe Sermons upon The Second of Haggai The Second Sermon. *And the Desire of all nations shall come.* [Haggai 2:7]",

This theological position was far removed from that of the reformers. Lake generously termed it "a correction". Previously, he pointed out, referring to the late mediaeval rite, the offering of a ceremonial sacrifice in worship was condemned not because of any fundamental flaw but because of the lack of any accompanying spiritual offering. This was not now the case. The spiritual aspect was firmly established. Yet the reformers had taken this component of worship to an extreme and made it the sole constituency of the offering. The balance now needed to be restored. For the offering of the sacrifice to be complete, the ceremonial component must be returned to its rightful place. An offering of a sacrifice that was purely spiritual, as the reformers had insisted, was an impoverishment and needed correction. Before the reforms of the mid-sixteenth century, God had accepted the ceremonial offerings as exercises of faith, Lake noted, and provided that due diligence was paid to the spiritual element, God accepted these sacrifices as true sacrifices.[16] These physical aspects of worship had always been a source of delight for God.[17] Doubtless there had been corruptions in the past. Gifts of beauty had been offered at the expense of the spiritual gifts of the heart and soul, and material gifts alone were but a partial offering, their incompleteness making them unacceptable to God. Many of the Persian kings and Grecians, for example, gave their goods but not themselves to God. However, after the coming of Christ, it was otherwise. "Great personages gave themselves first", said Lake, and "then their goods unto Christ." The wise men, for example, first prostrated their bodies and worshipped and only then did they open their treasures and offer them to Christ.[18]

Works in worship to be of the highest quality

With the acceptance of works as a necessary component of worship, attention turned to the necessity for them to be of the highest quality: "We must think that nothing we have is too good for God, and we must make

---

in Lake, *Sermons*, pp. 66–7.

[16] Lake, *Sermons*, pp. 236–7.
[17] Lake, *Sermons*, p. 496. Cf. Judges 9:12.
[18] Lake, *Sermons*, p. 67.

our Offerings of the best."[19] This principle was evident from the time of the ancient sacrifices. Bullocks were accounted the fairest offering, and St Paul's mention of the offering of the calves of our lips was taken by Lake as a reference to the offering of the bullocks, and if bullocks, it followed that the offering to God must be the most beautiful and glorious possible, both spiritual and physical, or as Lake had it, moral and ceremonial.

Works in worship are to be perfect
Not only must the offering of works be the finest, most beautiful and most glorious possible, it must be perfect. We first receive grace from God, said Lake, and then we give glory to God. Were the grace we receive imperfect, then it would not matter if the glory we give is also imperfect. However, since the grace we receive is perfect then the glory we offer must also be perfect, at one with the glory which is offered in the Church Triumphant.[20] In pursuit of this perfection, we are assured that, provided our sacrifice is solid and full, God will find it pleasing and we shall hear *Euge serve bone*, well done faithful and true servant, enter into your Master's joy. Such will be God's pleasure with the beauty of this offering that God will be prompted to do good to humanity in return. Here Lake attributes a propitiatory quality to the offering, a concept previously dismissed as odious to true faith.

God's gracious acceptance of the offering of worship
Lake also pointed out that as God was greater than humanity, so God's delight in humanity was greater than any delight ever known within human experience. This delight was neither gratuitous nor forced but genuine, for as God is all-sufficient and in need of nothing, so he is not reliant on anything humanity is able to produce. It is therefore thanks to God's favourable, paternal regard for his people that their offering of worship is accepted; not that the service deserves it, but that God respects

---

[19] Lake, *Sermons*, p. 237.
[20] Lake, *Sermons*, pp. 238–9.

it. The honour of humanity's offering depends on God's favourable aspect, which Lake describes as God's Acceptance.[21]

Offering of ornaments including music
There being no impediment to the offering of the earthly ornaments of the Church, Lake regarded it as crucial that all works of artistic merit were included. Their exclusion by the reformers he found deplorable. "The Church of Rome is plentiful in earthly ornaments of their Church", he noted, "and we are careful that the Word of God should dwell richly in ours; it were well if both were joined together; I wish we had more of their ornaments, and they had more of Christ's truth."[22] Included with those earthly ornaments was music. Music had been an accepted part of the sacrifices of the Old Covenant which Lake insisted were authentic types of the perfect sacrifice of Jesus Christ, and were therefore to be offered wholeheartedly:

> *Incensio* went before *Ascensio*, the Sacrifice was set on fire before it yielded an odour of sweet smell ascending unto God; besides the silver trumpets sounded aloud, with variety of other Musick while the Sacrifice was burning. These were but types whereof the moral was, that we must not be lither in devotion, but express a fervency therein.[23]

This fervency was commendable because "those things which we tender unto God are accepted of God".[24] The efficacy of Christ's sacrifice and his intercession before God was not a disincentive to the offering of prayer but rather showed how powerful prayer is with God and the power which our prayers have with him. Out of his goodwill God yields to our prayers

---

[21] Lake, *Sermons*, p. 236. *Condescensio paterna*: paternal condescension; *Non ex dignitate rei, sed ex dignatione sua*: Not out of the dignity of the thing, but out of its own dignity.

[22] Lake, *Sermons*, p. 82.

[23] Lake, *Sermons*, p. 536. "A Sermon preached at Paul's Cross on Luke 18:7-8, 1623". *Lither*: softer.

[24] Lake, *Sermons*, p. 539.

as parents yield to the petition of their children. The sacrifice offered to God was therefore "a thing that pleaseth him well, to be his delight, a savour of a sweet smell, a savour of rest".[25] Knowing what will prevail with God, "let us use that most which we are sure will please him best".

Music crucial in enhancing the sense of the words
Lake recalled that in offering his praises to God, David relied on the melody as much as the words.[26] Whilst the force of the words alone was not to be underestimated and Lake noted that David never endorsed a tune without a ditty, nevertheless it was important that the words were set to music. After writing a description of his conversion, David therefore passed the words over to the Master of the Quire, not only to be kept, but to be sung. As well, David himself joined the singers "in sounding and setting forth the righteousness of God".[27]

So Lake insisted that whilst it was necessary for prayer to come from the heart, for without the heart prayer was ineffectual, nevertheless music enhanced the words of prayer and was therefore to be welcomed. Moreover, with the whole person thus being involved, both body and spirit, then through music the whole range of human emotion was able to be expressed. Cheerfulness was mentioned in the Letter of James, for example. (Is any merry? Let him sing psalms' 5:13.) Mourning, joy, grief and contrition for sin were other emotions that were able to be represented in sound.[28]

In summary, Lake's advocacy of the all-embracing and enduring nature of divine forgiveness added to the gradual demolition of the reformers' obsession with God's anger and predilection for condemnation. His replacement of the concept of Original Sin with that of Original Righteousness allowed him to stress the participation of humanity in the grace and righteousness of Christ. Such a mutual participation enabled the works offered in worship to become united with the righteousness of Christ's perfect offering and therefore to become acceptable to God.

---

[25] Lake, *Sermons*, p. 540.
[26] Lake, *Sermons*, p. 193. "An Exposition of the one and Fiftieth Psalm".
[27] Lake, *Sermons*, p. 193.
[28] Lake, *Sermons*, pp. 62–3.

This being so, he believed that what was offered in worship should strive to be as perfect as that offered by Christ. These theological convictions informed Lake's desire for music to be fully incorporated into worship and for music to be of a beauty commensurate with the beauty of the offering to which it was united—that of the offering of Christ.

Lake's contribution to the theological issues concerning the offering of worship is significant and his views continue a dramatic departure from those of the reformers of the mid-sixteenth century.

Moreover, insisted Lake, every day must be a day where the sacrifice is offered. This was especially true for cathedrals, collegiate churches and monasteries, where the continued offering of worship was the primary purpose for which they had been founded.[29]

William Laud

William Laud (1573–1645), Archbishop of Canterbury from 1633 to 1645, aligned even more closely the offering of worship with the offering of Christ. The offering of worship to God, he argued, was not only expected but commanded by Christ in memory of his own perfect offering.[30] He reduced the nature of this sacrifice to three essential elements. There was the sacrifice offered by the priest only. This was the "commemorative sacrifice of Christ's death, represented in bread broken and wine poured

---

[29] Lake, *Sermons*, p. 236.

[30] William Laud: President of St John's College Oxford 1611; Bishop of St David's 1621; Dean of the Chapel Royal 1626; Bishop of Bath and Wells 1626; Bishop of London 1628; Chancellor of Oxford University 1628; Archbishop of Canterbury 1633; impeached by the Long Parliament 1640; executed 10 January 1645. William Laud, *A Relation of the Conference between William Laud, then Lord Bishop of St David's, now Lord Archbishop of Canterbury, and Mr Fisher the Jesuite* (1639), in *The Works of the Most Reverend Father in God, William Laud, D.D., sometime Lord Archbishop of Canterbury*, ed. W. Scott and J. Bliss (Oxford: John Henry Parker, 1847–60), Vol. II, p. 339. This passage is referred to in Darwell Stone, *A History of the Doctrine of the Holy Eucharist*, 2 vols (London: Longmans, Green, 1909), p. 269.

out".[31] The second sacrifice was offered by the priest and people together. This was the sacrifice of praise and thanksgiving for all the benefits and graces received by the precious death of Christ. The third sacrifice was that offered by "every particular man for himself only; and that is, the sacrifice of every man's body and soul, to serve Him in both all the rest of his life, for this blessing thus bestowed on him".[32]

Integration with the perfect offering of Christ
These three elements were designated by Laud as commemoration, praise and performance, and he believed they were all fully integrated within the one offering of worship. As a result, the third, performing element, the "sacrifice of every man's body and soul", became united with the sacrifice of Christ's death, the commemorative element. Thus integrated with the perfect offering of Christ's death, the performing dimension, both physical and spiritual, became acceptable to God. Laud's view of the offering of worship aligned with a status reminiscent of its pre-Reformation significance and stood in total contrast to that declared in the Book of Common Prayer.

This understanding of Laud's was opposed dramatically after a proposed new service book for Scotland underwent a final review by Laud and Matthew Wren and was approved by the king in April 1636. Soon after printing had been completed in the spring of 1637, riots broke out. Of particular concern was the restoration of the Prayer of Oblation to stand after the Words of Institution, prompting the criticism that it was placed there "for no other end but that the memorial and sacrifice of praise mentioned in it may be understood according to the popish meaning ... not of the spiritual sacrifice, but of the oblation of the body of the Lord".[33] Laud's actual position was more refined than his critics allowed. The sacrifice offered in worship, he declared, was not a reproduction of Christ's original sacrifice with all its propitiatory authority, yet it was so faithfully aligned with that original sacrifice

---

[31] Laud, *Works*, Vol. II, p. 340.
[32] Laud, *Works*, Vol. II, p. 341.
[33] Laud, *Works*, Vol. III, pp. 343, 353. Discussed in G. J. Cuming, *A History of Anglican Liturgy* (London: Macmillan, 1969), pp. 144–5.

that it was able authentically to represent it. This degree of theological sophistication was shunned by his critics and the book was abandoned. Works being included in what Laud identified as the performance aspect of worship meant that music was accepted as an integral part of worship, and Laud ensured that the standard of music in cathedrals was maintained. In his arch-episcopal *Visitation Articles* and *Injunctions* of 1634, he demonstrated a particular interest in the quality of the music, the skill of the choristers, lay-clerks and singing-men, the condition of the instruments and the suitability of the conditions under which the musicians performed. He pointedly enquired of the dean and prebendaries of Canterbury whether it be the custom for the singing men to be absent every third week, with the warning to "provide carefully that no such abuse be suffered hereafter".[34] That the wages of the choristers were not infringed was of sufficient importance for Laud that he demanded to know why the bursar of the choristers was maintained out of the boys' wages.[35] In 1634, the Dean and Chapter of Salisbury were asked "whether the quire be sufficiently furnished with able singers according to the foundation of the church?"[36] Also in 1634, they were confronted with another set of *Articles* demanding details of the entire musical establishment. *Article I* requested the number and names of all the vicars-choral, priests-vicars, singing-men, choristers and any other persons involved with the performance of music in the cathedral. *Article II* enquired "whether is the full number of them kept according to the first foundation thereof?" *Article VIII* indicates Laud's concern that the range of voices be maintained to enable the performance of works requiring several parts. It was clear that Laud was not impressed with works either limited to one part only, or with an imbalance in the force of the voices. He demanded assurances that "men of skill and good voices are chosen into your quire, and that the voices be seated every one in his place, so that there be not more of tenors therein, which is an ordinary voice, than there be of basses and counter tenors, which do best furnish the quire".[37]

---

[34] Laud, *Works*, Vol. V, ii, p. 455.
[35] Laud, *Works*, Vol. V, ii, p. 456.
[36] Laud, *Works*, Vol. V, ii, p. 459.
[37] Laud, *Works*, Vol. V, ii, p. 461.

In the same *Article VIII*, Laud indicated his support for instrumental music. He asked "whether have you in your quire a fair and tuneable pair of organs, and a skilful organist to play thereon?" *Orders* to the Dean and Chapter of Lichfield in 1635 required that "the two pair of organs in your church, which are much defective, be speedily amended, and if it will stand with the grace of your church, and be more convenient and useful for your quire (as we conceive it will) that ye put them both in one, and make a choir organ of them".[38]

Orders of 1634 to the Dean and Chapter of Peterborough reveal Laud's determination to maintain high musical standards. It was required that "those of your quire, who are defective in skill or voice, be removed, and some others more worthy taken into their places, unless they use means to better their own ability".[39] *Orders* to be observed by the Dean and Chapter of Worcester, issued in 1635, demanded that "none be admitted into any place of your Quire, before he be first approved of for his voice and skill in singing by such of your church as are able to judge thereof".[40]

Foulke Robarts

The efficacy of divine forgiveness and the ability for works to be incorporate in the offering of worship was also advocated by Foulke Robarts (*c*.1580–1650). Robarts was Prebendary of Norwich Cathedral 1616, from where he was ejected during the Civil War.

Given that divine forgiveness could absolve human sin and that therefore it was possible to include works in the offering of worship, Robarts pointed out that logically worship could not be restricted to a spiritual offering. The body as well as the soul must be engaged. Whilst worship was unable to consist entirely of physical gestures, this did not mean worship was the prerogative of the soul alone. The soul may well be thought to be the most excellent part but "the expressions of the body unto God" are crucial. The body is an essential part of the human being

---

[38] Laud, *Works*, Vol. V, ii, p. 484.
[39] Laud, *Works*, Vol. V, ii, p. 487.
[40] Laud, *Works*, Vol. V, ii, p. 481.

and must bear its part with the soul in God's worship. If the body acts alone, maintained Robarts, "then doth God say, Man, where is thy soule? If the soule alone take all upon it; then saith God, where is, or what doth thy body?" God has made his intentions clear, said Robarts: "Thy whole man is to be imployed in my worship."[41]

Both body and soul are involved in the offering of worship
This uniting of body and soul is pleasing, he claimed, both from the standpoint of the divine and the human: "How decent a thing it is in the eye of man, to behold bodies and soules accord and join together, in the holy worke?"[42] By all means "speak to God with the intention, judgement and fervency of the soule" but also take care to "speake also by the expressions of the members of thy body". Therefore, "Speake by thy tongue; Speake by thine eyes; Speake by thine hand; and by thy knees." To pray with the soul alone, devoid of physical expression, was insufficient, for "the tongue interpreteth the meaning of the soul, by words".[43] By the outward gestures of the body, contended Robarts, "we declare that worship which is in the heart". Without that physical expression the worship of the soul is defective; "there is no devotion in the heart of that man, who maketh no expression thereof, in his outward behaviour."[44]

Music is crucial to the offering of worship
Robarts regarded the offering of music as integral to this physical expression of the worship of the soul. He was aware of objections to music as being reminiscent of the offering of a propitiatory sacrifice: "And now me thinks I hear some of our bretheren call upon me to listen to the sounde that is made in our Churches, by voices of singers, by Organes and other instruments of musique, and to tell how I can cleare this from being Popish or superstitious?"[45] However, he countered,

---

[41] Foulke Robarts, *Gods Holy House and Service, According to the primitive and most Christian forme thereof* (London, 1639), p. 3.
[42] Robarts, *Gods Holy House and Service*, p. 3.
[43] Robarts, *Gods Holy House and Service*, p. 4.
[44] Robarts, *Gods Holy House and Service*, p. 61.
[45] Robarts, *Gods Holy House and Service*, p. 54.

there was no law to ban music in the church service and being rightly used "it is very usefull and profitable, for the spirituall man, in that it stirreth up his Christian affection, the more chearefully to prayse God". When correctly ordered, music is "comely, profitable and pleasant", as was demonstrated by the Israelites when they thanked God with singing and musical instruments for their deliverance from the Egyptians at the Red Sea. The appropriateness of music had also been demonstrated when God had "given the life of Siserah into the hands of Jael, and peace to Israel ... then sang Deborah and Barak: praise ye the Lord for avenging Israel".[46]

How could these two isolated examples from the days of the Exodus and the Judges have any bearing upon the use of music in the present? The answer, proposed Robarts, was that these musical performances were done in the public worship of God by the people of God without breaking any divine rule; as a result, it is still lawful "to be done again as well twice as once; & as well constantly ... "[47]

The king and prophet David, zealous for the reputation of the house and honour of God to be upheld, had composed psalms "to be tuned and sung to severall instruments of Musique, for Gods honor". Not only did he bring this music into the Church, in Robarts's opinion he "erected the most glorious Quire that ever was under the cope of Heaven: *for song in the house of the Lord: with Cymballs, Psalteries and Harpes for the Service of the house of God*".[48]

To the charge that these were Old Testament occurrences and therefore irrelevant and undesirable Levitical ceremonies, Robarts responded that the charge was invalid because the command for the music to be played came from the king, not the Levites,[49] and royal wishes were never to be regarded as undesirable. Neither could there exist any fear of popery in the use of church music because it had its "first Institution in the dayes of David: 1500 yeares before any Popery began".

---

[46] Robarts, *Gods Holy House and Service*, p. 54. Exodus 15:21; Judges 4:21–4.

[47] Robarts, *Gods Holy House and Service*, pp. 54–5.

[48] Robarts, *Gods Holy House and Service*, p. 55.

[49] Robarts, *Gods Holy House and Service*, p. 55. 1 Chronicles 25:6.

So esteemed was the practice of music in the Church, Robarts declared, that Christ himself sang a psalm with his disciples at the end of the sacred Supper. St Paul also advocated the use of psalms, hymns and spiritual songs, a practice common in the days of the apostles.

Finally, Robarts offered his own assurance that the man who with "a devout hart not perverted with prejudice" will come to the Church where "music is rightly used . . . and attend unto the Prayses of God which are set out with Musique", and in consequence cannot but "feele his thoughts therewith elevated and enlarged, the more pathetically and feelingly, the more amplie, and fervently to acknowledge and magnifie the goodnesse of God".[50]

When the ancient Fathers condemned the use of music in God's worship, they were not condemning the right use of music, only its misuse. "In the right use therefore of church Musique", he concluded, "there is good profit, and edification to the affection but no Superstition."[51]

---

[50] Robarts, *Gods Holy House and Service*, p. 56.
[51] Robarts, *Gods Holy House and Service*, p. 56.

11

Christ's Offering—A Present Reality

Robert Sanderson, Herbert Thorndike, John Cosin

The shift towards an assurance of the reality of the divine being experienced in the offering of worship became increasingly marked. In worship, the divine was present, not merely remembered. Continued confidence in the efficacy of God's forgiveness ensured that the offering of worship could become united with the offering of Christ and therefore prove as acceptable to God as Christ's offering. This offering of worship was to be comprised of the physical and not constrained to the spiritual.

In worship, it was believed possible to be brought into living contact with the substance of the divine life and therefore to experience a reality transcending rational analysis or description. That worship should be restricted to propositional declarations gave way to an appreciation of worship as the embodiment of the divine presence, the reality of which the arts, such as music, could effectively express.

Robert Sanderson

Robert Sanderson (1587–1663) was Chaplain to Charles I (1631), Regius Professor of Divinity Oxford (1642), Bishop of Lincoln (1660) and Moderator at the Savoy Conference (1661–2).

In a sermon preached at Whitehall in July 1641, Sanderson set out his understanding of the dynamics of worship. The text was Romans 15:6: *That ye may with one mind and with one mouth glorify God, even the*

Father of our Lord Jesus Christ.[1] For Sanderson, the offering of worship consisted of thanksgivings, confessions, faith, charity, obedience and good works. He stipulated that all these aspects of offering were designed to glorify God and were represented most naturally in the formal liturgical worship of the Church.

Despite sin, offering of worship accepted

Sanderson accepted that humanity was evil, corrupt and insignificant. It might therefore be concluded, he suggested, that the offering of such glory to God could best be achieved by the heavenly, not the earthly, Church. Yet despite this burden of sin and its consequent rendering of human offerings imperfect in comparison to those of heaven, Sanderson was adamant that God accepted these offerings, and that God did so on the basis of their sincerity, not their perfection. The offering of worship was appreciated by God as a worthy offering, not because of the quality of its outcome, which might be variable, but because of the earnestness of its intention: "Whoso offereth praise glorifieth me, for so he intendeth it, and so I accept it."[2]

Offering to be of both mind and mouth

It was important for Sanderson that this offering be made with one mind and one mouth. It remained true that "the mind must be first, and before the mouth, in this service",[3] for without it the offering would be deprived of any understanding of the faith. Even the best music of David's tongue with lute and harp as well would be no better than sounding brass or a tinkling cymbal. However, the outward, physical worship of the mouth was essential; "though the mind is to go first, yet the mouth must bear a part too". More than that, glorifying God with the heart and mind only constituted an incomplete offering. "We may not think we glorify God sufficiently", he warned, "if with the heart we believe in Him, unless with the mouth also we be ready to confess Him." It was David who

---

[1] *The Works of Robert Sanderson, D.D.*, ed. W. Jacobson, 6 vols (Oxford: Oxford University Press, 1854), Vol. I, Sermon XIII, p. 329. Psalms 66:1; 138:5.
[2] Sanderson, *Works*, Vol. I, p. 330.
[3] Sanderson, *Works*, Vol. I, p. 343.

had declared the importance of the offering of the voice with his plea of "Open thou my lips, and my mouth shall show Thy praise" and his prediction that "my soul shall be satisfied as it were with marrow and fatness, whilst my tongue praiseth Thee with joyful lips".[4] In any case, Sanderson insisted, an offering of glory to God which excluded the offering of the voice was an impossibility, for the physical was nothing but the consequential manifestation of the spiritual. The offering of worship could be likened to the overflowing of the emotions of the heart which, "if there be much heat there, it will break out at the lips". Testimony that the voice was the inevitable expression of the fire of the spirit came from David himself: "My heart was hot within, and whilst I was musing, the fire kindled, and at last I spake with my tongue."[5] Heart and tongue, mind and mouth, "both must work together".

A broader interpretation of edification

In a sermon preached at Hampton Court on 26 July 1640, Sanderson denied that the intellectual understanding and the edification of the mind were to constitute the sole object of worship. Edification remained an essential aspect of the Christian faith.[6] However, Sanderson introduced a nuanced interpretation of the word "edification". Edification, he said, was not to be restricted to the enlightenment of the understanding, and in a pointed reference to the practices of the reformers he stated:

> I know not how it is come to pass in these later times that in the popular and common notion of this word, in the mouths and apprehensions of most men generally, edification is in a manner confined wholly to the understanding.[7]

Sanderson regarded such a limitation of edification as a grave mistake; an error "such as hath done some hurt too". It was this unbalanced interpretation which had provoked the condemnation of music in

---

[4] Sanderson, *Works*, Vol. I, p. 344. Psalms 51:15; 63:5.
[5] Sanderson, *Works*, Vol. I, p. 344. Psalm 39:3.
[6] Sanderson, *Works*, Vol. I, Sermon XII, p. 311.
[7] Sanderson, *Works*, Vol. I, pp. 311–12.

worship as either obscuring individual words or ignoring whole texts. With the words either not understood or entirely absent, the reformers had argued that there could be no edification of the mind, without which worship was invalid. It was this unwarranted restriction of edification to the understanding of the mind that had led to the rejection of music as not directly promoting the clear declaration of the words.

With singing condemned on these grounds, then instrumental music, which was entirely untexted, had attracted stinging criticism. Objections were made against instrumental music in the service of God, "and some other things used in the Church, that they tend not to edification, but rather hinder it, because there cometh no instruction, nor other fruit to the understanding thereby".[8] These were objections "which some have stood much upon", Sanderson noted, "though there be little cause why". He declared it to be an invalid argument that where the understanding is not benefited there is no edification. The offering of worship was not to be limited to edification in the sense of a purely intellectual appreciation of faith. Edification embraced a wide range of human initiatives, consisting of

> whatsoever thing any way advanceth the service of God, or furthereth the growth of His Church, or conduceth to the increasing of any spiritual grace, or enliving [enlivening] of any holy affection in us, or serveth to the outward exercise or but expression of any such grace and affection, as joy, fear, thankfulness, cheerfulness, reverence, or any other, doubtless every such thing so far forth serveth more or less unto edification.[9]

Edification possible through music

Moreover, Sanderson noted, as well as an error of theology, opponents of so-called unedifying music had committed an error of logic. "From the unserviceableness of any thing to edification", he pointed out, "we cannot reasonably infer the Unlawfulness thereof, but the Inexpediency

---

[8] Sanderson, *Works*, Vol. I, p. 312.
[9] Sanderson, *Works*, Vol. I, p. 312.

only."[10] Edification not being limited to that which can be conveyed by words alone, Sanderson understood music to be able to edify by means of its sounds, and this offering would be accepted by God because of the goodwill with which it was offered.

Herbert Thorndike

Herbert Thorndike (1598-1672) was Fellow of Trinity College Cambridge, Prebendary of Lincoln Cathedral 1636 and Prebendary of Westminster Abbey 1661.

Thorndike acknowledged that the sacrifice offered in the liturgy could not be the original sacrifice offered by Christ on the cross. That had happened once and could no more be repeated than "the present time can become the present time another time". To believe the original sacrifice of the cross could be repeated and Christ sacrificed anew in every Mass would be nothing but a prodigious conceit,[11] for such an offering "being an action done in succession of time, cannot be done the second time being once done, because then it should not have been done before".[12] This caution aside, however, he argued that for the body and blood of Christ to be present, the eucharist must of necessity be the offering of Christ on the cross. The question is, how is this offering represented? Given that it cannot be represented actually, then it must be represented mystically and spiritually, that is, in and by a sacrament,[13] and this sacramental representation of Christ's offering is effected by the consecration of the bread and wine to become the body and blood of Christ.[14] Hence, he declared, the term "a spiritual sacrifice of praise and thanksgiving".

---

[10] Sanderson, *Works*, Vol. I, p. 312.

[11] *The Theological Works of Herbert Thorndike* (Oxford: Parker Society, 1854), Vol. V, p. 547.

[12] *The Theological Works of Herbert Thorndike*, Vol. V, p. 174.

[13] *The Theological Works of Herbert Thorndike*, Vol. IV, p. 98.

[14] *The Theological Works of Herbert Thorndike*, Vol. IV, p. 101.

Christ's offering—the representation is a reality

Further, because it is a representation not a repetition of the original sacrifice, there is no disparagement of Christ's offering, and in the sense that Christ's offering is repeated, it is repeated not actually but sacramentally.[15] Nevertheless, that it is represented sacramentally, not actually, is no reason it should be regarded as less properly a sacrifice.[16] It is a representation and commemoration of Christ's original offering which, when applied by celebrating and receiving the sacrament, becomes united with Christ's original offering.[17]

Being a representation of Christ's offering did not diminish the reality of the offering. The consecrated elements "are truly the sacrifice of Christ upon the cross, inasmuch as the Body and Blood of Christ crucified are contained in them".[18] The eucharist is the sacrifice of Christ on the cross in that the sacrifice of Christ is represented, renewed, revived and restored by it. This is made possible because every representation is the same thing with that which it represents, "taking 'representing' here, not for barely signifying, but for tendering and exhibiting thereby that which it signifieth".[19]

The sacrifice offered in worship gained its identity, not at the consecration but at the offering; not when the bread and the wine are consecrated but when they are offered. He believed the crucial moment occurred at the words, "We offer unto Thee this bread and this cup, beseeching Thee that they may become the body and blood of Christ to the soul's health of them that receive." Here was evidence for Thorndike that the sacrifice occurs, not at the consecration of the gifts, but at the offering of the gifts. Nowhere is it said, he noted, that "we offer unto Thee the body and blood of Christ", but that "we offer unto Thee . . . this reasonable service", which are the prayers of the liturgy. The elements of

---

[15] *The Theological Works of Herbert Thorndike*, Vol. IV, p. 102.
[16] *The Theological Works of Herbert Thorndike*, Vol. IV, pp. 103–4.
[17] *The Theological Works of Herbert Thorndike*, Vol. V, p. 174.
[18] *The Theological Works of Herbert Thorndike*, Vol. IV, p. 112.
[19] *The Theological Works of Herbert Thorndike*, Vol. IV, pp. 112–13.

the eucharist are therefore accounted oblations or sacrifices before they are consecrated.[20]

The debates concerning the connection between the bread and wine and the body and blood are then for Thorndike irrelevant because the sacrifice is achieved as the gifts are offered, not when they are consecrated. Further, although the eucharist is a sacrifice "in a general notion, in regard of the prayers which it is presented to God with", yet there remained what Thorndike called a more particular reason why it is so. There is, firstly, the offering and presenting of the elements by the people to be consecrated and made that sacrament, and secondly the "representation and commemoration of the Passion of Christ" which is the same as that "always offered to God within the veil, as the Apostle to the Hebrews shows".[21]

The present reality of Christ's offering

So Thorndike concluded that in the eucharist we "participate of the sacrifice of Christ upon the cross", the same sacrifice which is "carried by our Lord within the veil, into the most holy place of the heavens, to be presented to God, as it is declared in Hebrews.ix.11–26".[22] Therefore the eucharist is a sacrifice "which is the same one individual sacrifice of Christ upon the cross".[23] Being the same sacrifice did not for Thorndike mean it was an identical sacrifice. An identical sacrifice would have implied a theory of transubstantiation. It was, however, the same sacrifice because it was a remembrance of Christ's sacrifice, and this took place by virtue of a renewing of the covenant of grace which facilitated the unity of Christ's offering on the cross with the offering of the bread and wine on the altar. Through this offering God becomes propitious to us and we obtain at his hands the blessings of grace.[24] Or, as Thorndike reiterated, the eucharist may very properly be accounted a sacrifice "propitiatory and impetratory both ... because the offering of it up unto God, with

---

[20] *The Theological Works of Herbert Thorndike*, Vol. IV, p. 106.
[21] *The Theological Works of Herbert Thorndike*, Vol. I, pp. 860–1.
[22] *The Theological Works of Herbert Thorndike*, Vol. I, p. 476.
[23] *The Theological Works of Herbert Thorndike*, Vol. I, p. 477.
[24] *The Theological Works of Herbert Thorndike*, Vol. IV, pp. 103–4.

and by the said prayers, doth render God propitious, and obtain at His hands the benefits of Christ's death which it representeth".[25] There was therefore no doubt that the eucharist was an offering "whereby God is rendered propitious to, and the benefits of Christ's death obtained for, them that worthily receive it".[26]

Human offering united with the divine offering
As the body and blood of Christ is in the eucharist, sacramentally, then it is nothing less than the offering of Christ upon the cross; therefore God hears our prayers as though they were Christ's and accedes to our requests. "The only powerful means to commend the prayers of the Church unto God, and to obtain our necessities at His hands" occurs when the Church celebrates the remembrance of the sacrifice of the cross and offers and presents it to God.[27]

Singing of psalms
That the offering of the liturgy had a propitiatory status informed Thorndike's attitude to music in worship, particularly the singing of the psalms. He noted that from the time of the apostles, it was the custom, after the bishop had begun the psalms, for them to be sung by the whole congregation. However, Thorndike then cited Philo's account of hymn singing by the Essenes in Alexandria of Egypt, where the custom was for the congregation to remain silent until the ends and burdens (refrains) of the hymns, when all present joined in.[28] Thorndike thought that these burdens cited by Philo corresponded to the end-verses of the psalms

---

[25] *The Theological Works of Herbert Thorndike*, Vol. IV, p. 108. (Impetratory: to obtain by request.)
[26] *The Theological Works of Herbert Thorndike*, Vol. IV, p. 109.
[27] *The Theological Works of Herbert Thorndike*, Vol. I, p. 477.
[28] *The Theological Works of Herbert Thorndike*, Vol. I, p. 321. "And after him (the President) then others also arise in their ranks, in becoming order, while every one else listens in decent silence, except when it is proper for them to take up the burden of the song, and to join in at the end; for then they all, both men and women, join in the hymn." Philo, *De Vita Contemplativa*, in *The Works of Philo*, tr. C. Yonge (Peabody, MA: Hendrickson, 2011), p. 705.

referred to in the Constitutions of the Holy Apostles and in the canons of the Council of Laodicea, and were similar in character to the *Gloria Patri* sung at the end of each psalm. That the congregation was directed to join in the end-verses convinced Thorndike that the people should participate only at the end of each psalm, and that only those he refers to as the canonical singers should go up to the desk and sing in the church. Clearly, from early on, he claimed, there was "inconvenience found" in the congregations joining in the singing of the psalms, as a result of which the church singers alone assumed the responsibility of their musical rendition.[29] This restriction of the congregation to the *Gloria Patri* he claimed had ancient authority and permitted the congregation "to join in the praises of God with most comeliness". To have the choir alone sing the psalms offered the greater opportunity for worship to be offered with decorum and beauty.

Thorndike therefore had nothing but harsh words for those who set out to extinguish the beauty of the singing of the psalms "which this Church and the whole Church appointeth for devotion", and to turn them into lessons of instruction only. This was the motive underlying the move to abandon the old translation with pointings for chanting and to replace it with metrical psalms or, as Thorndike had it, "crowd in the Psalms in rhyme, instead of the Psalter". Things had come to such a pass, he noted, that in some cathedral churches, if the congregation was too small to sustain the singing of metrical psalms, they were read rather than given over to the choir. This suppression of the choral singing of the Psalter was for Thorndike a betrayal of "all use which the Church hath always made of it".[30] The appreciation of the Psalter purely as a means of devotion was one "which all Christendom before the Reformation hath always owned" but was now threatened because of partiality and faction. However, anyone aware of this ancient tradition "will never think it reason to put this part of God's service to silence, whosoever they be that desire or design it".[31]

---

[29] *The Theological Works of Herbert Thorndike*, Vol. I, pp. 321–2.
[30] *The Theological Works of Herbert Thorndike*, Vol. V, p. 467.
[31] *The Theological Works of Herbert Thorndike*, Vol. V, p. 468.

Ironically, observed Thorndike, the chanting of the psalms was easier from a musical point of view than the singing of metrical psalms. He regretted that this fact had been lost on those who are "keenly set against" any desire for compromise or forbearance. Without a commitment to the principle of forbearance commanded by St Paul (Romans 15:1), it was not possible, he believed, "either for this Church, or for any part of the Reformation, long to subsist". Should the current destructive tendencies persist, Thorndike feared nothing less than "the utter loss of religion, for my dearest country, and for the dearer Church of God in it".[32]

John Cosin

John Cosin (1594–1672) was Master of Greatham Hospital 1624; Prebendary of Durham Cathedral 1624; Master of Peterhouse 1634; Vice-Chancellor of Cambridge University 1639; Dean of Peterborough 1640; Chaplain to Charles I 1640; ejected from Peterhouse 1644; exiled in Paris until consecrated Bishop of Durham 2 December 1660; and a leading participant at the Savoy Conference 1661–2.

Cosin held that the offering of worship was not merely a commemoration but a continuation of the effect of Christ's original offering. This view is expressed throughout his *"Notes and Collections on the Book of Common Prayer"* written on the sheets inserted between the pages of two Books of Common Prayer (1604) published in 1619 and 1638.[33]

---

[32] *The Theological Works of Herbert Thorndike*, Vol. V, pp. 468–9.

[33] John Cosin, "Notes and Collections on the Book of Common Prayer", in *The Works of John Cosin*, Library of Anglo-Catholic Theology, 5 vols (Oxford: John Henry Parker, 1843–55), V, p. 106. Also in "Notes and Collections in an Interleaved Book of Common Prayer 1619", *The Works of the Right Reverend Father in God, John Cosin, Lord Bishop of Durham*, Vol. V (Oxford: John Henry Parker, 1855).

Offering of the Church in worship as effective as Christ's offering

Cosin referred to John Chrysostom, whom he thought detected a distinction between the sacrifice of Christ offered once for all upon the cross and the sacrifice of the Church, which consisted of the application of that original sacrifice in the offering of worship.[34] This sacrifice offered by the Church was not unique. It was, however, commemorative and its effect was as sufficient, true, real, efficient and propitiatory for human sin as Christ's original sacrifice. Referring to Juan Maldonado, Cosin argued that Christ's sacrifice was profitable only when brought into effect and that this was precisely what is achieved by the sacrifice of the Church.[35] The Church's sacrifice made Christ's sacrifice available. Both sacrifices were therefore propitiatory, claimed Cosin, for they possess both the force and the virtue to appease God's wrath against this sinful world.[36] The sacrifice offered by the Church was not a new sacrifice but the same which was once offered and which continues to be offered to God every day by Christ in heaven—a view for which he gathered support from the Flemish theologian Georg Cassander.[37]

Cosin therefore understood the sacrifice offered by the Church to be neither a new act of propitiation nor a new remission of sins. It was the making effectual of that offering once perfectly achieved by Christ. The sacrifice which Christ offered continually to the Father was continued on earth by means of the mystical representation of it in the eucharistic liturgy. The Church did not enact a new propitiation of its own creation; rather did it "make effectual" and "in act apply" that which was once obtained by the sacrifice of Christ upon the cross.[38] So the essential quality of the sacrifice offered in worship was one of propitiation. Its

---

[34] *Works of John Cosin*, Vol. V, pp. 106-7. Chrysostom: *Hom. Contra. Jud*, Part 2, Book IV. *Adversus Judaeos*.

[35] *Works of John Cosin*, Vol. V, pp. 107-8. Juan Maldonado (1533-83): Spanish Jesuit theologian, *Disputationum ac controversiarum decisarum et circa septum Ecclesiae Romanae Sacramenta* (2 vols, 1577), Vol. I, pp. 322-3.

[36] *Works of John Cosin*, Vol. V, p. 108.

[37] *Works of John Cosin*, Vol. V, p. 108. Georg Cassander (1513-66), *De articulis religionis inter Catholicos et Protestantes controversis consultatio* (1577).

[38] *Works of John Cosin*, Vol. V, p. 108.

true nature "in the offertory, is to acknowledge God's majesty and our misery, and to appease His wrath towards us, to get blessings from Him, to make Christ's bloody sacrifice effectual unto us".[39]

So Cosin maintained that the offering of the eucharist was not merely a "type and figure" offered in recognition and memory of Christ's offering but a discrete act effective in commending humanity to God. Although not a replication of Christ's offering, this offering was the instrument which brought the original offering into effect. In so doing, it assumed the force of Christ's own offering.

Prayer of Oblation

It was this understanding of sacrifice which prompted Cosin's advocacy for the Prayer of Oblation to be placed directly after the Prayer of Consecration as in the proposed Book of Common Prayer of 1637 for the use of the Church of Scotland. The point of this placement, he claimed, was "to make an offering of it (as being the true public sacrifice of the Church) unto God, that by the merits of Christ's death, which was now commemorated, all the Church of God might receive mercy".[40] Cosin noted that John Overall always used the Prayer of Oblation in what he considered to be its rightful place,[41] which was

> when he had consecrated the Sacrament to make an offering of it (as being the true public sacrifice of the Church) unto God, that

---

[39] *Works of John Cosin*, Vol. V, p. 118.

[40] The Prayer of Oblation begins "O Lord and heavenly Father, we thy humble servants entirely desire thy fatherly goodness mercifully to accept this our sacrifice of praise and thanksgiving", and contains the phrase 'And here we offer and present unto Thee, O Lord, ourselves, our souls and bodies, to be a reasonable, holy, and lively sacrifice unto thee." *Works of John Cosin*, Vol. V, pp. 114–15.

[41] John Overall (1560–1619): Fellow of Trinity College Cambridge 1591, Regius Professor of Theology Cambridge 1595–1607, Dean of St Paul's London 1602, Bishop of Coventry and Lichfield 1614, Bishop of Norwich 1618.

by the merits of Christ's death, which was now commemorated, all the Church of God might receive mercy.[42]

Cosin again referred to the placement of this prayer in his notes attached to a Prayer Book printed in 1638: "The Prayer of Oblation, which by the first ordering of this Book in the time of King Edward VI was appointed to be said before the distribution of the Sacrament. And it would not have been amiss if that order had continued so still."[43]

Cosin was insistent that he had not returned to that understanding of sacrifice characteristic of the late mediaeval Church. Emphatically he maintained that the sacrifice offered in the liturgy was not a reiteration of the sacrifice offered by Christ. "We do not hold this celebration", he insisted, "to be so naked a commemoration of Christ's Body given to death, and of his Blood there shed for us, but that the same Body and Blood is present there in this commemoration."[44] Such a sacrifice he dismissed as unacceptable because it could not be achieved without killing Christ again.

Christ's offering not replicated but brought into being

That said, the sacrifice which was offered, although not the original sacrifice of Christ, possessed a propitiatory quality. Christ did not die again and his sacrifice remained a past event, but the presentation of that past event in the context of the offering of praise and thanksgiving so united the one offering with the other that a propitiatory effect was achieved. We do not say, said Cosin, that what is offered in worship is "so nude a sacrifice of praise and thanksgiving as would disallow the offering and presentation of the death of Christ to God, that for His death's sake we may find mercy".[45] The true and proper nature of a sacrifice was the offering to God of some real and sensible thing,[46]

---

[42] *Works of John Cosin*, Vol. V, pp. 114–15. Quoted and discussed in G. J. Cuming, *A History of Anglican Liturgy* (London: Macmillan, 1969), p. 141.
[43] *Works of John Cosin*, Vol. V, p. 347.
[44] *Works of John Cosin*, Vol. V, p. 336.
[45] *Works of John Cosin*, Vol. V, p. 336.
[46] *Works of John Cosin*, Vol. V, p. 115.

designed neither to displace nor to re-create but to obtain and bring "into act" that propitiation which was once made by Christ.[47] Christ's sacrifice was not replicated in the liturgy; it was brought into being in order to be made effective in the present. This sacrifice was to be offered by means of "certain mysterious rites and ceremonies, which Christ and his Church have ordained".[48] There was historical precedence for this, Cosin added, for "the general form of a sacrifice ... consisted always in some ceremonious offering of it, the better to express the mystery contained in it", and without such a ceremonious offering the sacrifice was improper.[49] For this reason, tenths and first-fruits were offered to God, yet because they were not offered up *ritu mystico* they were not proper sacrifices.[50] These ceremonial offerings, with their accompanying rituals and ornaments, had been endangered by those returning from abroad at the accession of Elizabeth. "For the disuse of these ornaments", Cosin complained, "we may thank them that came from Geneva, and in the beginning of Queen Elizabeth's reign, being set in places of government, suffered every negligent priest to do what him listed."[51] These reformers professed an indiscriminate "difference and opposition" to every ceremony associated with the Church of Rome, no matter how lawful or relevant many of them remained.

Christ's offering present, not just a memory

In his *Particulars to be Considered, Explained and Corrected, in the Book of Common Prayer*, Cosin continued his advocacy for what he considered to be a proper recognition of the offering of worship. He recommended that in the Prayer of Consecration the words "and sacrifice" be added to the phrase "and in his holy Gospel command us to continue a perpetual memory of that his precious death".[52] The words "and sacrifice" had been

---

[47] *Works of John Cosin*, Vol. V, p. 120.
[48] *Works of John Cosin*, Vol. V, p. 115.
[49] *Works of John Cosin*, Vol. V, p. 116.
[50] *Works of John Cosin*, Vol. V, pp. 116–17.
[51] *Works of John Cosin*, Vol. V, p. 42.
[52] These recommendations of Cosin's are bound up at the end of an interleaved Book of Common Prayer published in 1619.

inserted in the 1637 Book of Common Prayer devised for the Church of Scotland.

Music as part of the offering of worship

Cosin was emphatic that music was to be reckoned amongst the mysterious rites and ceremonies of the offering of worship. Beautiful music afforded God much pleasure, therefore beautiful music needed to be included in the sacrifice, whose purpose was to please God. Cosin believed the antiquity of the use of hymns in the Christian Church could be traced to Christ himself, who with his disciples had sung a hymn at the Last Supper before leaving for the Garden of Gethsemane.[53] Cosin also cited Paul's instructions for hymns to be used in the Church of Colossae[54] and also in the Church in Alexandria founded by St Mark.[55] In any case, Cosin argued, Christ and St Paul were by no means the first to use hymns in worship. They were merely following a long-standing Jewish custom. After the apostles, Christians continued to use hymns, as was testified by Pliny, the Emperor Trajan's vicegerent, who testified that of all the churches in Pontus and Bithynia, the "only crime he there knew of them was that they used to meet together and to praise Christ with hymns as a God".[56] St Hilary made a book of "ecclesiastical hymns and songs for the Church" and St Ambrose introduced this book into the Church in Milan. From here came "all hymns for the most part to be called *Ambrosiani*, because from him they began to be spread all over the Latin Church".[57]

Alternatim singing of psalms

Cosin declared the practice of singing the psalms *alternatim*, "by course and sides", to be very ancient, having its origin in Antioch, according to Theodoret and Socrates. Theodoret had identified Flavian and Diodore as the initial practitioners of this style of singing, whereas Socrates declared Ignatius to be its founder based on a vision of angels he claimed

---

[53] *Works of John Cosin*, Vol. V, p. 59.
[54] Colossians 3:16.
[55] *Works of John Cosin*, Vol. V, p. 59.
[56] *Works of John Cosin*, Vol. V, p. 60.
[57] *Works of John Cosin*, Vol. V, p. 62.

to have had, who were glorifying God according to this method.[58] The authenticity of Socrates's vision was predictably "derided by our new masters", observed Cosin. However, "whether the story be true or no", he noted, "I am sure the thing itself is good, and if Ignatius did not hear the angels sing so, that which is better, the prophet Isaiah did". That Isaiah recorded that the seraphim stood upon the throne and cried to one another, saying, "Holy", convinced Cosin that they were singing by sides.[59] This practice of the singing of psalms by side was so steeped in the ritual of worship that it ought never to be relinquished. St Ambrose and St Augustine, for example, had sung the canticle *Te Deum* "one answering another *alternatim*, and verse by verse, as if God had from heaven taught them what to say".[60]

Instruments to be accepted in the offering of worship

Support for instruments had prevailed from the earliest times, claimed Cosin. The use of instrumental music was a tradition as ancient as Moses when he came out of Egypt with the Israelites.[61] This practice continued steadily until the time of David when as a result of his inspiration the number of instruments used in worship grew immeasurably.[62] After David, instruments continued to receive support from kings and prophets up to the time of Christ who, Cosin noted, "gave us an example to do as they did still".[63]

That the early Christians restricted the use of instruments as accompaniment to their singing is attributable to their fear of discovery and subsequent persecution, claimed Cosin, and is no reason for instruments not to be used in later times when the Church is settled and flourishing. Further, that there are examples in the Gospels of

---

[58] Theodoret (*c*.393–*c*.458/466): Bishop of Cyrus 423–57; Socrates (*c*.380–450) "Scholasticus": Greek Church historian; Flavian (*c*.320–404): Bishop of Antioch 399–404; Diodorus (*d*.390): Bishop of Tarsus 378–90.
[59] *Works of John Cosin*, Vol. V, pp. 53–4.
[60] *Works of John Cosin*, Vol. V, p. 64.
[61] *Works of John Cosin*, Vol. V, p. 60.
[62] *Works of John Cosin*, Vol. V, p. 61.
[63] *Works of John Cosin*, Vol. V, p. 60. Cf. Footnote 63.

congregations singing without instruments is likely to be because they could not do all at once, rather than they did not wish to".[64]

In his commentary on the Prayer Book instruction that "to the end the people may the better hear, in such place where they do sing, there shall the lessons be sung in a plain tune after the manner of distinct reading", Cosin admitted that this was the reason for singing in a plain and audible tone. The words of worship should be audible and comprehensible. However, he added, mere reading was inadequate. It lacked "the force to affect and stir up the spirit, which a grave manner of singing has". To avoid the compromising of edification, however, singing "needs to be tempered with that gravity which becomes the servants of God in the presence of his holy angels", and for this reason the Church has insisted that lessons and prayers are sung "as may make most for the dignity and glory of God's high and holy service". That said, the Church also recognizes music as a "means to inflame men's affections, to stir up their attentions, and to edify their understandings".[65]

Condemnation of metrical psalms

Cosin condemned the practice of the congregations in Geneva of rendering the psalms into verses and setting them to a variety of melodies to be sung by the whole congregation. He deplored this practice, known as metrical psalmody, considering it to be not only contrary to the tradition established by the early Church but unseemly because of its lack of musical quality. With contempt he described how "ill displeasing [and] harsh the effeminate Geneva tunes were to the gravity and ears of the ancient Church and how jointly esteemed the solemn music of the Christians was by all pious and learned men, even in primitive times".[66] Cosin spoke sharply against "our new masters and mistresses at

---

[64] *Works of John Cosin*, Vol. V, p. 61. Cosin is possibly referring to examples of the use of instruments attributed to the sayings of Jesus: Matthew 24:31 ("And he shall send his angels with a great sound of a trumpet"); and Luke 7:32 ("They are like unto children sitting in the marketplace, and calling one to another, and saying, We have piped unto you, and ye have not danced").

[65] *Works of John Cosin*, Vol. V, p. 58.

[66] *Works of John Cosin*, Vol. V, p. 63.

Geneva" whose despicable policy it was "to thrust out the solemn music of David's own psalms, and other glorious hymns of holy men, from the Church, and to give us songs of their own altering and composing to be sung instead of them". The metrical versions of the psalms which were usurping the place of solemn music offered by choirs was of such reduced quality that it was now produced by "a company of rude people, cobblers and their wives, and their kitchen-maids and all, that have as much skill in singing as an ass has to handle an harp".[67]

Music at Durham Cathedral

Cosin's desire for music to assume a more appropriate role in the offering of worship became dramatically evident during 1628 and 1629, when he was indicted before the Archbishop of York on charges of introducing ritualistic practices to the worship of Durham Cathedral. These indictments were brought by Peter Smart, a fellow prebendary. Amongst a number of complaints, Smart accused Cosin of having "converted divers prayers in the Book of Common Prayers into hymns, to be sung in the choir, and played with the organ",[68] and of allowing one particular morning service in the cathedral to consist chiefly of singing and playing on the organs.[69]

In response, Cosin compiled a series of arguments for the inclusion of music in worship. Solemn singing roused the spirit of the listeners; praise was rendered to God more easily and pleasantly when the liturgy was seasoned with a joyfulness of song; the singing of the psalms,

---

[67] *Works of John Cosin*, Vol .V, p. 63.

[68] *Works of John Cosin*, Vol. I, p. xxiv.

[69] *Works of John Cosin*, Vol. I, p. xxv. Peter Smart (1596–c.1652), a prebendary of Durham Cathedral since 1614, on 27 July 1628 preached a sermon condemning the liturgical practices of John Cosin, then also a prebend of Durham. Smart's sermon was subsequently published later that year as "The Vanity and Downfall of Superstitious Popish Ceremonies". Smart's charges against Cosin are quoted in P. Le Huray, *Music and the Reformation in England 1549–1660* (Cambridge: Cambridge University Press, 1978), pp. 48-9, and are to be found in G. Ornsby (ed.), "The Correspondence of John Cosin, D.D.", Surtees Society LII (1868 and 1870), p. 144.

lessons, readings and prayers represented a lively witness to the fact that Christians did not find the divine law troublesome and boring but rather a source of pleasure and an inducement to love.

Cosin's final argument was that the liturgy was a service offered to God and, as such, it was necessary for that service to be perfect in every respect. It was to constitute an offering to God of the most perfect human gifts, gifts characterized by Cosin as prayer from the soul and music from the body.[70]

---

[70] Cosin, "Notes and Collections on the Book of Common Prayer", p. 52.

1 2

Participation in the Worship of Heaven

Anthony Sparrow, Giles Widdowes, Thomas Westfield

As the unity of the divine and human offering continued to be appreciated, the offering of worship was seen as not merely a remembrance of Christ's offering but a continuation of it. Earthly worship was understood to be united to heavenly worship, and the elements of worship, such as ritual, the arts and music, came to be valued as embedded in this unity of the divine and the human. As such their beauty was regarded as significant, for as beauty was an inherent quality of the worship of heaven, so beauty was to be an inherent quality of the worship of the Church. The commonality of that beauty between the human and the divine corresponded to a commonality of holiness, contributing to a developing understanding of the unity of the divine and human in worship.

Anthony Sparrow

Anthony Sparrow (1612–85) was Canon of Ely Cathedral 1661, President of the Queen's College, Cambridge 1662, Vice-Chancellor of the University of Cambridge 1664, Bishop of Exeter 1667 and Bishop of Norwich 1676.

Offering of worship identical to the offering of the cross
What is offered in the offering of worship, declared Sparrow, is not restricted to a spiritual sacrifice of prayer, praise and thanksgiving, but is the commemorative Sacrifice of the Death of Christ. This commemorative offering "shows forth the death of Christ as those Sacrifices under the

Law did foreshow it".[1] As the words which "God our Saviour spake are the same which the priest now uses, so is the Sacrament the same".[2] Just as Christ consecrated the bread and wine at the Supper, so he consecrates the bread and wine of the eucharist. It "becomes God's Service and Worship by his own Law, as well as the Lamb was his Sacrifice, Exod. Xxix".[3] The origin of this sacrifice could not be ascribed to human fancy but God's will. It was "commanded by God to be offered up to him in the Behalf of the Church".[4]

Because of its participation in the perfect offering of Christ, the worship of the Church, in all its forms, was so pleasing to God that its offering was not simply requested, but commanded. "Prayers, Thanksgivings, Confessions, Lauds, Hymns, and eucharistical Sacrifices", Sparrow insisted, "are commanded to be offer'd up in the Name of Christ, in the Virtue and Merits of that immaculate Lamb".[5]

As a result of this divine authorization, Sparrow reckoned this propitiatory significance to have raised the offering of the daily public worship of the Church into as effective an offering as had once been true of the burnt sacrifices of the Old Covenant. The recitation of Morning and Evening Prayer was agreeable to God's own Law as stated in the book Exodus 29:38: "Thou shalt offer upon the Altar two Lambs of the first

---

[1] Anthony Sparrow, *A Rationale, or practical Exposition of the Book of Common Prayer* (London, 1722), p. 251. Although there are no copies in existence of a date earlier than 1657, *A Rationale, or practical Exposition of the Book of Common Prayer* is thought to have been first published in 1655. It is a significant and courageous document to have appeared during the Commonwealth period.

[2] Sparrow, *Rationale*, pp. 173–4. Chrysostom, *Second Epistle to Timothy*, second homily: "For as the words which God spake are the same which the Priest now utters, so is the Offering the same, and the Baptism, that which he gave." *A Select Library of the Nicene and Post-Nicene Fathers of the Christian Church*, ed. Philip Schaff (New York: The Christian Literature Company, 1889), Vol. XIII, p. 483.

[3] Sparrow, *Rationale*, p. 4.

[4] Sparrow, *Rationale*, p. 6.

[5] Sparrow, *Rationale*, p. 3.

Year, Day by Day continually; the one Lamb in the Morning, the other at Evening."[6] God requires a "daily publicke Worship, a continual Burnt Offering, every Day, Morning and Evening", which constitutes a sacrifice with undoubted propitiatory qualities, for God receives that offering as "a sweet Savour, or Savour of Rest, as it is in the Hebrew". It was a sacrifice without which God could not rest satisfied.

This appreciation of worship as an offering able to elicit approval and satisfaction from God inspired Sparrow's reverence and affection for churches and oratories which, he claimed, were originally built to provide appropriate places for the offering of worship. Set aside for such a holy use, these buildings were to be suitably adorned and beautified so that the sacrifice could be offered "in the beauty of holiness".[7]

Offering of worship

That divine authority granted to this offering held important consequences for Sparrow. Firstly, the liturgy must constitute the "only true and right publicke Worship" which could be offered. The private prayers of isolated individuals could never be regarded as an acceptable offering.[8] Secondly, this worship is received by God despite the shortcomings of those responsible for its offering. Even when offered by such notorious sinners as King David it lost none of its efficacy. That King David had prayed "Let the lifting up of my Hands be an Evening Sacrifice" was evidence that his offering was as surely accepted as that original sacrifice of the Lamb.[9] Thirdly, the offering of worship was effective for the whole people of God, not just for those who were the immediate participants: "This publicke Service is accepted of God not only for those that are present, and say Amen to it, but for all those that are absent upon just cause." The sacrifice was offered on behalf of all the faithful and so it was accepted by God in the name of all the faithful. Just as the Lamb "offered up to God by the Priest, Exod. xxix. was the Sacrifice of the whole Congregation of the Children of Israel", so the liturgy is the common service of them all,

---

[6] Sparrow, *Rationale*, p. 2.
[7] Sparrow, *Rationale*, p. 237.
[8] Sparrow, *Rationale*, p. 6.
[9] Sparrow, *Rationale*, p. 7.

commanded to be offered up in the names of them all and agreed to by all of them to be offered up for them all, and "therefore is accepted for them all, though presented to God by the Priest alone".[10] Finally, it was essential for Sparrow that worship be made fitting and acceptable to God. Since God had commanded the offering of this sacrifice, he is bound to accept it and so "it must needs be most acceptable to him, which is so appointed by him: for what he commands, he accepts most certainly".[11]

In worship the divine and human meet
Sparrow was in no doubt that the offering of worship had propitiatory status with God: "Good reason therefore it is", he declared, "that this sweet-smelling Savour should be daily offered up to God Morning and Evening, whereby God may be pacified, and invited to dwell amongst his People."[12] In response to the offering of this sacrifice God would be "as gracious and bountiful to us in the Performance of this Service, as he promised to be to the Jews in the offering of the Lamb, Morning and Evening, Exod. xxix. 43, 44". In consequence, God and man could be reconciled and become one. Through worship God would "meet us, and speak with us, that is, graciously answer our Petitions: he would dwell with us, and be our God".[13] The divine and the human would be united.

This appreciation of worship as an offering united with Christ's offering rendered it an integral and effective constituent of the worship of heaven. So Sparrow acclaimed the sung parts of the liturgy, for they constituted a human representation of the divine. He drew attention to the "Angelical Hymn, GLORY BE TO GOD ON HIGH, &c., wherein the Ecclesiastical Hierarchy does admirably imitate the heavenly, singing [those words] at the Sacrament of his Body, which the Angels did at the Birth of his Body". Sparrow found singing in the liturgy therefore to be authenticated not only because it was in imitation of the singing of the angels, but also because it followed the example of Christ. After the receiving of the holy sacrament "we sing an Hymn, in imitation of our

---

[10] Sparrow, *Rationale*, p. 7.
[11] Sparrow, *Rationale*, p. 6.
[12] Sparrow, *Rationale*, p. 7.
[13] Sparrow, *Rationale*, p. 9.

saviour, who after his Supper sang an hymn, to teach us to do the like".[14] In worship, at the uniting of the human with the divine, human singing became united with heavenly singing.

Value of music extends to edification

Sparrow therefore regarded music as integral to the offering of worship. Singing brought great benefit to the liturgy, especially in the hymns, in that they "inkindle an holy Flame in the Minds and Affections of the Hearers". Like others before him, he referred to Augustine and his confession that he had been so deeply moved by the beauty of music in worship that he had wept, "being enforc'd thereunto by the sweet Voices of thy melodious Church".[15] Furthermore, it was by means of the beauty of music that the essence of the divine was able to be conveyed to the human understanding. Quoting from the same commentary of St Basil's on Psalm 1 as had Richard Hooker before him, and using Hooker's exact words, Sparrow wrote that it pleased the Wisdom of the Spirit

> to borrow from Melody that Pleasure, which mingled with heavenly Mysteries causes the smoothness and Softness of that which touches the Ear, [to convey] as it were by Stealth, the Treasure of good Things into Men's Minds.[16]

For Sparrow, the beauty of music in worship became united with the beauty of heaven, and in the unity, or mingling, it was possible for the divine to enter into the human experience.

---

[14] Sparrow, *Rationale*, p. 181.
[15] Sparrow, *Rationale*, p. 33.
[16] Sparrow, *Rationale*, p. 33. *A Select Library of the Nicene and Post-Nicene Fathers of the Christian Church*, eds P. Schaff and H. Wallace (New York: The Christian Literature Company, 1890), Series II, Vol. 8, p. 77. Richard Hooker, *Of the Laws of Ecclesiastical Polity*, Book V, p. 153. Everyman II, p. 148.

Giles Widdowes

Giles Widdowes (1588–1645) was Fellow of Oriel College and from 1619 Rector of St Martin's Carfax, Oxford.

He preached a sermon at St Mary's Witney on the text "Let all things be done decently, and in order" (1 Corinthians 14:40). It was published in 1631 with the title *The Schismatical Puritan*. In it he challenged the view that the ceremonies of worship did not edify and were therefore illegitimate. He found it distressing that there were still those for whom edification consisted of a simple and uncritical acceptance of the words proclaimed in worship. These were they, he scorned, who were content simply to believe without demur or question. They were "afraid of essentiall and demonstrative exposition" and dismissive of profound consideration of the faith, preferring the type of edification which is superficial, factious and hostile to Church decency and order.[17] Beyond this level of so-called edifying "they never intend to proceed, like S. *Pauls* silly women, who are ever learning but never able to come to the knowledge of the truth".[18] As a result, "the able gracious practice of the church is neglected by them" and components of the liturgy such as ceremonial and music are dismissed out of hand. Not only choral music, but organs, "the musicall instruments of the churches gracious practice", are also tedious to them because it is claimed they do not edify.[19] Even "to ring the Church-bells in peale on the Lords day ... the saperatists call profaning of the Sabbath". All this is due to their ignorance,

> being unable to tell the difference betweene the worlds servile works, which are forbidden by the fourth commaundment, and betweene Churches musicall works, which in their due time done, doe praise the Lord.[20]

---

[17] Giles Widdowes, *The Schismatical Puritan. A Sermon Preached at Witney concerning the lawfulnesse of Church-Authority, for ordaining, and commanding of Rites, and Ceremonies, to beautifie the Church* (Oxford, 1631), F 3v.

[18] 2 Timothy 3:7. Widdowes's italics.

[19] Widdowes, *The Schismatical Puritan*, F 3r.

[20] Widdowes, *The Schismatical Puritan*, F 3r.

Rites and ceremonies are representative of heaven

As well as edifying in a more profound sense than a superficial reception of the stated word, rites and ceremonies, by means of their innate beauty, were a representation of the worship of heaven.[21] So for Widdowes, the Puritan was an enemy of worship and its accompanying ritual, impelled by an indiscriminate desire for God's ministers and his house to be naked, without any external beauty whatsoever.[22] These Puritans, he argued, were especially mistaken when they advanced the curious argument that the rites and ceremonies of the temple only existed because they signified "Christ to come", and then at Christ's coming they were to be repealed. Because Christ had now come, it was said, there was no longer any need for a sign that Christ was to come, therefore ceremonies were redundant. To the contrary, insisted Widdowes, ceremonies are not signs of the coming of Christ, but "signes of church beauty for morall ornament", and their beauty is to be found in the representation of the Lord Jesus as king of heaven and earth and of the triumphant and militant Church.[23] Moreover, this beauty of ceremonial was not optional but obligatory, as was everything pertaining to the beauty of the church, including music. "Church Organs are musicall signes of our exultation: they are the lowd, and as sweet as lowd, expressions of the Churches greatest joy towards God."[24]

The phrase "Let all things be done decently and in order", he declared, was Paul's authority for the Church to legislate ceremonies that enhanced the service of God.[25] These ceremonies had scriptural authority, "not in expresse sentence, but by pregnant consequence". To deny the Church the discretion to use such ceremonies would be to deprive her of Christian liberty.[26] "If Church-ceremonies were dumbe, non-significant, they might bee well condemn'd for unlawfull", but being significant, they are lawful. Whilst not of themselves sacraments, these ceremonies and other works

---

[21] Widdowes, *The Schismatical Puritan*, D 2v.
[22] Widdowes, *The Schismatical Puritan*, C 2r.
[23] Widdowes, *The Schismatical Puritan*, E 1v.
[24] Widdowes, *The Schismatical Puritan*, E 1r–E 2v.
[25] 1 Corinthians 14:40.
[26] Widdowes, *The Schismatical Puritan*, E 3v–r.

of beauty are signs of the glory of God. Here is the "similitude betweene the triumphant and militant Church", maintained Widdowes, and the ceremonies of the one are signs of the glory of the other. The sounds of organs and bells were therefore signs of the glory of heaven: "Let the Lord bee praised upon Church organs, and on the Sabbath and Holy-dayes", and "let him bee magnified with the musicall sound of all Church-bells".[27] Music was therefore a necessity in terms both of beauty and decency.

All of which led Widdowes to the unflattering conclusion that "Nonconformists have not the spirit of God to guid[e] them. For they are troublesome inventers of division."[28]

Thomas Westfield

Thomas Westfield (1573–1644) was Prebend of St Paul's Cathedral 1614, Archdeacon of St Albans 1631, and Bishop of Bristol 1642.

In his major work, *The White Robe, or the Surplice Vindicated*, published in 1660, he continued the break from the mindset of the reformers with a forceful account of God's promise of unconditional forgiveness.

Divine forgiveness

Westfield declared this forgiveness to be so comprehensive that humanity could be restored to a cleanliness which made divine acceptance not only possible but inevitable. No longer was it necessary to cringe in shame from God, for even though that sin be of a "double dye", it was forgiven entirely. Irrespective of the depths to which humanity had fallen, it was possible to be excused. Though our sins were red as scarlet, declared Westfield, God's forgiveness rendered us whiter than snow.[29] Thus forgiven, we are restored and being restored are made worthy, and being made worthy are able to offer our works to God, for it is said, "Go & eat

---

[27] Widdowes, *The Schismatical Puritan*, E 4r.
[28] Widdowes, *The Schismatical Puritan*, F 4v.
[29] Thomas Westfield, *The White Robe: or, The Surplice Vindicated* (London, 1660), pp. 55–6. Westfield's reference is to Isaiah 1:18.

thy bread with joy and drink thy wine with a cheerful heart: for God now accepteth thy works."[30] This assurance of divine forgiveness invested the offering of works with the confident expectation that worship would be enhanced by their beauty and they would become an adornment rather than an impediment.

Worship of heaven on earth
Further, being fellow servants of the same God, both angels and men found a common purpose as together they sang Hallelujahs. They became united in their worship of the one God. This unity with the angels in worship was humanity's most treasured vocation,[31] for it allowed the offering of worship on earth to be understood as participation in the worship of heaven.

This unity between the worship of the Church on earth and the Church in heaven was confirmed by the outward appearance of the worshippers. The members of the Church Triumphant praise God in white, he noted, and the Church Militant, exemplified by the Levites that brought the Ark of God into the appointed place, followed this example (2 Chronicles 5:12).[32]

For Westfield the implications for the ceremonial of worship, in particular music, were profound. Because of the unity of the human offering of worship with Christ's offering, music was as indispensable to the worship of the Church Militant as it was to the worship of the Church Triumphant. This had been the case throughout the history of God's people. "O what glorious things are spoken of thee, O thou city of God", he declared, for "here be the Angels singing Hallelujahs, all Praise, and Glory, and Honour be to God in the highest ... the 24 Elders in the Revelations, all of them in white apparel ... sang praise to God, to him that sate upon the throne".[33] It was through music that

---

[30] Westfield, *The White Robe*, pp. 57–8. Ecclesiastes 9:7.
[31] Westfield, *The White Robe*, pp. 45–6.
[32] Westfield, *The White Robe*, p. 54.
[33] Westfield, *The White Robe*, pp. 31–2.

the Levites, which were the singers, all of them of Asaph, of Heman, of Jeduthan, with their sons, and their brethren, being attired in white linen, having Cymbals, and Psalteries, and Harps, stood at the east of the Altar, and with them an hundred and twenty Priests, sounding with trumpets.[34]

That music, vocal and instrumental, particularly of such an exotic nature, was able to be united with the worship of heaven was a direct consequence of the offering of humanity being made acceptable by being united to Christ's perfect offering. Thus could God say to the Church of Sardis, "They shall walk with me in white, for they are worthy." This blessing was given, not according to their own worthiness, but by "the greatest acceptation of God; he is pleased to accept them worthy in Christ".[35] It followed that if humanity was worthy, then his offering had to be worthy and would be accepted by God.

Offering to be of the greatest beauty
To give God the greatest pleasure the offering had therefore to be of the greatest beauty. Westfield specified the fragrance of oils and perfumes as some of the natural delights capable of arousing pleasure. He drew an analogy between a dove being anointed with sweet ointment in order to draw other doves into the dovecot, and with Christ being similarly anointed to draw people to the Church of God. Both doves and humans were attracted by that which was beautiful and delightful.[36] For this reason, God had provided humanity not only with the necessities of life but also with such "refreshments", as Westfield had it, as were consistent with a restored relationship with the divine. Such is the goodness of God, he pointed out, that

---

[34] Westfield, *The White Robe*, p. 54.
[35] Westfield, *The White Robe*, pp. 60-1.
[36] Westfield, *The White Robe*, pp. 121-2.

he allows us not onely cloathes to put on, to keep our bodies from the injury of the weather in winter, and the parching heate of summer, but oyntments to set out nature, befitting glory.[37]

God not only allows us meats to nourish us but has created many other things to delight us:

> To what end serve the variety of colours in birds and beasts, and stones, but to delight the eye? ... to what end serves the variety of delicate tastes in the meat, but to delight the palate? ... to what end serves the variety of smells of aromatick Gumms, Flowers, and Oyntments, but to delight the smell?[38]

The sense of hearing had also been granted by God so that the beauty of music could be experienced. "To what end", asked Westfield, "serves the variety of musical notes, but to delighte the ear?" It was God's will that pleasure should be found in the beauty of colours, tastes, aromas and music. That God attributed such significance to beauty in all its forms and equipped humanity to delight in it clearly indicated that God welcomed works of beauty in worship.

The ultimate authority for the offering to God of all that would bring God delight, however, was Christ's anointing as King, Priest and Prophet.[39] The "Oyle of Gladness" with which he was anointed was not confined to Christ alone but was extended throughout the whole Church, incorporating even its lowest member. The ointment that was poured on the head of Aaron ran down his beard to the skirts of his clothing. Here was an analogy of the meanest member of the Church being able rightfully to claim to be anointed by God. This being so, these members were expected to be true to the four-fold nature of their appointed vocation and to the responsibilities those offices required. For priests, it was the offering of their bodies as a living sacrifice to God; the offering of a contrite heart in sorrow for sin; the offering of praise and

---

[37] Westfield, *The White Robe*, pp. 122-3.
[38] Westfield, *The White Robe*, p. 123.
[39] Westfield, *The White Robe*, pp. 132-3.

thanksgiving, singing psalms, hymns and spiritual songs; and the offering of prayer: "Let my prayer ascend up as incense, and the lifting up of my hands as a sacrifice."[40] Just as Christ's priestly offering of himself brought pleasure to God as though it were "an oyntment poured out, as sweet as hony in all meats, as sweet as music, a banquet of wine",[41] so the sacrifice of worship offered by humanity, being united to that of Christ's, must be as beautiful and as pleasurable to God as well. So did works of beauty, including music, become for Westfield an essential element of the offering of worship for, united with Christ's perfect offering, human worship was able to participate in the worship of the angels.

---

[40] Westfield, *The White Robe*, pp. 149–50. Psalm 141:2.
[41] Westfield, *The White Robe*, p. 152.

13

The Beauty of Holiness and the Holiness of Beauty

Robert Skinner, Jeremy Taylor, John Gauden

With the establishment of the principle that divine forgiveness entirely prevails over human sin it became possible for works, previously discredited, to be included in the offering of worship, and for that offering to become at one with the perfect offering of Christ. In both its physical and spiritual aspects, worship became the means of becoming absorbed in the divine presence and so being raised from the human to the divine. Moreover, Christ being a priest forever made it possible for his offering of himself to be made permanently effective through the worship of the Church, of which the priesthood and all who partake of Christ's intercession are enablers.

The offering of worship and the offering of Christ now being united, it followed that the worship of the liturgy becomes at one with the worship of heaven and able authentically to declare the effect of Christ's continual pleading to the Father, together with the resulting divine acceptance and forgiveness. The worship of heaven being imbued with a holiness in which the quality of beauty is inherent, so increasing attention was paid to beauty in worship, for beauty being in holiness meant that holiness was inherent in beauty.

Robert Skinner

Robert Skinner (1591–1670) was Chaplain to the King, later Bishop of Bristol (1637), Bishop of Oxford (1641), and Bishop of Worcester from 1663.

In a sermon delivered before the king at Whitehall in 1634, Skinner preached on Psalm 96:9: "O worship the Lord in the beautie of Holinesse."[1] From this text, he drew four particulars.

Firstly, *adorate*, worship: this was a humble, devout, religious act. Secondly, *Dominum*, Lord: here was specified the object of worship. Thirdly, in *atrio sancto*, a place of holiness: the place of worship must be a holy place. Fourthly, in *decore sanctitatis*, in the beauty of holiness: the whole offering of worship had to embody beauty, for beauty is holy.

The text, for Skinner, was self-explanatory: "O worship the Lord in the beautie of holinesse" could bear no other interpretation but that the Lord will be worshipped in a place of Holiness; and a place of Beauty, as well as Holiness.[2] It is a holy place, "a place of Holinesse; and a beautifull place, the very beautie of Holinesse". We are to worship "*In atrio Sancto*, or *in Sanctuario*, In his holy Courts, or in his holy Sanctuary; for who can doubt but the *beautie of Holinesse* must needs bee *holy*?"[3] These places of worship are holy because they have been "solemnly *hallowed* and *devoted* in the name of God, and to the glory of God", but also because "our Lord God, most holy, doth inhabite and possesse [them] . . . as his proper Mansion, or dwelling House".[4] These places are holy because of God's gracious presence. They are "indeed Heaven upon Earth, and here *the Tabernacle of God is with men, and God himselfe is with them, Revel. 21*", and because the Lord is there by his holy presence, "*Holy* then we see".[5]

---

[1] Robert Skinner, *A sermon preached before the King at White-Hall, the third December* (London, 1634).

[2] Skinner, *A sermon preached before the King*, p. 15.

[3] Skinner, *A sermon preached before the King*, p. 20. Skinner's italics.

[4] Skinner, *A sermon preached before the King*, pp. 21–2. Skinner's italics.

[5] Skinner, *A sermon preached before the King*, p. 23. Skinner's italics.

Worship to be in holy and beautiful places

Worshipping in a place which is holy is vital, insisted Skinner. He avowed himself free of prejudice against private prayer and gave examples of those who called upon God from various, disparate places and were all heard by God: "Moses in the Sea, Job on the Dunghill, Jeremie in the Dungeon, Daniel in the Den, Jonas in the Whale, the Children in the Furnace, S. Peter and Paul in Prison." Moreover, the apostle Paul himself "would have men pray everywhere, lifting up holy hands *1 Tim.2*". Whilst this was all very well for those who were able to pray with holy hands, the question then became "what shall the sinner doe that is destitute of *holy hands*?" The answer was that the prayers of the righteous, when offered in a holy place, were able to accommodate, or, as he put it, to "make way" for the sinner.[6]

As to this holy place, it must be beautiful as well as holy, for it is in the beauty of holiness that we worship. Skinner noted the various expressions used to describe the holiness of churches: some say "*in Sanctuario magnifico*, in the stately Sanctuarie; Some, *in magnificentia Sanctitatis*, in the sumptuousness or magnificence of Sanctitie; Some, *in splendore Sacrarii*, in the splendour or glory of his holy Place; Some, *in decore Sanctitatis*, in the comelinesse or Beautie of holinesse".[7] Put them all together and the place of worship is holy, comely, stately, sumptuous and glorious, but not more holy than comely, nor more sacred than sumptuous, for if one is separated from the other, both are diminished. Where holy is separated from stately and beauty is separated from sanctity—where "they part and goe asunder, both abate of their perfection".[8] Beauty is so much a part of sanctity that sanctity is diminished where beauty is excluded.

As a result, worship is enhanced by the beauty of the building. The comparison between coming into "a naked, deformed, ruinous Temple, adorned with nothing but dust and cobwebs", and "a goodly reverend beautifull Church" marked by a "devout Magnificence" is striking, remarked Skinner, for does not the "very Fabricke and fashion, and

---

[6] Skinner, *A sermon preached before the King*, p. 24. Skinner's italics.

[7] Skinner, *A sermon preached before the King*, p. 27. Skinner's italics.

[8] Skinner, *A sermon preached before the King*, p. 28.

solemne accommodation" of that which is beautiful "beget in our hearts a religious regard, and venerable thoughts?"[9]

With disdain he noted that some Christians think beauty distracting and superstitious. They imagine that God appreciates only the temples of their bodies and souls and has no regard for their temples of worship. But, he asked, how possibly could the inward grace of these living temples be thought prejudicial to the outward grace of the beauty of holiness? A satisfactory answer to this question he found to be "beyond my capacitie".[10]

Whether we look back to God's service under the Law or to the choicest times under the Gospel, "wee shall soone discover Beautie and Holinesse sweetly accorded".[11] The original Temple was beautiful. Its instruments and utensils were of pure gold, "even to the *Snuff-dishes*, Exod.25".[12] This Temple was a place of wonder and astonishment, "a glorious Spectacle of admiration to all the World", so that when the Queen of Sheba beheld it, the majestical beauty so filled her heart that she was overcome with amazement.[13] The beautification of a place of worship was of such importance that the Fathers and ancient men mourned and wept when the foundation of the later House was laid, because it was less glorious than the first (Ezra 3:12).[14] The reason for this magnificence, Skinner declared, is that God is great and above all gods and this glorious majesty of God continues to inspire the creation of so many stately monuments of piety all the world over.[15] In the cases where churches had been vandalized, "which infidels had desolated", they were restored to a more exquisite beauty than ever before.[16]

---

[9] Skinner, *A sermon preached before the King*, p. 29.
[10] Skinner, *A sermon preached before the King*, p. 30.
[11] Skinner, *A sermon preached before the King*, pp. 30–1.
[12] Exodus 25:38.
[13] Skinner, *A sermon preached before the King*, p. 31. 1 Kings 10:5.
[14] "But many of the priests and Levites and chiefs of the fathers, who were ancient men, that had seen the first house, when the foundation of this house was laid before their eyes, wept with a loud voice."
[15] Skinner, *A sermon preached before the King*, p. 32. 2 Chronicles 2:5.
[16] Skinner, *A sermon preached before the King*, p. 33.

The Jews, Skinner noted, had their beauty of holiness concentrated most conspicuously in the Tabernacle and the Temple, but Christians more especially in the diocesan and mother churches: that is, cathedrals. The example of the Jews, however, was exemplary. They did "excell in *bountie*", sending yearly contributions to Jerusalem for the maintenance of the Temple "because *they delighted in the stones thereof, and had pitie on the dust thereof, Psal.102*".[17] Skinner was delighted that the beauty of holiness in both city and country seemed to "revive and flourish as never more", proof that "Religion hath life in it, and that we are in love with Religion".[18]

As God was to be blessed for moving the king's heart to beautify the house of the Lord in Jerusalem (Ezra 7:27), so also to be blessed were those who strengthened the hands of the workmen involved in removing the abomination of desolation. Those who by their "cheerefull beneficence" support the work of beautifying the place of worship, even "to the poore widow, that shall *cast in her two mites*", will prosper upon earth and have their names recorded in the Book of Life. Moreover, Skinner continued, how desirable would it be that those who were present at the laying of the first stone "might live to behold the consummation, that they, and all the Benefactors, and above all our most *gracious Zerubbabel*, might (when all is finished) worship the Lord, in that beautie of Holinesse".[19] There can be no truer testimony or evidence of "our unfeined esteeme of Holinesse, of our love to God, of our zeale for his Gospell", he exhorted, than to reach out "a liberall hand to the supportation, and a bountifull hand to the exornation [ornamentation] of that sacred edifice where from age to age beyond all discovery Holinesse hath had her habitation".[20] Enemies of the beauty of holiness are properly shamed in order that

> all that lay claime to true Holinesse may preferre the beauty of Holinesse before all other beauties, and with cleane hands and

---

[17] Skinner, *A sermon preached before the King*, pp. 34–5.
[18] Skinner, *A sermon preached before the King*, p. 35.
[19] Skinner, *A sermon preached before the King*, p. 36. Cf. Ezra 3:8–13.
[20] Skinner, *A sermon preached before the King*, pp. 36–7.

pure hearts, delight to worship the Lord, in the proper place of his Worship, the beauty of holinesse.[21]

The only way to preserve religion and the truth untainted, Skinner concluded, is "to have Holinesse duely taught, in the beautie of Holinesse",[22] for that will allow for the authentic worship of truth, unity and piety where the God of truth and peace will bring us all in mercy from the Beauty of Holiness in the kingdom of Grace, to the Holy of Holies in the kingdom of Glory.[23] Far from being an impediment or even an optional ornament, works of beauty were commended by Skinner as a fundamental element of worship, for it was by means of the beauty of holiness on earth that the Holy of Holies in the kingdom of God could be revealed. Through the holiness which beauty embodied, the reality of the divine could be experienced.

Jeremy Taylor

Jeremy Taylor (1613–67), Bishop of Down and Connor 1658, then with Dromore 1661, and Vice-Chancellor of Dublin University 1660, acknowledged that the bedrock of the Christian faith was Christ's offering of himself on the altar of the cross, and because this sacrifice was perfect there could only be one of them, offered once.[24] However, he argued, because the needs of the world would last as long as the world itself, it was necessary that a perpetual ministry be established so that this one sufficient sacrifice of Christ's could be made eternally effectual. So Christ was made a priest for ever, with a priesthood initiated and consecrated

---

[21] Skinner, *A sermon preached before the King*, p. 37.
[22] Skinner, *A sermon preached before the King*, p. 41.
[23] Skinner, *A sermon preached before the King*, p. 43.
[24] Jeremy Taylor, "The Rule and Exercises of Holy Living and Dying", in *The Whole Works of The Right Rev. Jeremy Taylor, D.D.* (London: Longman, Brown, Green & Longmans, F. & J. Rivington, 1856), Vol. III, Chapter IV, Section X, pp. 214–15. Originally published as *The Rules and Exercises of Holy Living* (1650), and *The Rules and Exercises of Holy Dying* (1651).

on the cross, and because of this priesthood, Christ was able to offer continually to the Father the great sacrifice made for the atonement and expiation for all mankind.

Offering of worship is a copy of Christ's offering
For this ministry to be exercised on earth so that the effects of Christ's sacrifice could continue to be realized, Taylor believed that an order had been constituted which, by showing forth the Lord's death by sacramental representation, "may pray unto God after the same manner that our Lord and High Priest does, that is, offer to God and represent in this solemn prayer and sacrament Christ as already offered".[25] Therefore, as Taylor has it, the ministers of the sacrament present the sacrifice of the cross to God by being imitators of Christ's intercession. As a result, that which is offered is a copy of Christ's passion, not simply a remembrance.

Offering of worship includes all
The offering of this sacrifice was not restricted to the prayers and actions of the ministers of the sacrament but involved all the worshippers: "The people are sacrificers too in their manner: for ... by saying 'Amen' they join in the act of him that ministers and make it also to be their own."[26] This is possible because when the people eat and drink the consecrated elements worthily, they receive Christ within them. Their offering of obedience and thanksgiving to God must of necessity include the offering of Christ to God as Christ is now spiritually incorporate within them. By virtue of this indwelling of Christ, the offering of bodies and souls and services to God is made in Him, by Him and with Him, who is His Father's well-beloved, in whom He is well pleased. "This is the sum of the greatest mystery of our religion", asserted Taylor: the sacrifice offered to God in worship is the copy of the passion, and the ministration of the great mystery of our redemption. It is a celebration which is our manner of applying or using the sacrifice offered by Christ.

---

[25] Taylor, *Whole Works*, III, p. 214.
[26] Taylor, *Whole Works*, Vol. III, p. 215.

Offering is of both body and soul

In the offering of this sacrifice, Taylor insisted, God "requires of us to serve Him with an integral, entire, or a whole worship and religion",[27] which was to include the offering both of the body and the soul. The sacrifice of the heart remained essential. God could never be satisfied with the work of the hands when the affections of the heart were absent.[28] Serving God with the body alone, without the soul, would be deceitful. Yet God created the body to complement and support the soul and so the body must not be excluded from any offering that is made. It is not the soul alone which is involved in worship.

Moreover, the offering of the works of the body were not to be despised, for in the process of offering they assume the spiritual nature of the kingdom of the Father, which will be manifest at the day of judgement. Albeit imperfect, the works of the body shall be transformed to be at one with the soul, and in so doing become acceptable to God. God is therefore to be worshipped with all our faculties; with those of the body as well as of the soul, because united with the perfect offering of Christ they are made acceptable to God.

Invoking St Paul's plea in the *Epistle to the Romans* to "present your bodies a living sacrifice", Taylor applied Paul's subsequent qualification that this sacrifice must be "holy", ἁγίαν, and "an intelligent [reasonable] service", λογικὴν λατρείαν.[29] By rendering ἅγιος as "in holy offices", and λατρεία as "in the worship of God", Taylor could construe Paul's exhortation to mean "Your bodyes must be offered up as a Sacrifice in God's worship, that is in adoration (for that's God's worship Corporal) at the Altar (for it is a Sacrifice)." Further, by translating λογικὴ λατρεία as "a reasonable worship, or a worship according to right reason", Taylor was reversing John Jewel's interpretation of λογικὴ as "spiritual".

---

[27] Jeremy Taylor, "A Course of Sermons for All the Sundays in the Year", in *The Whole Works of The Right Rev. Jeremy Taylor, D.D* (London: Longman, Brown, Green & Longmans, F. & J. Rivington, 1856), Vol. IV, Sermon XII, Part I, p. 145.

[28] Taylor, *Works*, Vol. IV, Sermon XII, Part I, p. 147.

[29] Taylor, *Works*, Vol. V, p. 318. Romans 12:1.

If reasonable, continued Taylor, worship must therefore display reasonable characteristics. Firstly, we cannot hope to have our bodies glorified by God if we will not glorify God with our bodies. Secondly, we cannot fulfil the divine command for all the works of God to worship and praise him if our bodies, which are God's workmanship, do not. Thirdly, since the complete man is comprised of both soul and body, the rendering of adoration by both is required for there to be a complete liturgy. Fourthly, the second commandment, in prohibiting external worship of idols, by implication endorsed external worship to God, it being the idols which were the problem, not the external worship.[30]

Taylor was convinced that there were many places of scripture where we were called on to worship God, "to bow down to him, to fall down before his footstool, of external, or corporal adoration".[31] He referred to the use of the verb προσκυνέω, which occurred at the adoration of Jesus by the Magi at the crib and at the temptation of Jesus in the wilderness: "The wise men of the East came to the Babe lying in the Manger, καί πεσόντες προσεκύνησαν αὐτώ: They bowed downe, and worshipped him."[32] Πάντα σοι δώσω ἐάν πεσών προσκυνήσης μοι: "If thou wilt fall downe, and worship me", demanded the Devil. Christ's answer, κύριον τόν θεόν σου προσκύνήσεις, "we must adore, or worship God" indicated that as the Devil would have had Christ do to him, so we must do to Christ.[33] "I think it is clear", concluded Taylor, that

> worship of God supposes externall, and to worship God in spirit is not opposed to worship him in body . . . spirituall worship no more excludes bodily . . . unlesse we say that faith is no part of

---

[30] "Thou shalt not make to thyself any graven image, nor the likeness of any thing that is in heaven above, or in the earth beneath, or in the water under the earth. Thou shalt not bow down to them, nor worship them."

[31] Taylor, *Works*, Vol. V, p. 319.

[32] Taylor, *Works*, Vol. V, p. 318. "and having fallen down did homage to him". Matthew 2:11.

[33] Taylor, *Works*, Vol. V, p. 318. "The Lord your God you shall worship". Matthew 4:9–10.

divine worship: for if it be, then spirituall is not onely internall, or at last excludes not the other.[34]

God is most present in holy places

Once established that God was to be worshipped externally, publicly and bodily, this worship was to occur most properly in the place most hallowed by God's presence. Although God is present "in all places alike in respect of his essence", yet He is present most especially in "Holy places, places consecrate to the service of God by acts of publike, and religious solemnity, in them, and from them to heaven".[35] Throughout scripture, asserted Taylor, it is evident that in the places where he appoints himself to be worshipped, there he records his name, and there he promises his presence, and that will bring a blessing.[36] These places are holy. They are God's Sanctuary, he insisted, and "God's Sanctuary is called the beauty of Holinesse, and the beauty of Holinesse must needs be Holy, and therefore *Adorate Dominum*, worship the Lord in the beauty of Holinesse ... Holinesse for Holy places, *Sancta Sanctis*: Holinesse is its ornament, and beauty."[37] Where God is present, there he is to be worshipped, and worshipped according to what Taylor described as "the degree of his presence". So as God is especially present in holy places such as temples, churches, altars, "therefore these must be the places of our adoration",[38] for it is here that it is possible to behold the fair beauty of the Lord all the days of our life.[39]

Further, because God is present in these consecrated places, it must be that it is in such places that God is most delighted to hear the prayers that are made to Him,[40] and therefore be most likely to bestow special

---

[34] Taylor, *Works*, Vol. V, p. 319.
[35] Taylor, *Works*, Vol. V, pp. 319–20.
[36] Taylor, *Works*, Vol. V, p. 321. Exodus 20:24: "Wherever I cause my name to be invoked, I will come to you and bless you."
[37] Taylor, *Works*, Vol. V, p. 321. Psalms 96:9; 93:5.
[38] Taylor, *Works*, Vol. V, p. 325.
[39] Taylor, *Works*, Vol. V, p. 329. Psalm 27:4.
[40] Jeremy Taylor, "Of the Religion of Holy Places", Discourse VIII, in "The Great Exemplar of Sanctity and Holy Life according to the Christian Institution",

blessings and graces.[41] These are therefore places of advantage to our devotions in respect of acceptance and benediction.[42]

A place of worship is the image of heaven

In fact, Taylor added, the devotions offered in these holy places, these churches and oratories, are even more efficacious because, being the residence of God's name on earth, they are regions and courts of angels and of archangels. A place of worship was the court of God and the image or representation of heaven itself.[43] It was therefore to be held in the highest regard and treated with the greatest devotion. Reverence my sanctuary, Taylor quoted from Leviticus, "for what God loves in an especial manner, it is most fit we should esteem accordingly".[44] Taylor recalled the observation of St Gregory, that

> the church is heaven within the tabernacle, heaven dwelling among the sons of men, and remember that God hath studded all the firmament and paved it with stars, because he loves to have His house beauteous and highly representative of His glory;

The Whole Works of the Right Rev. Jeremy Taylor, D.D., Vol. II (London: Longman, Brown, Green & Longmans, F. & J. Rivington, 1850), Part II, Section XI, p. 315.

[41] Taylor, *Works*, Vol. II, p. 314.
[42] Taylor, *Works*, Vol. II, p. 315.
[43] Taylor, *Works*, Vol. II, p. 321. Chrysostom, Homily xxxvi, *I Corinthians*. "The Homilies of Saint John Chrysostom Archbishop of Constantinople, on the Epistles of Paul to the Corinthians", in *A Select Library of the Nicene and Post-Nicene Fathers of the Christian Church*, ed. Philip Schaff (New York: The Christian Literature Company, 1889), Vol. XII, p. 220. "For the church is no barber's or perfumer's shop, nor any other merchant's warehouse in the market-place, but a place of angels, a place of archangels, a palace of God, heaven itself... In truth, the things in this place are also a heaven."
[44] Taylor, *Works*, Vol. II, p. 322. Leviticus 19:30: "Ye shall keep my sabbaths, and reverence my sanctuary: I am the Lord."

I see no reason we should not do as Apollinaris says God does, "in earth do the works of heaven".[45]

Works of beauty

For Taylor, all this was not only appropriate but necessary, for God is the God of beauty and perfection. This being so, the offering of works in worship is essential. They must not be present in worship for their own benefit, signifying only themselves, for then they would be nothing more than the vain imaginations that were forbidden in the second commandment. Yet when they can be made useful and are innocent in themselves, they are acceptable, as they adorn the worship of God. They are good ministers of edification and are of themselves fit to minister to religion.[46]

Worship and music

On this basis Taylor welcomed music. He argued strongly that music was capable of enhancing the process of edifying, for it could stir up the affections and make religion increasingly pleasurable and acceptable to more of the human faculties. He regarded the singing of psalms as particularly valuable, as was vocal music in general. Being natural to the human condition, vocal music constituted one of the opportunities for pleasure with which humanity was endowed, and being able to invest religion with the experience of that human pleasure heightened the efficacy of worship.

Taylor was less supportive of the use of instruments. He believed they needed to be treated with caution for of themselves they lacked

---

[45] Taylor, *Works*, Vol. II, p. 325. Gregory of Nyssa (335–95). Cf. A. Conway-Jones, *Gregory of Nyssa's Tabernacle Imagery in its Jewish and Christian Contexts* (Oxford Scholarship Online, 2014).

[46] Jeremy Taylor, "Of the Power of the Church in Canons and censures, with their Obligations and Powers over the Conscience", in "Ductor Dubitantium or, The Rule of Conscience", Part II, Book III, Chapter IV, in *The Whole Works of the Right Rev. Jeremy Taylor, D.D.*, ed. Alexander Taylor (London: Longman, Brown, Green & Longmans, F. & J. Rivington, 1855), Vol. X, Part II, Section XI, pp. 408, 411.

the immediacy of human expression. He conceded that they may add "some little advantages" to singing by guiding the voice and so on this basis their use should be permitted, yet his concern was that, lacking a text, instrumental music was of itself unable either to provide instruction or convey wisdom.

Taylor concluded that instrumental music had been permitted in ancient worship only because the use of the voice alone to praise God was in its infancy and the choral skill required was undeveloped. Instruments had therefore been necessary as an accompaniment to support the voice. Once the singers had become more competent, however, the value of choral music was more properly appreciated and, if done well, Taylor deemed it to constitute a far greater contribution to the offering of worship than that of simple speech. This could never be said of instrumental music and so its use was to be restricted to the accompaniment of the voices. Taylor included a quotation from Justin Martyr in support of simple and plain singing in worship, which

> stirs up the mind with a certain pleasure unto an ardent desire of that which is celebrated in the song; it appeases the desires and affections of the flesh; it drives away the evil thoughts of our enemies that are invisible and secretly arise; it makes the mind irriguous [well-watered] and apt to bring forth holy and divine fruits; it makes the generous contenders in piety valiant and strong in adversity, and it brings a medicine and remedy to all the evil accidents of our life.[47]

Such a celebration of the word of God in mind, song and verse then assumed the force of what St Paul described as the sword of the spirit, which had the power to banish evil spirits and perfect the pious mind in virtue. Yet, innately cautious, Taylor remained wary lest the musical rendering of the psalmody "pass further into art than into religion and serves pleasure more than devotion; when it recedes from that native simplicity and gravity which served the affections and holy aspirations of

---

[47] Taylor, *Works*, Vol. X, p. 412. Justin Martyr, *Quaest. cvii. ad orthod.* [p. 468 A].

so many ages of the church".⁴⁸ Music's role ceased to be acceptable when it was made so curious that only musicians could participate and the style of singing became so removed from what he termed "recitative" that the words were not expressed clearly enough to be understood. Taylor drew on the same reference to Basil of Caesarea as had been used by Hooker and Sparrow, yet quoted only the final sentence where Basil, after having expressed his satisfaction with "the delight of melody mingled with heavenly mysteries" added that it was the "tunes of harmonious psalms" which allowed those who sang to be instructed in the faith as the words were plainly articulated.⁴⁹

Curious music supported

Regarding those cathedrals, churches or other institutions with musical establishments where so-called "accurate and curious" music was performed so that "none can join in it but musicians", Taylor was extremely accommodating. "But in this and all things like this", he declared, "the rulers of churches are to do that which most promotes the end of their institution," and if by this means even one person is brought to an appreciation of the Christian faith then this style of singing is to be tolerated. The rule *Salus populi suprema lex esto* was "the rule which in this affair hath no exception: the salvation of one soul is more than all the interests in the world besides".⁵⁰

Over-reach of the reformers

Taylor's defence of the rites and ceremonies of the liturgy and his appreciation of the role of music within it was sharpened in his *Apology for Authorized and Set Forms of Liturgy*. The liturgical reform which had resulted in the First Edwardian Prayer Book of 1549 he believed to be moderate and discreet. Whereas the first reflexions of a crooked tree are not to straightness, he observed, but to a contrary incurvation, the efforts of those reformers were cautious and conservative, being concerned to

---

⁴⁸ Taylor, *Works*, Vol. X, p. 412.

⁴⁹ Basil the Great, *Commentary on the Psalms*, Homily 10.

⁵⁰ Taylor, *Works*, Vol. X, p. 413. *Salus populi suprema lex esto*: "The welfare of the people should be the supreme law."

retain rather than discard elements deserving of further consideration. However, in a fevered desire for a more thorough reformation, the compilers of the Second Prayer Book of 1552 had "cast out something that might with good profit have remained".[51] In their concern to satisfy the world of their zeal to reform and "to avoid their being charged in after ages with a *crepusculum* of religion, a dark, twilight, imperfect reformation, they joined to their own star all the shining tapers of the other reformed churches".[52]

Regrettably, many of these zealots, as he called them, who had fled abroad to avoid the "funeral piles kindled by the roman bishops in Queen Mary's time", agitated for even further liturgical reform. However, the Prayer Book of 1552, even though more extreme than the book of 1549, survived in 1559 with a few Elizabethan modifications. Had it not, Taylor judged that much more of value would have been lost. The canon of the communion, for example, would have been pared away if the Church of England "had mended her piece at the prescription of the Zuinglians"; the service of baptism would have been severely compromised "if she had mended by the rules of the Anabaptists"; east-end stone altars would have remained "by the example of the Lutherans"; and as for the Calvinists, they would simply have "stripped the Church of decency".[53]

Edification and singing of psalms

Embedded in the Prayer Book was the priority given to edification in the faith and Taylor believed this was expressed effectively through the singing of psalms and hymns. He understood the authenticity of this practice to lie deep in religious history. Hezekiah and the princes made it a law in their church to sing praises to the Lord with the words of David and Asaph the seer.[54] Moreover, Christ and his apostles "after the manner

---

[51] Jeremy Taylor, "The Preface to the Apology for Authorized and Set Forms of Liturgy", *The Whole Works of the Right Rev. Jeremy Taylor, D.D.*, ed. Alexander Taylor (London 1853), Vol. V, p. 234.

[52] Taylor, *Works*, Vol. V, p. 234. *Crepusculum*: twilight, dusk.

[53] Taylor, *Works*, Vol. V, p. 235.

[54] Taylor, *Works*, Vol. V, p. 238. "Hezekiah the king and the princes commanded the Levites to sing praise unto the Lord with the words of David, and of Asaph

of the Jews in the feast of passover, sung their hymns and portions of the great Allelujah in the words of David and Asaph the seer too". This tradition was "ready at hand for the use of the church" so that St Paul could observe of the churches in Corinth that "every man had a psalm". Further, Taylor noted that "the church did also make hymns of her own, in the honour of Christ, and sung them; such as was the *Te Deum* made by S. Ambrose and S. Augustine".[55]

Taylor denounced attacks on the established liturgy. The policies of the dissidents, he complained, were being "forced violently by the strength of fancy, or driven on by jealousy and the too fond openings of troubled hearts and afflicted spirits", and such changes as they might achieve would provide only a "fantastic and groundless comfort".[56] The divine liturgy had for Taylor a numinous quality which set it apart from earthly constraints and he saw the Temple at Jerusalem as providing the inspiration for worship which partook of the worship of heaven:

> the order of her services, the beauty of her buildings, the sweetness of her songs, the decency of her ministrations, the assiduity and economy of her priests and Levites, the daily sacrifice, and that eternal fire of devotion that went not out by day nor by night.[57]

Worship and the beauty of holiness

The essence of Taylor's position was that Christ's offering is eternally effective. He argued that this was because Christ dwells in us, and in offering our body and soul we are offering that which is of Christ in us. This offering is therefore embodied in Christ's offering. More, the body is an essential part of this offering, as God is to be worshipped with all human faculties and with everything able to be created to the honour of God. Consequently, works have a place in worship because of their beauty, which is essential to holiness. So God is to be worshipped most obviously in churches, which are dedicated to the presence of Christ and

---

the seer." 2 Chronicles 29:30.
[55] Taylor, *Works*, Vol. V, p. 239.
[56] Taylor, *Works*, Vol. V, p. 232.
[57] Taylor, *Works*, Vol. V, p. 232.

are therefore the most holy places; and being the most holy, they are also the most beautiful. Worship is to be offered in the beauty of holiness and so there is to be no stinting in the provision of works of beauty. Regarding music, whilst it has an obligation for the words which are sung to be clearly articulated, musical establishments accustomed to "accurate and curious" music were to continue without hindrance as part of the offering of beauty, which in itself is holy.

The sacramental representation of Christ's sacrifice, he claimed, was assured by the institution of the priesthood. Through the priesthood the offering of worship was united with that which Christ had already offered, so that what was offered in worship was not a simple remembrance but an actual copy of Christ's sacrifice. Therefore, the offering of the bodies, souls and services in worship must of necessity be accepted by God as they were inexorably united with the sacrifice of Christ. Those works—bodies, souls and service—were an integral work of the sacrifice. Rather than demean and invalidate worship, they enhanced it.

John Gauden

John Gauden (1605–62), Bishop of Exeter (1660) and Bishop of Worcester (1662), expressed his understanding of the offering of worship most fully in his work entitled *The Tears, Sighs, Complaints, and Prayers of the Church of England*.[58] Through liturgical worship, which Gauden referred to as "Devotionals of the Church of England in its public worshipping of God", offering was made to God by means of "Confessions, Prayers, Praises, Psalmodies, and other holy Oblations of rational and Evangelical Services".

Ceremonial as the embodiment of the divine reality
This offering comprised the whole of humanity, and it included works, which Gauden termed "inventions". The reality of the divine was able to be experienced symbolically in the ritual and ceremonial of worship. In

---

[58] John Gauden, *The Tears, Sighs, Complaints, and Prayers of the Church of England* (London, 1659), p. 87.

direct opposition to the reformers, Gauden maintained that "it doth no where appear that our blessed God is so *Anti-ceremoniall a God* as some men have vehemently fancied and clamoured, rather than proved". It is evident, he argued, that

> the God of heaven instituted many ceremonies in the ancient, religious services required of the Jewish Church, and this God would not have done if such ceremonies had been so utterly Antipatheticall against the Divine nature, or contrary to that spiritual sincere worship which he anciently required (beyond all doubt) of the Jew as well as the Christian, as all the Prophets witnesse.[59]

Whilst it was true the Mosaic rites and ceremonies were rendered obsolete when Christ appeared, this was not a reason for the abolition of ceremonial, for these ceremonies were the legitimate shadows of the substance which "follow, attend upon, and betoken the Sun's being now risen and present with his Church". The Church had now incorporated these ceremonies into its own worship, publicly acknowledging them to be the religious, visible and social service of the transcendent divine reality, and the representation of the spiritual and inward worship of God to be appreciated in the faculties of men's souls.[60]

Even if some ceremonies would appear to bear no great fruit, Gauden believed they were not to be discarded for they may well fulfil a role in worship akin to that of hedges, acting as both "a fence and an ornament to Religion".[61] For if some ceremonies were not immediately appreciated as "herbs of grace" or as the "most fragrant and cordial sorts of flowers" yet they were to be retained on the grounds that they would undoubtedly be a means of grace for some of the worshippers at least. Even those ceremonies whose worth was queried "were never found to be so noxious and unsavoury weeds as some pretend".[62]

---

[59] Gauden, *The Tears*, p. 97.
[60] Gauden, *The Tears*, p. 99.
[61] Gauden, *The Tears*, p. 102.
[62] Gauden, *The Tears*, pp. 101–2.

In a direct attack on the reformers' determination to abandon all forms of ceremonial in worship, Gauden retorted that the violent removal of such ceremonies had brought "infinite greater mischiefs *upon Religion & the whole Church*".[63] Experience has already taught us, he added, "that the authentick *ceremonies of the Church of England* were either no hindrances at all, or far lesse, as to the advance of piety, holiness and charity, than the taking away of them".[64] True worshippers, as distinct from those who had perverted the traditions of the authentic Church, were those who "love to serve God in the beauty of holiness and handsomeness, [and] who are ambitious to honour God and his worship with our substance".

It was God's delight to dwell in the sons of men and the meeting of God and man was to be the occasion not only of the offering of humble spirits, contrite hearts and believing souls, but also of such "visible manifestations as are specially circumscribed by times and places".[65] The offering of worship was therefore not to be purely spiritual but was to include visible, physical offerings. As Christ had honoured humanity with the offering of himself at his incarnation, so it was expected that humanity should honour God with the offering of works in proportion to the bounty of God.[66]

The offering made by the Gentiles to the infant Christ was an example of a proper offering to God and so Gauden urged the offering of "Gold, Myrrh, Frankincense, and things equivalent" as a proportionable and acceptable service. God deserved to be worshipped with the best that could be presented, even though God stood in no apparent need of such an offering. Gauden recalled the pouring of the costly ointment on Christ's head, which offering was neither what he needed nor required. What mattered was that he deserved it, as a token of love, honour and gratitude. Far from criticizing the content and expense of this offering, Christ welcomed it; he "accepted it kindly, he justified it publickly, and

---

[63] Gauden, *The Tears*, p. 100. Gauden's italics.
[64] Gauden, *The Tears*, p. 101.
[65] Gauden, *The Tears*, p. 350.
[66] Gauden, *The Tears*, p. 353.

commended it highly ... that it might be an everlasting example of generous Grace and liberal Love".[67]

The holiness of beautiful buildings

The holiness of God could be experienced in the beauty of places of worship, and Gauden reserved some of his harshest criticisms for those whose intention was "to reduce all our material churches, or Houses of God in the Land, to sordid deformities". The very barns and stables of these "thrifty reformers", he complained, were more substantial and in better repair, more decent and cleaner than our churches. Unashamed, "these Church-worms, these moths of Reformation" are constantly murmuring at the large amounts spent on the upkeep of places of worship, even though it is given by others, some long dead. With "supercilious demurenesse and affected zealotry (the better to colour over or conceal their sacrilegious spirits) they are heard very oft to cry out, To what purpose is this waste, this excessive, yea, superstitious cost?"[68] Their blatant hypocrisy was mercilessly exposed when it was revealed that "there is no end of the Cost and Curiosity, the Beauty and Richness of their private Dwellings".

Poetry and music

Gauden advocated the inclusion into worship of two works in particular. In his view, poetry and music were the art forms most essential for the experience of the transcendent, the numinous, in worship. It was therefore a matter of profound regret, he noted, that it was only in heathen worship that the art of poetry had received due recognition. If the use of verse had inspired respect and veneration towards pagan gods, there ought to be no impediment to its inclusion in the offering of Christian worship.[69] As well as poetry, Gauden urged the use of music, vocal as well as instrumental. In an eloquent passage of his *Hieraspistes: A Defence by Way of Apology for the Ministry and Ministers of the Church of*

---

[67] Gauden, *The Tears*, p. 354.
[68] Gauden, *The Tears*, p. 349.
[69] Gauden, *The Tears*, p. 353.

England, he commended singing, melody and music in general, whether oral or organical, in consort or solitary, as crucial. It was through music that the great Creator could be experienced and glorified, both in private and public, either by the skilful practitioners, or those Christians who lack musical ability but who nevertheless with David have harmonious souls joined in devout and gracious hearts. It was nothing short of despicable, he claimed, that music had fallen victim to the "sad severity and moroser humor of some men" who would utterly banish it from all devout and pious uses, "as if all Musick and Musical Instruments had been prophaned ever since the Dedication of Nebuchadnezzar's golden Image".[70] Moreover, together with poetry, praying and preaching, music was a gift bestowed by God in order that humanity might be better disposed to heavenly service, either in more spiritual, holy, humble and calm affections or in more flaming devotions and sweet meditations "which are the usual effects of good and grave Musick on sober and devout souls".[71] Only a religion "flattened with vulgar fears" would forbid Christians to make the best use of music and direct it to the highest end, that is, God's glory.

Offering of good Musick

Further, it was not only through congregational participation in psalms, hymns and spiritual songs that the mind and spirit could be enlightened by the divine truth. Of equal importance was singing "which is sensible in good Musick". The melodious delectation, as Gauden described it, of music which is offered by a choir as distinct from the music of congregational singing has "a secret, sweet, and heavenly virtue to allay the passions of the soul, and to raise up our spirits to Angelical exaltations, by which we may more glory and praise God".[72] That there are those for whom such "good Musick" makes no impression and is unappreciated constitutes no reason for its abandonment. "The immusical rusticity of

---

[70] John Gauden, *Hieraspistes: A Defence by Way of Apology for the Ministry and Ministers of the Church of England* (London, 1653), p. 254.
[71] Gauden, *Hieraspistes*, p. 255.
[72] Gauden, *Hieraspistes*, p. 255.

some men of more ferine (feral) spirits, which no harp can calm", he declared,

> must not prejudice the use and liberty of those Christians who are of more sweet and harmonious tempers, even in this particular gift and excellency of Musick, than which nothing hath a more sensible, and nothing a less sensual delectation.[73]

"If there be not Musick in Heaven, sure there is a kind of heaven in Musick", he stated. The mystery of the divine reality, which defied rational explanation, could be experienced most vividly through the arts, in particular poetry and music, which made the immoderation and violence of those who sought to banish the arts from worship even more intolerable. Their opposition "hath in it a vein of the old Picts and Scythian barbarity", and their efforts "to deprive men and Christians of one of the divinest Ornaments, most harmless contentments and indulgences, which in this world they can enjoy" marked them indelibly as an enemy to humanity and divinity alike. There is no more blatant example of "the rude and unreasonable transports to which men are subject in what they call religious Reformations". For example, he warned, the misplaced vigour and severity with which these reformers were prohibiting the art of music from worship would only have the disastrous effect of making religion "more sour and heavy than God in his Word hath required". Since God specifically commands singing to his praises and loves a cheerful temper in his service, it makes no sense to be an enemy of "the right and sanctified use of melody or music". Music being "of all sensible beauty, the most harmless and divin[e]", there can be no reason, he concluded, "why [music] should be thought to deform us Christians or be wholly excluded from making a part in the beauty of holiness".[74] Gauden unleashed a fierce denunciation of those who had so wilfully denuded worship of the beauty of its music and the dignity of its ceremonial:

---

[73] Gauden, *Hieraspistes*, p. 255.
[74] Gauden, *Hieraspistes*, p. 256.

No men are branded with blacker and juster marks of Vilenesse and Unworthinesse, than those who either grudged at, or secretly defrauded, or forcibly took away what was once dedicated or given to the Worship of God, the Honour of Christ, and the Benefit of his Church.[75]

In his *Considerations touching the Liturgy of the Church of England*, Gauden continued his attack on those who condemned music, particularly in cathedrals and other great churches. The music to which objection was made, Gauden pointed out, was as lawful as any of the metrical psalms, hymns and "singing to tunes" so wholeheartedly accepted by the detractors. There should be no scruple that "*Musick* of voice and instruments may be so *gravely* and *solemnly* applyed, as may very much fit the temper of mens spirits ... when either sad or solemne with grief, or *chearfull* and *exalted* with joy".[76]

Gauden judged this to be an impressive precedent for the acceptance of music. David and the whole Church of the Jews served God in spirit and truth "amidst those joyful and harmonious noises", and they used both singers and musical instruments. Music had been so embedded in the worship of God throughout the ages, so sweet, so angelical, so heavenly and divine, that "it is a pity God should not have the *glory* and *honour* of it in his service, and the *Church* an *holy comfortable use* of it". Gauden thought it a complete nonsense that such an orient pearl as music should be used only at civil conventions or debased by being applied to "wanton carols" and "vain effusions". He found such misuse akin to putting a jewel in a swine's snout. As such a jewel, however, church music was to be treated with the utmost respect for it had its birth at Christ's nativity with the heavenly choir of angels.

Gauden conceded that some discreet regulations and emendations might be introduced, such as not singing the creeds or commandments, the lessons and those parts of the liturgy "which are most *plain, doctrinall,* and *fundamentall,* which ought to be fitted to the meanest auditors

---

[75] Gauden, *Hieraspistes*, p. 352.

[76] John Gauden, *Considerations touching the Liturgy of the Church of England* (London, 1661), p. 35. Gauden's italics.

ears and understanding".[77] These concessions were acceptable and in a reference to the canticles at Morning and Evening Prayer he pointed out that there are already opportunities for music to be offered "in the pauses or intervals of the lessons, and in the close of Divine Service".

A place for excellent music
As well, the psalms, hymns and holy and devout anthems may be aptly used, with settings that are not restricted to rendering the words as though they were read, or plainly sung, but "advanced with *excellent Musick*". It was important that such music should be included in worship for not only did it "suit with and regulate the *common peoples* tunes and *singing*", but it was also able "to be elevated to those *perfections* of Skill, which are worthy of the best Quires, and those *chief singers*, or Masters of *Symphony*, which were and still are in the Church of *England*".[78] The debasing and exclusion of music as an art and a science from the worship of the Church was due entirely to "those mens rudeness to abandon Church Musick" and their grim determination "to fill all things with the alarums of war, and crys of confusion". However, ceremonies that even some grave and learned men initially found objectionable were ultimately accepted "not as any Sacramentall signes conferring any grace ... but meerly as visible tokens or memorials, apt by a sensible sign to affect the *understanding* with something worthy of its thoughts as signified thereby".[79]

These theologians—Skinner, Taylor, Gauden—all contributed to the dismantling of the reformed position that sin had so corrupted works as to disqualify them from worship and that therefore the sacrifice had to be the offering of the spirit alone. This theological revision was a pivotal factor in the acceptance of works in worship. At the same time, the restrictive definition of edification, so beloved of the reformers, continued to be reconstructed in more generous and inclusive terms.

The argument that the offering of worship became united with Christ's offering on the cross was pursued with increasing vigour, giving

---

[77] Gauden, *Considerations touching the Liturgy*, pp. 35–6. Gauden's italics.

[78] Gauden, *Considerations touching the Liturgy*, p. 36. Gauden's italics.

[79] Gauden, *Considerations touching the Liturgy*, p. 36. Gauden's italics.

strength to the conviction that the worship of the Church participated in the worship of heaven. As earthly worship engaged with heavenly worship it assumed the holiness of the divine. Beauty was increasingly acknowledged to be an inherent quality of the divine holiness and so it followed that holiness had to be an inherent quality of beauty. This in turn meant that holiness was to be found in the beauty of what was offered in earthly worship. As a result, the beauty of the elements of worship—music, ceremonial, art, stained glass and architecture—assumed critical importance, for in their beauty could be perceived the holiness of God. The offering of worship became holy by participation in the offering of Christ and had therefore to be of the most exquisite beauty possible, for holiness could be perceived through beauty and God was to be worshipped in the beauty of holiness.

This growing theological appreciation of the beauty of holiness gave rise to a vivid acknowledgement of the holiness of beauty and such was the force of this coherence of beauty with holiness that the reinstatement of the offering of worship with propitiatory significance became increasingly acknowledged.

Conclusion

Fundamental theological positions enshrined in the sixteenth-century Prayer Books were vigorously contested, both up to and immediately beyond the Restoration of 1660, particularly those concerning the so-called fatal corruption of humanity, the inability of anything other than a spiritual offering to be acceptable, the impossibility of the offering of worship being united with Christ's offering, and the aversion to any sense of the divine presence being embodied in worship. Any idea of worship constituting a unity of heaven and earth had been dismissed as illusory. As a result, there was no attempt to realize a sense of otherness or transcendence, for there was no otherness or transcendence to realize. The point of worship was not to embody Christ's offering but simply to remember it.

Scholarship that emerged in critical response to the theology of the reformers demonstrated that it was possible in worship to be brought into a living experience rather than a simple remembrance of the divine, thereby investing the offering of worship with a significance far removed from the predilections of the reformers.

Such revisions made it possible for the offering of worship to be invested with a character more sympathetic to being united with the perfect offering of Christ, as a result of which the worship of the liturgy became at one with the worship of heaven and was able authentically to declare the effect of Christ's continual pleading to the Father, together with the resulting divine acceptance and forgiveness. This understanding of worship allowed for a broader acceptance of the worth accompanying ritual and ceremonial, including music, and more appreciation of the beauty of holiness and the holiness of beauty. In both its physical and spiritual aspects, worship was once again seen to embody the divine presence. Moreover, Christ being a priest for ever made it possible for his offering of himself to be made permanently effective through the worship of the Church.

The worship of heaven being imbued with a holiness in which the quality of beauty is inherent, so increasing attention was paid to beauty in worship, for beauty being inherent in holiness meant that holiness was inherent in beauty. The realms of beauty and holiness became intertwined.

This realignment of the nature of worship is consistent with an authentic Anglican position which has consistently embraced the view that the offering of worship enables entry into another dimension of experience, another consciousness, and facilitates an engagement with a deeper, more fundamental reality than that which could ever be expressed in terms of rational explanation or statements of doctrinal propositions.

Through worship it would once again be possible to be incorporated into the divine web of ultimate reality, an environment in which it is possible to experience, in the words of Anselm of Bec, the presence of "something-than-which-nothing-greater-can-be-thought".[1]

Being an embodiment rather than a remembrance of the divine, worship evoked a consciousness of a mystery, incomprehensible and enigmatic.[2] This experience has been described as the *numinous*, the wholly other, a *magisterium*, an experience of the divine beyond rational explanation.

It testifies to a realm of experience beyond all known thoughts and understandings. It is a dimension inspired and inhabited by the eternal God. In monastic terms, the liturgy is the path towards an exalted "ecstasy", a flight into the cloud of unknowing, the place where God is and where the true contemplation of the creative stillness of God is possible. It is an embodiment which has been described as the *splendor veritatis*, the radiance of truth and a declaration of "the immutable values

---

[1] Rudolf Otto, *The Idea of the Holy: An Inquiry into the Non-Rational Factor in the Idea of the Divine and Its Relation to the Rational*, tr. John W. Harvey, 2nd edn (Oxford: Oxford University Press, 1958).

[2] Otto, *The Idea of the Holy*.

of a transcendental order".[3] The effect of the transcendence and otherness of God is poignantly expressed by Eliphaz the Temanite in his response to the prophet Job: "A spirit passed before my face; the hair of my flesh stood up."[4]

This is the appreciation of worship affirmed by John Donne: "Of Christ it is said, Without a Parable spake he not", and it was this "darke way" that increased the desire to penetrate the mystery of God.[5] The God of our salvation, according to Donne, "calls us to Holinesse, to Righteousnesse, by Terrible things ... Terrible, that is, stupendious, reverend, mysterious".[6]

This is an understanding of worship which is appreciative of the beauty of holiness and the holiness of beauty and values the arts—music being one of the most significant—as part of that offering. It is the manifestation, the actualization in the present of the Kingdom which is to come—"that which is above time and belongs to another aeon".[7] The time of the liturgy is the fulfilment of time itself, the time of salvation.[8]

This reversal of crucial theological principles underpinning the Book of Common Prayer undermines any claims that those principles continue to represent a determinate position in any final or authoritative sense, and

---

[3] Otto von Simson, *The Gothic Cathedral: Origins of Gothic Architecture and the Medieval Concept of Order*, 3rd edn (Princeton: Princeton University Press, 1988), pp. v and xx. Reference to von Simson's account of perfect proportions is found in Robert A. Scott, *The Gothic Enterprise* (Berkeley, CA: University of California Press, 1985), pp. 121–33.

[4] Job 4:15. Quoted by A. E. Housman, *The Name and Nature of Poetry* (Cambridge: Cambridge University Press, 1939), p. 46.

[5] *The Sermons of John Donne*, ed. E. M. S. Simpson and G. R. Potter, 10 vols (Berkeley, CA: University of California Press, 1953), Vol. 7, Sermon 12, p. 16.

[6] Donne, *Sermons*, Sermon 12, p. 15.

[7] Alexander Schmemann, *Introduction to Liturgical Theology*, tr. A. E. Moorhouse (London: Faith Press, 1970), p. 63.

[8] Alexander Schmemann, *For the Life of the World: Sacraments and Orthodoxy* (Crestwood, NY: St Vladimir's Seminary Press, 1973), p. 57.

that the offering of worship according to the Book of Common Prayer is only to be interpreted through that original lens.

The reluctance to countenance such a living experience in worship reflects an aversion to engage with the *mysterium* and numinous character of the divine that defies easy characterization, instead seeking refuge in a perceived propositional security.

The theological and liturgical principles expressed in the Prayer Books of the sixteenth century were a phenomenon of their time and cannot lay claim to be the sole lens through which the worship of the Anglican Church is in perpetuity to be understood. An appreciation of the dynamics of worship continued to evolve, embracing a more thorough awareness of the reality of the Divine and a deeper recognition of the experience of transcendence.

Index

Aaron   20, 122, 147, 241
Abel   123, 151
Act of Uniformity   22, 45, 53–54, 57
Adam   25, 29, 129, 166–67, 175, 187
Alberic of Monte Cassino   6
Alexander the Great   65, 106
Amalar of Metz   10–11
Ambrose of Milan   107, 226, 227, 258
Andrewes, Lancelot   162
   on acceptability of the offering in Christ   146–50
   on divine mercy   144–45
   liturgical priorities of   150–51
   on music in worship   154–55
   offertory, prioritizing over alms collection   151–52
   place of worship, reverence for   153–54
angels   15, 79, 134, 179, 190, 200, 228
   in places of worship   135, 253
   singing of the angels   108, 114, 226–27, 234, 239
   worship of the angels   130, 239, 242
Anselm of Bec   269
Apollinaris of Laodicea   254
Aquinas, Thomas   6
Ashewell, Thomas   20
Athanasius of Alexandria   48, 75
Audley, Thomas (Lord Audley)   91
Augustine of Hippo   48, 61–62, 65, 66–67, 75, 104–5, 227, 235, 258

Bale, John   60, 61n6, 79, 83
Banester, Gilbert   20
Barthelot, John   98–99
Basil of Caesarea   88, 89, 102–3, 106, 140, 141, 235, 256

Basilius Magnus   114
beauty of holiness   3, 133, 261, 269
   beauty in worship, appreciation of   231, 241, 243, 267, 268
   holy places, God as most present in   252–53
   music, role in the holiness of beauty   264, 270
   works of beauty, condemnation of   39–42
   worship in a beautiful place   233, 244, 245–48, 258–59, 262
Becon, Thomas   26, 33, 35, 68, 77
   on David's offering to God   42–43
   music, abhorrence for   63–65, 70, 76
   musical performers, antagonism toward   81–83
   on silent prayer of the heart   71–72
   on works of man not equal to the sacrifice of Christ   31, 41
Bentham, Thomas   59
Berengar of Tours   5–6
Bernard of Clairvaux   103
Book of Common Prayer   46, 76, 80, 114, 116, 166, 228, 229
   1549 Prayer Book   24, 45, 52, 54, 151, 256, 257
   1552 Prayer Book   22, 45, 49, 52, 54, 57, 116n16, 150, 151, 257
   1559 Prayer Book   53–54, 57, 257
   1637 Prayer Book   206, 223, 226
   The Book of Common Prayer Noted   47
   corruption and   23–24
   Notes and Collections on The Book of Common Prayer   221
   Prayer of Consecration in   225–26

INDEX

Prayer of Oblation in 206, 223–24
worship dynamics of 270–71
Browne, John 20
Buckeridge, John
 on the offering of works as persuasive 163–65
 on physical as well as spiritual offering 158–61, 162–63
 on the unity of human and divine 156–57
Bullinger, Heinrich 54–55, 61–62, 67–69, 73–76, 82–83, 86, 97–99

Calfhill, James 37–38, 40, 43, 65–66
Calvin, John 49, 112–13, 116, 193
Cartwright, Thomas 116, 119, 121
 cathedrals, decrying 117–18
 liturgical changes, supporting 111, 112
 singing, opposition to 113–14, 122–23
Cassander, Georg 222
cathedrals 83, 118, 208, 221, 247
 cathedral choirs 84, 107, 110, 220
 cathedral worship 80, 82, 205
 music in 91–92, 117, 207, 229–30, 256, 265
  Winchester Cathedral 76–77, 84
Cecil, William 96, 99
Celestine I, Pope 8–9
Chrysostom, John 37, 103, 222
Cole, Henry 78
Comfortable Words 29, 44
Common Prayer 58, 64, 76, 80, 96–97
Conyers, Thomas 94–95
Cooper, Thomas 33–34, 35–36, 41
Cornysh, William 21
Cosin, John 46, 221–30
Council of Trent 8
Cranmer, Thomas 24, 28, 32, 34, 45
Crowley, Robert 50, 95
Cyprian of Carthage 159–60

David 62, 107, 133, 149, 155, 186
 Andrewes, in praise of 153–54
 Asaph the seer and 257–58
 instruments, utilizing 105, 119–20, 121, 227
 as a poet 102, 137–38
 psalms of 101, 103, 104, 185, 189, 229
 song, use of 112, 119–20, 204, 210, 213–14
 temple, building for God 147–48
 worship offered by 42–43, 197, 233, 263, 265
Day, John 89, 95, 100n41
Dean, Nowell 84
Diodore of Tarsus 226
Donne, John 181, 192, 196, 270
 ceremonies, likening to shadows 186–87
 on divine forgiveness 166, 168–69, 172
 faith and works, on the complementarity of 179–80
 on human sin and corruption 166–67
 on incorporation into Christ 172, 173–74, 175
 on music for worship 187–91
 on the mystery of the divine 182–83
 on Original sin 169–70, 171
 on parable use by Christ 183–84
 psalms, on the singing of 193, 194
 reformers, on their goal of destruction 185–86
 transubstantiation, distinguishing from propitiatory sacrifice 176–77
Dunstable, John 19
Durand, Guillaume 81

edification 2, 3, 61, 79, 105, 112, 118, 211, 228, 235, 254
 Cartwright on music as negating edification 111, 113–14
 clarity in words and 96, 122
 edifying music 120–21, 139–41, 215–16
 musicians, edification of 51–52, 84, 85n99

reformers as focused on 97, 153, 266
Sanderson on edification 214–16
singing of psalms and 87, 103–4, 142, 193, 257–58
style of singing as enabling 45–50
vernacular use for 44–45, 68
Widdowes on edification beyond words 236, 237
Edward VI, King 52, 53, 54–55, 224
Eliphaz the Temanite 270
Elizabeth I, Queen 53, 54, 55–57, 70, 92, 93–94, 98, 154, 225
Erasmus 49n15, 74, 75
Essenes 219
Eusebius of Caesarea 35–36, 105, 108, 160
Evening Prayer 87, 150, 232–33, 266

faith 29, 50, 73, 75, 82, 92, 125
 in Christ 1, 33, 91, 248
 complementarity of faith and works 179–80
 edification as an aspect of faith 2, 44, 45, 214, 215, 236, 257
 God, faithfulness of 171–72
 liturgical practices not detrimental to 112–13
 music accused of interfering with 61, 67, 77, 79, 80, 86, 118
 music as stimulating faith 104, 110, 111, 120, 140, 141, 256
 musicians, teaching in the faith 51–52, 84–85
 psalm singing as an expression of faith 87–88, 89
 works of beauty as obscuring true principles of faith 39, 40
 worship, faith expressed through 69, 107, 201, 202, 213, 233, 251–52
Fawkyner, John 20–21
"Fifteen Oes of St Bridget" 12
Flavian of Antioch 226
Flavius Josephus 105
forgiveness 72, 166, 190, 204

potency of divine forgiveness 168–69
sacrifice, forgiveness through 32, 77
 of sin 151, 168–69, 170, 171, 173, 196, 208, 238, 243
Westfield on divine forgiveness 238–39
works and forgiveness 3, 164, 196, 208, 212, 243
worship, forgiveness through the offering of 2, 43, 131, 268
Fourth Lateran Council 7

Gardiner, Stephen 16, 17, 18, 52
Gauden, John 259–67
Gregory Nazianzus 63, 88, 89, 253–54
Grindal, Edmund 27, 55, 59, 84, 97, 98
Gualter, Rodolph 97, 99
Guest, Edmund 59, 60–61, 69

Hampton, John 20
Hannah 71, 115n10
Henry VIII, King 21, 45, 53
Hilary of Poitiers 226
Holgate, Robert 49, 51
Holy Spirit 29, 62, 118, 168, 175, 192
 divine truth, using music to convey 140–41, 187
 music as a gift of 102–3, 189–90
 sacrifices made by the grace of 37–38
homilies 24–25, 28, 66–67, 102–3, 140. See also sermons
Hooker, Richard 256
 Christ's offering, on participation in 126–29, 130
 music, on its role in worship 135–41, 235
 psalms, on the singing of 142–43
 on salvation by Christ 124–25
 on the unity of worship 131–34
 works, on the acceptance of 125–26
Hooper, John 24, 25–26, 29, 31, 68
Hopkins, John 50, 95
Horne, Robert 76, 80, 84, 90, 97, 98
Howard, Henry 111, 119–23
Humphrey, Laurence 97, 99

INDEX

Ignatius of Antioch 108, 114, 226–27
Injunctions 59, 69, 90, 92
   music, on the style and quality of
     49, 207
   musicians, on the education of 51, 84
   organs, on restricting the use of
     79–80
   Royal Injunctions 57, 80
   on singing to resemble speech
     76–77
Innocent III, Pope 7

Jerome of Stridon 72, 81, 132, 133–34
Jesus Christ 1, 40, 164, 170, 191, 192, 260
   anointing of Christ 123, 145–46,
     146–50, 240, 241, 261–62
   blood of Christ 12, 127, 148, 171,
     178, 182, 223
   body of Christ 4, 5, 6, 126, 129,
     131, 158, 176, 177, 185, 224
   body and blood of Christ 1, 3,
     4, 5–6, 7–8, 10, 11, 14–15, 17,
     176–77, 216, 217–18, 219, 224
   coming of Christ 188, 201, 237
   crucifixion of Christ 12, 14, 56,
     127, 157, 176
   death of Christ 31, 32–33, 38, 41,
     91, 171–72, 178, 180, 206, 219,
     223, 224, 231
   divine nature of Christ,
     incorporation into 172, 173–74,
     175
   eucharist, presence of Christ in
     5–6, 7, 60
   hymns, Jesus as singing 73–74, 211,
     226, 257–58
   at the Last Supper 36, 226, 232,
     234–35
   liturgical reality of Christ's presence
     181, 216
   musical instruments and 190, 227
   parables, Jesus speaking in 182, 270
   priesthood of Christ 13, 156, 198,
     242, 243, 248–49, 268–69
   putting on of Christ 172–73
   righteousness of Christ 30, 175,
     197–98, 204
   sacrifice of Christ for our sins
     29–31, 32, 33, 36, 126, 176
   salvation through Christ 14, 15, 22,
     30, 31, 35, 124–25, 126, 162
   worship of Christ 72, 159, 251–52
   See also offering of Christ
Jewel, John 30, 33, 35, 56, 66, 67, 71, 250
   1559 Prayer Book, pleasure over
     restoration of 54–55
   cathedral churches, distaste for 83
   Holy Spirit, on sacrifices made by the
     grace of 37–38
   on humanity as sinful 26–27
   organs in the church, against 78
   psalms, on the singing of 87–89, 90
   works of beauty, condemning 40, 43
Judas 148, 149, 150
justification 124–25, 179–80, 198
Justin Martyr 255
Justinian, Emperor 68

Kilwardby, Robert 6
Kingdom of God 248, 250, 270

Lake, Arthur 196–205
Lanfranc of Bec 6
Laud, William 205–8
liturgy 88, 180, 230, 235, 251, 270
   all believers, liturgy offered up for
     233–34
   Andrewes, liturgical priorities of
     150–51, 152, 155
   eucharistic liturgy, sacrifice of Christ
     in 222, 224–25
   liturgical practices 11, 61, 111,
     112–13, 123
   liturgical prayers 217–18
   liturgical reform 2–3, 53, 256, 257
   liturgical singing 19, 75, 97
   liturgical worship 1, 75, 213, 259
   mediaeval liturgy, reformers
     condemning 36, 43
   music as a component of 45, 53,
     91–92, 229, 236

offering of Christ, liturgical
    re-enactment of   10–11, 224
presence of Christ in the liturgy   8,
    59, 181, 216
propitiatory status of liturgical
    offering   219, 224–25
Queen Elizabeth, liturgical
    preferences of   56–57
sixteenth century, liturgical
    principles in   21, 271
Taylor, defence of the liturgy   256, 258
worship of the liturgy united with the
    worship of heaven   243, 268

Maldonado, Juan   222
Martyr, Peter   55–56, 70, 83, 87–88
Mary I, Queen   52–53, 257
Mary Magdalene   71–72, 123, 146,
    149–50
Merbecke, John   41, 47–49, 62, 73, 77,
    78, 86
mercy   32, 42, 150, 173, 190, 191, 196,
    248
    as available to all   170–71
    in Book of Common Prayer   151
    through Christ's death   223–24
    divine mercy   144–46, 168, 176, 197
    God's judgement, as ever tempering
        169–70
    human mercy   128–29
metrical psalmody   50, 194, 265
    Cosin as condemning the practice
        of   228–29
    edification of the faith and   87–88
    Hooker on the use of   139, 141
    improvement in quality of   89–90
    Parker as supporting   94–96,
        99–103
    Thorndike on chanting vs. singing of
        psalms   220–21
Morning Prayer   54, 87, 150, 151, 153,
    232–33, 266
Moses   71, 123, 154, 182, 189, 227, 245
Mundy, William   53
music   90, 192, 203, 212, 236, 241, 268

alternatim singing   107, 113–14,
    226–27
antagonism toward musical
    performers   81–83
Augustine on sin as linked with
    melodious music   61–62
as benefitting the human experience
    188–90
in cathedrals   91–92, 117, 207,
    229–30, 256, 265
church music   88, 139, 194–95
church organs, in praise of   237–38
David as using song in worship
    112, 119–20, 204, 210, 213–14
edifying music   45–49, 120–21,
    139–41, 215–16
elimination of music   45, 80, 97, 118
exquisite singing   97, 98, 121, 123
faith, teaching to musicians   84–85
good music, on the offering of
    263–66
holiness of beauty, music's role in
    259, 264, 270
instrumental music   77–80, 138,
    208, 215, 227–28, 255
liturgy, music as a component of
    45, 53, 91–92, 229, 236
music of the spheres   190, 191
a place for excellent music   266–67
poetry and music   262–63
the power of music   103–7
psalms, singing of   100–101, 107–9,
    142–43, 219–20, 226–27
reformers on the use of   2, 21,
    61–70, 77–80, 86, 93, 97–99, 104,
    112, 113, 121–22, 264
sense of the words and   66–67,
    109–10
singing during worship services   48,
    76–77, 113–20
singing in the spirit   70–76
solemn music of early Christians
    228–29
as transcending words   137–39
as uniting earth and heaven   187–88

whole of humanity, music engaging 135–37
worship, music as a component of 19–21, 57, 58, 107, 110, 122–23, 154–55, 209–11, 226, 231, 239–40, 242, 254–56, 267
Myrc, John 13

Nathan 120, 147
Nero, Sextus, Emperor 65
Nettesheim, Henrich Cornelius Agrippa von 64
Nicephorus I, Patriarch 107–8
Nowell, Alexander 27, 40, 56–57

offering of Christ 124, 131, 182, 261
　as brought into being 224–25
　commemoration of 156–57, 160, 162
　as a continual offer 13–14, 15, 205, 222
　on the cross 231–33, 248, 266–67
　efficacy of 175, 203, 222, 243, 248–49, 258
　eucharist as memorializing 14–15, 163, 205–6, 223, 232
　liturgical re-enactment of 10–11, 224
　participation in Christ's offering 126–29
　as a perpetual memory 205, 225–26
　in Prayer of Consecration 225–26
　as propitiatory 4, 15, 29–30, 32–34, 34–36, 53, 61, 130, 176, 206, 222, 224
　remembrance of 2, 12, 22, 34, 36, 43, 44, 66, 143, 218, 219, 231
　representation of the original sacrifice 8, 217–18
　righteousness of 30, 198–99, 204
　sacramental representation of 15, 157, 259
　salvation through 15, 35, 125
　as unique 29–31, 32, 43, 78, 216
　works incorporated in 144, 165
　worship in unity with 3, 9, 16, 53, 57, 157, 234, 242, 266–67

as acceptable to God 146–50, 212, 240, 250
as an authentic representation of Christ's offering 206–7
ceremonial of heaven and earth, as conjoined with 135
continuation of offering through worship 221, 231
Donne on 195
Hooker on 130
Lake on 196–205
Laud on 205–8
negation of 22, 28, 59, 268
Robarts on 208–11
worship as a copy of Christ's sacrifice 249, 259
Overall, John 223–24

Parker, Matthew 136
　Advertisements 96–97, 98, 99
　alternatim singing, defending 113–14
　cathedral music, helping to shape 91–92
　metrical psalms, version of 99–103
　on the power of music 103–7
　psalms, on the method of singing 107–9
　sense of the words, on music enhancing 109–10
　on the understanding of words during worship 94–97
　Whythorne as serving under 93–94
Parkhurst, John 54, 69
Paschasius Radbertus 5
Paul 115, 182, 202, 221, 236, 245, 250, 255, 258
　on the faithfulness of God 171–72
　on hymns and spiritual songs used in worship 75, 102, 211, 226
　musicians as memorizing Epistles of 51–52, 85
　on singing with the spirit and the mind 71, 73
Pelagius 133
Philip, King 65

Philo of Alexandria 101, 105, 219–20
Pliny the Younger 226
poetry 102, 137–38, 262–63, 264
Prayer of Consecration 10, 223, 225
Prayer of Oblation 206, 223–24
private devotions 45, 54, 75, 108, 123, 233, 245
Prosper of Aquitaine 8–9
Puritans 111, 237
Pythagoras 106

Rabanus Maurus 62, 76, 140
Ratramnus of Corbie 5
reconciliation 15, 28, 29–30, 33, 34, 43, 176
the Reformation 1, 185, 220, 221
reformers 29, 43, 52, 119, 124, 144, 146, 161, 163, 170
  as anti-ceremonial 225, 260, 261
  beautiful buildings, against the use of 117, 262
  desolate understanding of human nature 28, 35, 166
  Donne as departing from views of 180, 181, 185–86, 196
  edification, giving prominence to 84, 153, 214–15, 266
  frustration experienced by 55–57
  Hooker as countering 125, 126, 128, 130, 137, 139, 143
  Lake as correcting views of 196, 201, 203, 204, 205
  mediaeval liturgy, condemning 36, 43
  musical performers, antagonism toward 81–83
  negation of worship united to the offering of Christ 59, 268
  optimism of reformers 53–55
  over-reach of 256–57
  reversal of basic theological positions held by 2–3
  sacrifice, reformed interpretation of 35, 37, 156
  singing of psalms by sides, not favoring 107, 114
  singing resembling speech, promoting 76–77
  on the use of music 2, 21, 61–70, 77–80, 86, 93, 97–99, 104, 112, 113, 121–22, 264
  vernacular, preference for 67–69
  words of worship, on the comprehension of 66–67, 87, 110
righteousness 1, 23, 26, 41, 141, 170, 184, 245, 270
  of Jesus Christ 29, 30, 175
  Original Righteousness 197–98, 204
  sacrifice of righteousness 198–99
Robarts, Foulke 208–11

sacraments 12, 53, 131, 153, 155, 156, 181, 185, 218, 249, 257
  Christ in the eucharistic sacrament 5, 7, 176, 177–78, 219
  Holy Communion 29–30, 162
  hymn singing after receiving sacrament 234–35
  music and the sacraments 64, 237, 266
  "Of Common Prayer and Sacraments" homily 66–67
  Order of Communion and 44
  Parker on the administration of prayer and sacraments 96–97
  Prayer of Oblation before distribution of the Sacrament 223–24
  reformers' stance on 112, 180
  sacramental representation of Christ's offering 216, 217, 259
salvation 12, 25, 160, 176, 197, 256
  through Jesus Christ 14, 15, 22, 30, 31, 35, 124–25, 126, 162
  music, role in 155, 190, 191
  negation of salvation through propitiatory music 63–64
  time of liturgy as time of salvation 270
Sampson, Thomas 56, 70, 97, 99
Sanderson, Robert 212–16

Sandys, Edwin   26, 30, 38–39, 41, 56, 59, 60, 76, 77, 80, 82
sermons   24, 25, 28, 65, 69, 70
　by Andrewes   144–46, 152, 153, 154
　on the beauty of holiness   244–48
　cross and saints, on relinquishing   56–57
　by Donne   173–74, 194
　on metrical psalms   87, 90
　on the Schismatical Puritan   236–37
　on worship   212–13, 214–15
Sheppard, John   53
sin   28, 42, 91, 100, 112, 125, 204, 241, 245, 266
　of Adam   167, 187
　divine forgiveness for   151, 168–69, 170, 171, 173, 196, 208, 238, 243
　God's displeasure with   24, 25
　gravity of sin   22, 124
　melodious music, sin as linked with   48, 61–62
　no sacrifice to God as appeasing sin   34–35
　offering of Christ for our sins   15, 29–31, 32, 33, 36, 126, 176
　offering of worship for human sin   2, 222
　Original sin   23, 26, 167, 168, 169–70, 171, 190, 191, 197, 198, 204
　sacrifices of the Old Law for forgiveness of sin   77–78
　works, no remission of sins for   28, 41, 165
　worship offered by sinners   213, 233
Skinner, Robert   244–48, 266
Smart, Peter   229
Socrates Scholasticus   108, 226–27
Song of Deborah   189, 210
Sparrow, Anthony   231–35, 256
Sternhold, Thomas   50, 89, 95

Tallis, Thomas   19n62, 20, 53, 109
Taverner, John   19n61, 20, 46
Taylor, Jeremy   248–59, 266
Te Deum (canticle)   46, 94–95, 227, 258

Theodoret of Cyrus   226
Thorndike, Herbert   216–21
Timotheus the musician   103
transubstantiation   6, 7–8, 176–78, 218
Tye, Christopher   50, 53, 91

Valens, Emperor   88
Vitalian, Pope   78

Walton, Izaak   194–95
Westfield, Thomas   238–42
White, Robert   53
Whitgift, John   111, 112–13, 114, 115–17, 118, 119
Whythorne, Thomas   93–94
Widdowes, Giles   236–38
Wisdom, Robert   68, 81
Withers, George   98–99
Wylkynson, Robert   20

EU GPSR Authorized Representative:

LOGOS EUROPE, 9 rue Nicolas Poussin, 17000 La Rochelle, France

contact@logoseurope.eu

www.ingramcontent.com/pod-product-compliance
Lightning Source LLC
Chambersburg PA
CBHW061435300426
44114CB00014B/1702